ENV BOOKS SERIES

SOIL CONTAMINATION AND CONSERVATION

Editors

Dr. Ezeaku Peter Ikemefuna
Department of Soil Science
University of Nigeria, Nsukka, Enugu State, Nigeria

Dr. Pawan Kumar 'Bharti'
Vice President (Executive)
Society for Environment, Health, Awareness of nutrition & Toxicology (SEHAT)
1775, Sohan Ganj, Near Clock Tower, Delhi-7, India
E-mail: *gurupawanbharti@rediffmail.com*

DISCOVERY PUBLISHING HOUSE PVT. LTD.
NEW DELHI-110 002

Published by:
Tilak Wasan
DISCOVERY PUBLISHING HOUSE PVT. LTD.
4383/4B, Ansari Road, Darya Ganj
New Delhi-110 002 (India)
Phone : +91-11-23279245, 43596064-65
Fax : +91-11-23253475
E-mail : discoverypublishinghouse@gmail.com
sales@discoverypublishinggroup.com
web : www.discoverypublishinggroup.com

***First Edition:* 2015**

ISBN: 978-93-5056-737-1

Soil Contamination and Conservation

Printed at:
Infinity Imaging Systems
Delhi

SOIL CONTAMINATION AND CONSERVATION

ENV Books Series, India

Calls lengthy and error free chapters for further volumes of books on various environmental issues. (Send your manuscripts to envbooks@gmail.com)

Founding Editor (Editor-in-Chief)

Dr. Pawan Kumar 'Bharti'

Society for Environment, Health, Awareness of Nutrition & Toxicology (SEHAT-India)

1775, Sohanganj, Near Clock Tower, Delhi-7, India

E-mail: *gurupawanbharti@rediffmail.com*

Other titles by Editor-in-Chief:

1. **Advances in Agriculture and Ecology (2013)**
   Bharti, P.K.; Chauhan, A. and Ezeaku Peter Ikemefuna (eds.)
   (ISBN: 978-93-5056-362-5).
2. **Advances in Biotechnology and Ecological Sciences (2013)**
   Bharti, P.K., Chauhan, A. and Ray, J. (eds.)
   (ISBN: 978-93-5056-358-8).
3. **Agriculture and Environmental Biotechnology (2014)**
   Bharti, P.K. and Chauhan, A. (eds.)
   (ISBN: 978-93-5056-479-0).
4. **Agriculture Ecology and Environment (2014)**
   Bharti, P.K. and Olubukola O. Babalola (eds.)
   (ISBN: 978-93-5056-480-6).
5. **Agro-forestry and Climate Change (2014)**
   Bharti, Pawan K. and Singh, Narayan (eds.)
   (ISBN: 978-93-5056-514-8).
6. **Aquaculture and Fisheries Environment (2014)**
   Gupta, S.K. and Pawan K. Bharti (eds.)
   (ISBN: 978-93-5056-408-0).
7. **Aquatic Biodiversity and Pollution (2013)**
   Bharti, P.K.; Chauhan, A. and Kaoud, H.A.H. (eds.)
   (ISBN: 978-93-5056-359-5).

8. **Aquatic Ecology and Biotechnology (2014)**
Bharti, P.K. and Zaki, M.S.A. (eds.)
(ISBN: 978-93-5056-451-6).

9. **Aquatic Environment and Toxicology (2013)**
Bharti, Pawan K. (ed.)
(ISBN: 978-93-5056-236-9).

10. **Biodiversity of Aquatic Ecosystem:**
***Significance, Threat and Conservation* (2013)**
Bharti, P.K. and Kaoud, H.A.H. (eds.)
(ISBN: 978-93-5056-297-0).

11. **Clean Technologies and Environmental Protection (2015)**
Chauhan, A.; Sharma, S. and Bharti, P.K. (eds.)
(ISBN: 978-93-5056-731-9).

12. **Climate Change and Agriculture (2012)**
Bharti, P.K. and Chauhan, Avnish (eds.)
(ISBN: 978-93-5056-148-5).

13. **Climate Change and Biodiversity (2013)**
Bharti, P.K. and Chauhan, Avnish (eds.)
(ISBN: 978-93-5056-360-1).

14. **Conservation and Cultivation of Medicinal Plants (2015)**
Bharti, P.K. and Narayan Singh (eds.)
(ISBN: 978-93-5056-740-1).

15. **Eco-toxicology and Eco-technology (2013)**
Bharti, P.K. and Zaki, M. (eds.)
(ISBN: 978-93-5056-313-7).

16. **Environmental Biotechnology and Application (2013)**
Bharti, P.K. and Chauhan, Avnish (eds.)
(ISBN: 978-93-5056-262-8).

17. **Environmental Conservation and Biotechnology (2014)**
Chauhan, A. and P.K. Bharti (eds.)
(ISBN: 978-93-5056-512-4).

18. **Environmental Health and Problems (2013)**
Bharti, P.K. and Gajananda, Kh. (eds.)
(ISBN: 978-93-5056-263-5).

19. **Environmental Pollution and Biodiversity (2012)**
Bharti, P.K.; Chauhan, Avnish and Kumar, P. (eds.)
(ISBN: 978-93-5056-149-2).

20. **Fisheries and Toxicology (2014)**
Zaki, M.S.A.; Bharti, P.K. and Chauhan, A. (eds.)
(ISBN: 978-93-5056-452-3).

21. **Freshwater Ecosystem and Xenobiotics (2013)**
Bharti, P.K.; Zaki, M. and Chauhan, A. (eds.)
(ISBN: 978-93-5056-299-4).

22. **Limnology and Aquatic Science (2015)**
Sharma, S. and Bharti, P.K. (eds.)
(ISBN: 978-93-5056-735-7).

23. **Medicinal Plants: *Distribution, Utilization and Significance* (2015)**
Sharma, P.; Bharti, P.K. and Narayan Singh (eds.)
(ISBN: 978-93-5056-734-0).

24. **Microbial Applications and Environment (2014)**
Bharti, Pawan K. (ed.)
(ISBN: 978-93-5056-515-5).

25. **Microbial Ecology and Habitat (2014)**
Bharti, Pawan K. (ed.)
(ISBN: 978-93-5056-514-8).

26. **Prakriti me Aushadhi (*in Hindi*) (2012)**
Singh, J.R.; Bharti, P.K. and Bharti, B.
(ISBN: 978-93-5056-200-0).

27 **Seed Technology, Plant Growth and Cropping System (2015)**
Tyati, P.K., and Bharti P.K., (eds.)
(ISBN: 978-93-5056-738-8).

28. **Soil Quality and Contamination (2013)**
Bharti, P.K. and Chauhan, Avnish (eds.)
(ISBN: 978-93-5056-361-8).

29. **Water Resources and Agriculture (2014)**
Bharti, P.K. and Ezeaku Peter Ikemefuna (eds.)
(ISBN: 978-93-5056-481-3).

30. **Waste Disposal and Management (2015)**
Bharti, P.K.; Tabassum, B. and Bajaj, P. (eds.)
(ISBN: 978-93-5056-729-6).

Preface

With the rise of concrete buildings and roads, one part of the Earth that we rarely see is the soil. It has many different names, such as dirt, mud and ground. However, it is definitely very important to us. The plants that feed us grow in soil and keeping it healthy is essential to maintaining a beautiful planet. However, like all other forms of nature, soil also suffers from pollution. The pollution of soil is a common thing these days, and it happens due to the presence of man-made elements.

The main reason why the soil becomes contaminated is due to the presence of man-made waste. The waste produced from nature itself such as dead plants, carcasses of animals and rotten fruits and vegetables only adds to the fertility of the soil. However, our waste products are full of chemicals that are not originally found in nature and lead to soil pollution.

Soil contamination or soil pollution is caused by the presence of xenobiotic (human-made) chemicals or other alteration in the natural soil environment. It is typically caused by industrial activity, agricultural chemicals, or improper disposal of waste. The most common chemicals involved are petroleum hydrocarbons, polynuclear aromatic hydrocarbons (such as naphthalene and benzo(a)pyrene), solvents, pesticides, lead, and other heavy metals. Contamination is correlated with the degree of industrialization and intensity of chemical usage.

The concern over soil contamination stems primarily from health risks, from direct contact with the contaminated soil, vapors from the contaminants, and from secondary contamination of water supplies within and underlying the soil. Mapping of contaminated soil sites and the resulting cleanup are time consuming and expensive tasks, requiring extensive amounts of geology, hydrology, chemistry, computer modeling skills, and GIS in Environmental Contamination, as well as an appreciation of the history of industrial chemistry.

Soil pollution can be caused by due to these reasons:

- Accidental Spills
- Acid rain

- Intensive farming
- Deforestation
- Genetically modified plants
- Nuclear wastes
- Industrial Accidents
- Landfill and illegal dumping
- Agricultural practices, such as application of pesticides, herbicides and fertilizers
- Mining and other industries
- Oil and fuel dumping
- Buried wastes
- Disposal of coal ash
- Drainage of contaminated surface water into the soil
- Electronic waste

The most common chemicals involved are petroleum hydrocarbons, solvents, pesticides, lead, and other heavy metals.

Contaminated or polluted soil directly affects human health through direct contact with soil or via inhalation of soil contaminants which have vaporized; potentially greater threats are posed by the infiltration of soil contamination into groundwater aquifers used for human consumption, sometimes in areas apparently far removed from any apparent source of above ground contamination.

Effects occur to agricultural lands which have certain types of soil contamination. Contaminants typically alter plant metabolism, often causing a reduction in crop yields. This has a secondary effect upon soil conservation, since the languishing crops cannot shield the Earth's soil from erosion. Some of these chemical contaminants have long half-lives and in other cases derivative chemicals are formed from decay of primary soil contaminants.

Environmental remediation is analyzed by environmental scientists who utilize field measurement of soil chemicals and also apply computer models (GIS in Environmental Contamination) for analyzing transport and fate of soil chemicals.

Soil conservation is a set of management strategies for prevention of soil being eroded from the Earth's surface or becoming chemically altered by overuse, acidification, salinization or other chemical soil contamination. It is a component of environmental soil science.

Decisions regarding appropriate crop rotation, cover crops, and planted windbreaks are central to the ability of surface soils to retain their integrity, both with respect to erosive forces and chemical change from nutrient depletion. Crop rotation is simply the conventional alternation of crops on a given field, so that nutrient depletion is avoided from repetitive chemical uptake/deposition of single crop growth.

Soil is an indispensable foundation of life for humans, animals and plants. It provides foodstuffs and raw materials, stores and filters water and decomposes contaminants. It offers areas for settlement, transport and leisure activities and is an archive of natural and cultural history. However, soil cannot fulfill all these functions at the same time. In addition, some of these functions are hampered by pollution, erosion, decreasing humus layers and compaction. Damage cannot be remedied in the short term as fertile soils are the result of slow physical, chemical and biological processes: it takes 200 to 300 years for one centimeter of soil to build up.

It is cause for concern that the use of soil for settlements and transport makes it increasingly lost for other functions. Every second, an area of around 11 square meters is turned over to settlements or transport in Germany. Almost half of this area is sealed. Natural soil functions such as permeability, the ability to store water, fertility and provision of habitats for organisms are lost through surface sealing.

This book will provide comprehensive coverage of the fundamental principles and current practices and trends in the field of conservation and protection of soil quality. This book updates the subject matter, illustrations and problems to incorporate new concepts and issues related to soil science, land degradation, lithosphere and edaphic components.

The book includes chapters contributed by outstanding scholars and scientists from different institutions of Nigeria and India. We hope this book will provide a multi-disciplinary forum to explore emerging areas in the field of soil science, land degradation, lithosphere and edaphic environment.

–Editors

(envbooks@gmail.com)

Contents

Pages: 1-11

SOIL CONTAMINATION AND CONSERVATION

Edited by: Dr. Ezeaku Peter Ikemefuna; Dr. Pawan Kumar 'Bharti'

ISBN: 978-93-5056-737-1

Edition: 2015

Published by: Discovery Publishing House Pvt. Ltd., New Delhi (India)

Evaluation of Heavy Metal Concentrations in Soils at Mechanic Village Abakaliki, Southeast Nigeria and the Implication for Agricultural Landuse Planning

*Okolo C.C[1]., Nwite J.N[2] and Ezeaku, P.I.[1]

ABSTRACT

Contamination is mainly as a result of anthropogenic activities especially from automobile servicing and seems to cause heavy metal pollution load in soils around mechanic village. High values of heavy metals is a source of concern to environmentalists as it may cause soil degradation and water pollution. Therefore a study was undertaken to determine the degree of contamination by heavy metals of Pb, Zn, Cu, Mn and Cd concentrations in the soils of Abakaliki mechanic village, Ebonyi State in south-eastern Nigeria. The area was characterized into heavy impact areas of battery contaminated, lubricant contaminated and paint contaminated region and low impact areas which were 100 cm each away.

A total of thirty-six (36) samples were collected at two depth intervals viz: surface 0-15 cm and sub-surface 15-30 cm. The soils were analysed in a

1 Department of Soil Science, University of Nigeria Nsukka, Nigeria.

2 Department of Soil Science and Environmental Management, Ebonyi State University, P.M.B 053, Abakaliki, Ebonyi State. Nigeria.

standard laboratory. Results obtained showed that soil at high impact areas had higher heavy metal concentrations relative to low impact areas at 0-15cm and 15-30 cm depths. The heavy metals at 0-15 cm increased by 60.27%, 6.47%, 36.54%, 39.21%, 24.46%; 15.58%, 54.22%, 77.67%, 41.07, 14.44% and 57.61%, 48.95%, 7.81%, 42.62%, 29.62% respectively for Pb, Zn, Cu, Mn and Cd at high impact areas over low impact areas for battery contaminated, lubricant contaminated and paint contaminated areas respectively. Similarly, heavy metal concentration was lower at sub soil than surface soil at high impact area and much lower at low impact areas.

Key words:, automobile servicing, heavy metals, mechanic village, soil.

INTRODUCTION

Heavy metals are trace metals with densities greater than 5 gcm^{-3} (Duffus, 1980). Although, heavy metals are ubiquitous in most natural materials, anthropogenic activities have resulted in elevated concentration of such metals in the environment (Ojanuga *et al.*, 1996; He *et al.*, 2004). The very low general levels of their content in soil and plants as well as the biological role of most of them make them microelements (Lacatusu, 1998). Heavy metals are deemed serious pollutants because of toxicity, persistence and non-degradability in the environment (Fang and Hang, 1999; Klavins *et al.*, 2000; Tam and Wong, 2000; Yuang *et al.*, 2004; Hakan, 2006). The metal is non-essential element to human and has a toxic potential for all biological systems if present in a large quantity (Mba and Ezeaku, 2010). Many metals are biologically essential, but all have the potential to be toxic to biota above certain threshold concentrations (David and Johanna, 2000).

Automobile servicing activities is one of the significant anthropogenic sources of heavy metals in the environment. In Nigeria motor mechanic workshops are concentrated extensively in an area known as mechanic village. Such village is located in such places where the surrounding lands are not used for crop production. However, the waste products of motor mechanic workshops (petrol, diesel, engine oil etc.) are dumped on these surrounding lands and are often released during combustion and spillage (Loranger *et al.*, 1994; Lytle *et al.*, 1995).

Lubricating oil spills and other chemical inputs as a result of automobile operation cause pollution problems with associated incidents of oil spillage around motor mechanic workshops, which result in metals contamination of soil (Osibanjo *et al.*, 1983; Oyido and Agboola, 1983; Onianwa *et al.*, 2001). This tends to aggravate the direct deposition of exhaust emission and scrap batteries and solder products from motor mechanic workshops. In particular, soils in the eastern region of Nigeria have been polluted from wide range of sources with Pb, Cd, Hg, As and other heavy metals (Nriagu, 1979). Studies of heavy metals in ecosystem have indicated that many areas near urban complexes, metalliferous mines or major express road system contain anomalously high concentrations of these elements (Alloway, 1996).

Soil being a complex porous material retains and transports hazardous pollutants to ground water (Pickett *et al.*, 2001; Liu *et al.*, 2006). Crops raised on metal-contaminated soils accumulate metals in quantities excessive enough to cause clinical problems both in animals and human being consuming those metal rich plants (Tiller, 1989; Rattan *et al.*, 2005). Thus accumulation of heavy metals in the soil have potentials to restrict the soil's function, causing toxicity to plants and contaminate the food chain. Heavy metals (metals and metalloids with an atomic density >6cm^3) from wastes and anthropogenic activities can accumulate and persist in soils at environmentally hazardous level (Alloway, 1996).

There has been little attention to vicinities of motor mechanic workshops, which are liable to pollution arising from automobile operations. Furthermore there is need to monitor the levels of heavy metals in these lands so as to know whether the status of these pollutants are at a level that should cause concern to the environmentalists. As a result it becomes imperative to carry out studies meant to assess the level of heavy metal concentration and contamination of soil in Abakaliki mechanic village.

MATERIALS AND METHODS

Study Area

The study area is mechanic village located along Ogoja road, near agro-rice milling industry Abakaliki in Ebonyi State. The area lies within latitude 06° 28^N and longitude 08° 03^E in the derived savannah zone of Nigeria. The rainfall regime is bimodal with peak periods in the months of July and September, with short spell in August normally called ''August break''. Dry periods starts appreciably in April and stops in October leaving a completely dry period between November and April. The area is characterized by high temperature and high rainfall (2000 mm) with mean monthly temperature ranging between 27°C and 31°C. Relative humidity is 65-80% at rainy season. Soils from Abakaliki area are majorly ultisol and classified as Typic Haplustult (FDALR, 1985).

Field/Soil Sampling and Laboratory Determinations

Field sampling was conducted using a free survey technique involving target sampling of soils from three sites viz, battery contaminated area (BCA), lubricant contaminated area (LCA) and paint contaminated area (PCA). Each of these areas had a heavy impact point which is high automobile activity and low impact point situated 100m away. On each area, six (6) soil samples were collected each at the surface (0-15cm) and sub-surface (15-30cm) using soil auger. Thus, twelve (12) samples were collected each from BCA, LCA and

PCA, giving a total of thirty-six (36) soil samples. The samples were taken to the research laboratory and air dried at room temperature between 25-29ºC. The dried samples were ground with mortar and pestle, and then sieved through a 2mm sieve. Thereafter the soils were analysed for heavy metals (Pb, Zn, Cu, Mn and Cu) using Atomic Absorption Spectrometer (AAS).

Statistical Analysis

The data was analysed using standard deviation and mean value for comparison.

RESULTS AND DISCUSSION

Standard minimum, maximum and average metal concentrations (mgkg^{-1} soil) in soils are shown in table 1.1 according to Marjanovic *et al.*, 2009.

Table 1.1

Concentration	Cd	Co	Cu	Pb	Mn	Zn
Minimum	1.1	4.4	8.8	<LOD[a]	281.8	63.2
Maximum	3.1	36.0	251.3	785.7	688.9	691.1
Average	1.8	16.5	46.3	298.6	417.6	174.2

a Limit of detection for Lead is 5mgkg^{-1} dry sample.

The results in Table 1.2 show that in general, the concentrations of lead (Pb) were high at the top soil(0-15cm) at High Battery Impact than when compared with the sub soil which had a lower concentration. The values of Pb at the top soils were 324.12, 146.02 and 209.21mgkg^{-1} respectively for HBI, HLI and HPI locations. These values are higher compared to the concentration of these metals at lower profile (15-30cm). The high impact of Pb at the three locations represent 60.27, 74.76 and 27.46% increments respectively compared to the sub soil values. The concentration of heavy metals at the topsoil (0-15cm) is in line with the observations of Nyanagabobo and Hamya (1986) and El-bassam *et al.*, (1979) as reported by Mbah and Ezeaku (2010) that top soils are better indicators of heavy metal burden than sub soils.

Highest Pb concentration within the three different locations was found at high battery impact location with a concentration of 324.12 mgkg^{-1} (0-15cm) while the lowest concentration (36.85 mgkg^{-1}) was found in 15-30cm soil depth. This represents percentage increase of 88.63%. The highest value of Pb observed, especially at HBI at both depths is within the normal range in soil (Marjanovic *et al.*, 2009).

The concentration of Zn at the surface (0-15cm) was high (257.37mg kg^{-1}) at battery impact location while subsoil (15-30cm) recorded low concentration of 252.56mg kg^{-1} (Table 1.2).This accounts for percentage increase of 1.86% in Zn at topsoil over subsoil. High lubricant impact location recorded a high concentration of Zn at the surface (0-15cm) with a concentration of 250.05 mgkg^{-1} while the subsoil (15 – 30cm) is 114.47 mgkg^{-1} representing a percentage increase of 54.22% compared to subsoil value. The same trend of increase of Zn was obtained at high paint impact location with 7.86% increase in level of Zn concentration at a depth of 0-15cm. High lubricant impact had the lowest concentration value of 114.47 mgkg^{-1} at a depth of 15-30cm. Similar observation has been reported by Marjanovic *et al.*, 2009.

The values of Cu obtained at three different locations signified that Cu concentration was high at the surface (Table 1.2). At high battery impact locations, the trend was from 266.13mgkg^{-1} at the surface to 203.38mgkg^{-1} at the subsurface. It was also a downward trend at high lubricant impact location, with the surface recording 304.23mgkg^{-1} while the subsurface recorded 67.92mgkg^{-1}. The topsoil of high paint impact had a concentration of 166.97mgkg^{-1} which reduced to 119.69 mgkg^{-1} in the subsoil. The common characteristic of Cu distribution in soil profiles is its accumulation in the top horizons (Kabata-Pendias and Pendias, 2001). The percentage increase was 28.32%. The high value of Cu observed especially in HLI at the surface was above the normal range in soil (Marjanovic *et al.*, 2009). This suggests that the range is abnormal for crop production.

The value of Mn at high battery impact location implies that the value was high at the surface with a concentration of 755.61mgkg^{-1} while that of subsurface was lower with a concentration of 749.39mgkg^{-1} (Table 1.2). The percentage increase were 41.07% and 3.95% respectively for HLI and HPI. HBI had the highest concentration of Mn at a depth of 0 -15cm with a concentration of 755.61mgkg^{-1} while HLI had the lowest concentration of 307.75mgkg^{-1}. The high value of Mn observed especially in HBI was above the normal range in soil (Marjanovic *et al.*, 2009), the range at which concentration is limiting crop production and pose danger to human health if in contact with the food chain.

The concentration of Cd at a high battery impact was 9.12mgkg^{-1} at a depth of 0-15 cm and decreased with depth of 15-30cm to 8.46mgkg^{-1}. Cd at HLI recorded a higher concentration at the surface and much lower at the subsurface with the following concentrations of 5.27mgkg^{-1} and 4.87mgkg^{-1} respectively. Highest Cd concentration was found at HPI location at both depth of 0-15cm and 15-30cm, and with both recording a concentration of 10.58mgkg^{-1}. Lowest concentration of 4.87mgkg^{-1} was recorded at a depth of 15-30cm. The percentage increase of Cd in HPI over LPI was 74.66%.The concentrations of Cd in the studied area was observed in HLI at both depths especially at HPI was far above the normal range in soil (Marjanovic *et al.*, 2009).

Table 1.2: Heavy Metal Concentration ($mgkg^{-1}$) Levels of Soil Around Mechanic Village at High Impact Points

Location	Depth (cm)	Pb	Zn	Cu	Mn	Cd
HBI	0 - 15	*324.12±61.67	257.37± 4.52	266.13 ±14.93	755.61±161.56	9.12± 87.12
	15 - 30	128.78 ±3.44	252.56 ± 6.12	203.38± 22.52	749.39±159.49	8.46± 87.01
Mean		226.45	254.97	234.76	752.50	8.79
HLI	0 - 15	146.02±18.10	250.05±16.64	304.23±46.70	522.20±119.35	5.27±2.020
	15 - 30	36.85±8.29	114.47±9.56	67.92±32.07	307.75±47.87	4.87±2.21
Mean		91.44	182.26	186.08	414.98	5.07
HPI	0 - 15	209.21±30.18	252.42±3.38	166.97±40.86	647.21±134.97	10.58±72
	15 - 30	151.76±11.03	232.58±3.24	119.69±25.11	621.64±126.45	10.58±70
Mean		180.49	242.50	143.33	634.43	10.58

Note: High Battery Impact (HBI), High Lubricant Impact (HLI) and High Paint Impact (HPI), Standard Deviation (±), * Actual values followed by standard deviation (±).

Pb and Zn values at topsoil in HBI were of normal values while Cu at HLI, Mn at HBI and Cd at HPI at 0-15 cm were above normal value (Marjanovic *et al.*, 2009). The values above normal range portend serious contamination to crop production and the use by livestock and humans.

Metal Levels in Soil of Mechanic Village at Low Impact Points

The results of the actual levels in the soils of mechanic village at low impact points are shown in table 1.3. It shows the concentrations of Pb, Zn, Cu, Mn and Cd in soil at low impacts point at three different locations. At LBI, surface soil had high concentration (237.94mgkg^{-1}) of Pb while the sub-soil had a lower concentration of 94.30mgkg^{-1}. These values are quite comparable to High Battery Impact location which also had a high concentration of Pb at the topsoil. This suggests that there might be other sources of Pb to soil apart from anthropogenic activities.

Low lubricant impact (LLI) location had a higher concentration of Pb at the surface but the concentration decreased with increase in depth at the sub-soil. The concentration varied from 36.85mgkg^{-1} to 31.11mgkg^{-1}. At low paint impact location, the top soil had a higher Pb concentration (59.38 mgkg^{-1}) which decreased (25.36 mgkg^{-1}) considerably at the sub-soil. The steadily increasing amounts of Pb in surface soils, both arable and uncultivated, have been reported for various terrestrial ecosystems (Huffman 1980) and this was evidently illustrated by Blum *et al.*, (1997).

At low battery impact, Zn concentration was high (141.10 mgkg-^{1}) at the surface (0-15cm) (Table 1.3). High level of Zn concentration at the surface may be attributed to topographical feature of sampling site which encouraged zinc concentration on soil surface (Carpe, 2010). At low lubricant impact location, surface soil also had a higher concentration than subsurface with concentration varying from 129.89 mgkg-^{1} to 70.53mgkg-^{1}, respectively. Low paint impact location recorded a high concentration of Zn at the surface (0-15cm) with a concentration of 87.17 mgkg-^{1} while the subsurface was much lower in concentration value of 44.50 mgkg-^{1}.

The level of Cu at the surface was 227.68mgkg-^{1} at the depth of 0-15cm and decreased at the sub-surface (144.48mgkg-^{1}) (Table 3). Low lubricant impact location had a Cu concentration of 86.29 mgkg-^{1} at the surface soil (0-15cm) which was higher in concentration (47.18 mgkg-^{1})than the sub soil (15-30cm). The common characteristic of Cu distribution in soil profile is its accumulation in the top horizons. Concentration of Cu at the top soil (0-15cm) in LPI was almost comparable with the value of sub-soil (15-30 cm) which is 23.72 mgkg-^{1}. Concentration of Cu in surface soils reflects the bioaccumulation of the metal and also recent anthropogenic sources of the element (Kabata-Pendias and Pendias, 2001). The concentration of Cu in the three studied impact locations within the depths (0-15 and 15-30cm) exceeded the normal range of Cu in soil (Table 1.1) and the concentration of copper in this study was higher than those reported by Bamgbose *et al.*, (1999) for contaminated sites.

Table 1.3: Heavy Metal Concentration ($mgkg^{-1}$) Levels of Soil Around Mechanic Village at Low Impact Points

Location	Depth (cm)	Pb	Zn	Cu	Mn	Cd
LBI	0 - 15	237.94±58.87	141.10±0.66	227.68±29.52	647.21±134.97	3.27±45.58
	15 - 30	94.30±11.00	131.97±2.38	144.48±1.79	621.64±126.45	2.47±45.28
Mean		166.12	136.54	186.08	634.43	2.87
LLI	0 - 15	36.85±44.43	129.89±9.72	86.29±1.81	255.50±54.59	3.67±53.49
	15 - 30	31.11±42.34	70.53±7.07	47.18±14.85	144.08±17.45	3.14±45.55
Mean		33.98	95.71	66.74	199.79	3.41
LPI	0 - 15	59.383±0.35	87.17±9.45	25.73±11.70	178.66±13.18	3.14±18.87
	15 - 30	25.36±11.15	44.50±4.77	23.72±11.03	108.61±10.17	2.21±18.56
Mean		42.60	65.84	24.73	143.64	2.68

Note: Low Battery Impact (LBI), Low Lubricant Impact (LLI), and Low Paint Impact (LPI), Standard Deviaton (±)All the metals are expressed in ($mgkg^{-1}$)

The value of Mn at the top soil (0-15cm) of LBI was 647.21mgkg-1, which was higher than the value (621.64mgkg-1) obtained at the sub-soil (15-30cm). The top soil (0-15cm) at low lubricant impact location recorded a higher Mn concentration of 255.50mgkg-1 than sub soil (15-30cm) which had a value of 144.08 mgkg-1 with a percentage increase of HLI over LLI as 41.07%. The value of Mn at the surface (0-15cm) in LPI was higher than the sub-surface (15-30cm) with values of 178.66 mgkg-1 and 108.61mgkg-1 respectively. Although Mn can be concentrated in various soil horizons, particularly in those enriched in Fe oxides or hydroxides, usually this element is also accumulated in topsoils as a result of its fixation by organic matter (Kabata-Pendias and Pendias, 2001).

Low battery impact location had Cd value high at the surface soil (0-15cm) with a concentration of 3.27 mgkg-1 and at the sub-surface (15-30cm) with a reduced concentration of 2.47mgkg-1 (Table 3). Low lubricant impact location recorded a high concentration value of 3.67 mgkg-1 at the surface soil (0-15 cm) with a decrease at the sub-surface (15-30 cm) with a concentration of 3.14 mgkg-1. At low paint impact location, the top soil had a high value of Cd compared with the sub-soil which had a lower value. These values varied from 3.14 mgkg-1 at the surface (0-15cm) to 2.21 mgkg-1 at the sub-surface (15-30 cm). Under man- induced condition, Cd is likely to build up in surface soils (Kabata-Pendias and Pendias, 2001). Moreso, Cd concentration in the soil is relatively low and is reported to range from 0.2 to 6 mgkg-1 (Kabata-Pendias and Pendias, 2001).

The studied heavy metals of Pb, Zn, Cu, Mn and Cu are generally high at topsoil (0-15 cm) depth relative to 15-30 cm depth at the three different locations of impacts. Generally, lower heavy metals at 15-30cm depth could be attributed to binding action of clay (Kabata-Pendias and Pendias, 2001). Thus accumulation of heavy metals the surface soil have potentials to restrict the soil's function, causing toxicity to plants and contaminate the food chain (Kabata-Pendias and Pendias, 2001).

CONCLUSION

Results from this study showed higher levels of heavy metals on top surface soil (0-15 cm) of high impact and low impact locations of the mechanic village. These heavy metals generally decreased with depth in both high impact and low impact locations. The values of heavy metals in the studied areas were generally higher than acceptable and permissible limits in soil in the 0 -15cm depth than subsoil (15 – 30cm). These values suggest a high degree of bioavailability and toxicity in the surface soils. The result is indicative of the fact that soils of these mechanic village require some remedial action before any form of chosen development can proceed on such land. The automobile servicing centre (mechanic village) represent potential source of heavy metals contamination to the ecosystem and threat to human and animal health, ground water and surface water.

Thus agricultural land use planning is imperative in order to reclaim and optimise agricultural productivity of the soils.

REFERENCES

Alloway, B.J. (1996). Heavy Metal in Soil. Halsted Press. John Wiley and Sons, London. p. 339.

Bamgbose, O; Odukoya, O and Arowolo, T.O.A. (1999). Earthworm as Bio-indicator of Heavy Metal Pollution in Dumpsite of Abeokuta City, Nigeria. *http:/rbt.ots. ac.cr/revista/ 48-1/zoobamb.htm:* p. 1-7.

Blum, W.E.H., Brandsetter, A., and Wenzel, W.W (1997). Trace Element Distribution in Soils as Affected by Landuse, in Biogeochemistry of Trace Elements, Adriano, D.C., Chen, Z.S., Iskadar, I. K., Eds., 61 pp.

Carpe, S.O (2010). Determination of Heavy Metals in Soil Around a Battery Manufacturing Industry.

David, H and Johanna, E (2000). Organochlorino, Heavy Metal and Polyaromatic Hydrocarbon Pollutant Concentrations Great Barrier Reef (Austraia). Environ: A Review, Marine Pollu, Bull, 4: 267-278.

Duffus, J. H (1980). Environmental Toxicology. Edward Arnold Publishers Ltd., London, 164 p.

El-Bassam, M; Tietja, C and Esser, J (1979). Long Term Studies on Application of Urban Wastes on Heavy Metal Inputs and Crop Ecology. Intern. Conf. Manag. and Contr. Heavy Metals in Environment. London J 1: 1-4.

Fang, T.H and Hang, E (1999). Mechanisms Influencing the Spatial Distribution of Trace Metals in Surficial Sediments Off the South-western Taiwan. Marine Bulletin, 38: 1026-1037.

Federal Department of Agricultural Land Resources (FDALR) (1985). The Reconnaissance Soil Survey of Anambra State Soil Report 1985. Federal Department of Agriculture and Land Resources. Lagos, Nigeria.

Hakan, P (2006). The Distribution and Sources of Heavy Metal in Izmit Bay Surface Sediment Affected by a Polluted Stream. Marine Pollution Bulletin.

He, Z.L; Zhang, M.L; Calvert, D.V; Stofella, P.J; Yang, X.E and Yu, S. (2004). Transport of Heavy Metals in Surface Run-off from Vegetation and Citrus Fields. Soil Serv. Soil.Am. J. 68: 1662-1669.

Huffman, M.K., Lepp, N.W., and Phipps, D.A (1980). Aerial Heavy Metal Pollution and Terrestrial Ecosystems, Adv. Ecol. Res., 11, 217.

Kabata-Pendias, A and Pendias, H (2001). Trace Elements in Soils and Plants.(3rd ed) CRC Press LLC, 2000 N.W Corporate Blvd., Boca Raton, Florida 33431. 106-285 pp.

Klavins, M; Briede, A; Rodinev, V; Kokorige, L; Parela, E and Klavins, I. (2000). Heavy Metals in Rivers of Latvia, Sci. Journ. Environ. 262: 175-183.

Lacatusu, R (1998). Appraising Levels of Soil Contamination and Pollution with Heavy Metals. In: Land Information System for Planning the Sustainable Use of Land Resources. Heinke, A.J; Eckel Man, W; Thomasson, A.J; Jones. R.J.A; Montanarella, L and Buckey, B (Eds). European Soil Bureau.

Liu, C.L; Chang, T.W; Wang, M.K and Haung, C.H (2006). Transport of Cadmium, Nickel and Zinc in Taoyyan Red Soil Using One-dimensional Convective Dispersive Model. Geoderma; 131-181.

Loranger, S; Zayed, J and Forget, E. (1994). Manganese Contamination in Montreal in Relation with Traffic Density, Water Air Soil Pollu.74: 385-396.

Lytle, C.M; Smith, B.N and Mcjinon, C.Z (1995). Manganese Contamination Along Road Ways. A Possible Indication of Motor Vehicle Exhaust Pollution. Sci Total Environ., 162: 103-109.

Marjanovic, M.D; Vukcevic, M.N; Anthonovic, D.G; Dimirtrijevic, S.I; Jovanovic, D.M; Matavulj, M.N and Ristic, M.D (2009). Heavy Metal Concentration in Soils from Parks and Green Areas in Belgrade. Journal of Serbian Chem. Soc. 74(6) 697-706.

Mbah, C.N and Ezeaku, P.I (2010). Physicochemical Characterization of Farmland Affected by Automobile Wastes in Relation to Heavy Metal. http//www.sciencepub.net/nature.httm; 8(10): 134-138.

Nriagu, J.O (1979). Copper in the Environment. Part II. Health Effects. John Wiley.

Nyanagabobo, J.T and Hanya, J.W (1986). The Decomposition of Lead, Cadmium, Zinc, and Copper from Motor Traffic on Biucharia erimi and Soil along a Major Bombo Road in Kampala City. Int. Journ. Env. Studies 27: 115-119.

Ojanuga, A.G; Lekwa, G and Okusami, T.A (1996). Distribution, Classification and Potentials of Wetland Soils of Nigeria. Soil Sci. of Nig. 1-24.

Osibanjo, O; Abumere, S and Akintola, F (1983). Disposal of Used Oil from Motor Garages and Petrol Stations in some Nigeria Coastal Towns.

Onianwa, P.C; Jaiveola, O.M and Egekenze, R.N (2001). Heavy Metal Contamination of Top Soil in the Vicinities of Auto-repair Workshop, Gas Stations and Motor Parks in a Nigeria City, Toxicol. Environ. Chem., 84: 33-39.

Oyido, C.O and Agboola, E.A (1983). Pollution Control in Petroleum Product Marketing Operations in Nigeria. In: Proceedings of the International Seminar on the Petroleum.

Pickett, S.T.A; Cadenasso, M.L; Grave, C.H; Nilon, R,V; Pouyat, W.C; Zipperer and Costanaza, R. (2001). Urban Ecological Systems Linking Terrestrial Ecological, Physical and Socio-economic Components of Metropolitan Areas. Annual Review. Eco. Sys. 32: 127-137.

Rattan, R.K; Datta, P.K; Chenkar, K; Suribabu and Singh, A.K (2005). Long Term Impact of Irrigation with Sewage Effluents on Heavy Metal in Soil, Crops and Ground Water. A Case Study. Agriculture, Ecosystem Environ., 109: 310-322.

Tam, N.F.V and Wong,Y.S. (2000). Spatial Variation of Heavy Metal in Surface Sediments of Hong Kong Mangrove Swamps. Environ. Pollu., 100: 195-205.

Tiller, K.G (1986). Essential and Toxic Heavy Metals in Soils and Their Ecological Relevance Trans XIII congr. Int. Soc. Soil Sci., 1: 29-44.

Tyler, G; Balsbey-Pabisson, A.M; Bongtsson, G; Bath, E and Tranvik, I (1989). Heavy Metal Ecology of Terrestrial Plants, Micro Organisms and Invertebrates. A Review.Water, Air and Soil Pollu. 47: 189-215.

Yuan, C.J; Shi, B; He, I; Elu, L; Liang and Jiang, G (2004). Speciation of Heavy Metals in Marine Sediments from the Fast China Sea by ICP-MS with Sequential Extraction. Environ. Int. 28: 1425-1433.

Pages: 12-35

SOIL CONTAMINATION AND CONSERVATION

Edited by: **Dr. Ezeaku Peter Ikemefuna; Dr. Pawan Kumar 'Bharti'**

ISBN: 978-93-5056-737-1

Edition: **2015**

Published by: **Discovery Publishing House Pvt. Ltd., New Delhi (India)**

Effect of Metal Sources and Incubation Period on Nickel and Copper Speciation in Polluted Soils Under Oxic and Anoxic Environment

Geeta Tewari

ABSTRACT

Copper (Cu) and nickel (Ni) are essential micronutrients for plant growth and required by the plant in very small amount. High amount of these metals may show toxic effect on plant growth and in turn animals and human. Concentration of copper and nickel was determined (by using Atomic Absorption Spectrophotometer) in sludge and inorganic salt amended soils incubated under two oxic (field capacity moisture level) and anoxic (flooding moisture level) environment for one and half year at nine time intervals (1 week (W), 2W, 4W, 6W, 8W, 16W, 32W, 48W, 16 month (M) by using different extractants (DTPA, $CaCl_2$ and speciation scheme). Copper (Cu)-P_1, Cu-P_2, Cu-P_4 and Cu-P_5 pools were observed to be highest under oxic environment as compared to anoxic environment while the reverse was true for Cu-P_3.

Department of Chemistry, D.S.B. Campus, Kumaun University, Nainital, Uttarakhand, India.

Inorganic source maintained higher mean content of Cu-P_1 pool as compared to sludge. The mean concentration of Cu-P_1, Cu-P_2, Cu-P_3 and Cu-P_5 pools decreased with the time of incubation. Oxic environment maintained higher Ni-mean content of P_1, P_2, P_3 pools as compared to anoxic environment. The mean concentration of P_1 pool was observed to be higher in inorganically polluted soils as compared to organically polluted soils. The mean concentration of Ni-P_1 and Ni- P_5 pools decreased with the incubation time.

INTRODUCTION

The pollution in the agricultural fields near Ramganga River is caused by effluent waters and sludge of nearly 450 electroplating industries and entire brass and stainless steel industry and untreated domestic waste (Sharma and Pande, 1998). Although sludge is a useful fertilizer for soils, it also contains toxic heavy metals, which may have some harmful and adverse effects on crops, animals and humans. According to Cheraghi et al. (2009), waste water used for irrigation containing creates metals have problems for vegetables and human health due to accumulation of heavy metals in soil and biological accumulation of these elements in food chain. In the soil, metals tend to partition themselves (heavy metals) among the solid and solution phases with higher preference to the solid phase. Metal partition in the solid phase can be determined by sequential extraction procedure. Knowledge of the relative content of different chemical pools of heavy metals in soil solution/ solid phase is very important in determining their mobility, bioavailability and long term impact on the concerned environment (Emmerich et al., 1984). Cadmium (Cd), nickel (Ni), lead (Pb), zinc (Zn) and copper (Cu) are among the most commonly found heavy metals in sewage sludge.

Rapid industrialization has produced a tremendous increase in the generation of industrial solid waste. Solid (both domestic and industrial sludge) and liquid wastes are generally disposed as land-fills or incinerated or dumped into the open spaces or road sides whereas, the sewage is used to irrigate agricultural fields (Jain, 1994). The utilization of these liquid and solid wastes as organic fertilizers in the agricultural soils leads to accumulation of heavy metals in the soils and crops to a concentration which is toxic to man and animals (Purves, 1985).

For evaluating potential hazards due to heavy metals accumulation in soil via sludge amendment requires knowledge of their chemical speciation in soils and the effects of soil properties on their behavior and bioavailability in the soil. Heavy metal distribution among different pools is governed by soil properties, moisture level, incubation period and the concentration of other metal species present in the soil (Han and Banin, 1997; 1999). Water soluble and exchangeable forms of metals are and the most readily available forms to the plants, whereas other forms such as carbonate bound, organic matter bound, reducible and residual are of minor importance as plant uptake is concerned (Dudka and Chlopecka, 1990).

Some studies revealed that water levels and time of incubation also affect metal availability to the plants. Silviera and Sommers (1977) reported that the transformation of Cu, Zn and Cd were similar in water-saturated and unsaturated soil-sludge systems. Sposito et al. (1983) reported that in the EDTA-extractable fraction (possibly carbonates bound) and/or the HNO_3-extractable fraction of heavy metals tended to increase with time in sludge-mended soils of California. McGrath and Cegarra (1992) found that the exchangeable and NaOH-extractable Ni and Zn fractions (primarily organically bound) decreased, while metal in the residual fraction increased during the 20 years after cessation of sludge application to field plots in England; thus, decreasing bioavailability of these metals.

In the light of the facts mentioned above, it is important to elucidate different chemical pools of heavy metals, in sludge and also in soils amended with sludge and inorganic salts and to examine their distribution among different pools.

Two metals were chosen for the present study; Cu and Ni. Ni is essential for plant growth while Cu provides a vital nutritional component for plants, animals and humans. This study might be helpful in assessing the long-term phyto-availability of nickel and copper in polluted soils.

MATERIALS AND METHODS

SITE OF COLLECTION

Composite surface (0-15 cm) soil and sludge (Karula nala) sample were collected from Moradabad (Figure 2.1).

SAMPLE PREPARATION

Physicochemical Characterization of Soil and Sludge Samples

The soil samples were shade-dried, ground into fine powder using pestle and mortar and passed through a 2 mm sieve. These processed soil samples (in triplicates) were used for determining the physicochemical properties such as pH (Jackson, 1958), organic carbon (%OC) by Walkley Black method (1934), texture and cation exchange capacity (CEC) (Bower et al., 1952) (Table 2.1).

Heavy Metal Analysis

For total, DTPA extractable, $CaCl_2$ extractable or residual metal (Ni and Cu) analysis in soil, the samples were digested with a 5:1 mixture (concentrated acid mixture) of hydrofluoric acid and perchloric acids (Page et al., 1982). The digests were analyzed for Ni and Cu by Atomic Absorption Spectroscopy (AAS).

Fig. 2.1: Site of Sludge Collection

Table 2.1: Physicochemical Properties of Soil Samples Used in the Study

General Soil Properties		Soil Sample
Mechanical analysis	Sand (%)	36.00
	Silt (%)	29.00
	Clay (%)	35.00
	Texture	Clay loam
Other soil properties	pH (1:2)	9.58
	O.C. %	0.80
	% $CaCO_3$	2.29
	Cation exchange capacity (c mol kg^{-1})	12.23
	Water holding capacity	50.05
Total metal content (mg kg^{-1})	Ni	56.08
	Cu	18.59

POOLS OF COPPER AND NICKEL

Enrichment of Sludge

Two thousand gram of sludge was mixed with 100 mL of solution containing 2000 mg L^{-1} Ni and 4000 mg L^{-1} Cu and left for one-month incubation.

Soil Amendment with Enriched Sludge and Inorganic Source

Fifteen gram of soil was treated with a dose of 10g metal-enriched sludge in 200 mL plastic cups. The contents of Ni and Cu added in the treatment amounted 40 and 80 ppm, respectively. In another series the similar level of both the metals through inorganic source were added and mixed thoroughly. The pots were prepared in triplicate.

Incubation Under Oxic and Anoxic Environment

Amended soil was incubated under oxic and anoxic environment: field capacity (oxic) and flooding (anoxic; 2.5 cm water level above the soil surface) at room temperature. The water content was maintained constant throughout the study.

Speciation of Heavy Metals at Different Time Intervals

The amended soils were incubated for period of 1W (Week), 2W, 4W, 6W, 8W, 16W, 32W, 48W and 16M (Month), three cups of each treatment combination were selected. Three gram wet soil portions were taken into 50-ml polycarbonate centrifuge tubes. Exact dry weight of soil transferred was determined after oven drying an equivalent aliquot of soil for 48hr at 105°C. Wet soil samples taken in centrifuge tube were sequentially extracted as per the scheme given by Ahnstrom & Parker (1999) to obtain the following five pools:

All the slurries from each pool were centrifuged at 5000 rpm for 20 minutes and the supernatants were filtered (Whatman #42) and stored into plastic vials. Fractions 1 to 3 were acidified to 0.16M HNO_3. A drop of toluene was added to the F_4 extracts to check bacterial growth. There were total 108 pots (2 metal source X 2 moisture levels X 3 replicates X 9 time of incubation X 3 soils). Copper and nickel in solutions of each pool were analyzed by Atomic Absorption Spectroscopy.

Total and Residual Metal Analysis

Total content of Cu and Ni in soil samples were estimated in digests by Atomic Absorption Spectroscopy (GBC-902 and Avanta sigma model). The measuring conditions were as under (Table 2.2).

Table 2.2: Measuring Conditions of Atomic Absorption Spectrophotometer

Element	Wavelength (nm)	Lamp Current (mA)	Slit (nm)	Flame Type
Cu	324.7	3.0	0.5	-do-
Ni	232.0	4.0	0.2	-do-

INCUBATION STUDY AND TIME DEPENDENT DTPA AND $CACL_2$ EXTRACTION OF COPPER AND NICKEL

At the end (1W, 2W, 4W, 6W, 8W, 16W, 32W, 48W, 16M) of incubation, soil from each plastic cup was also analyzed for DTPA and $CaCl_2$ extractable copper and nickel using Atomic Absorption Spectrophotometer.

DTPA Extraction

Soil samples were extracted for 0.005 M DTPA extractable Cu and Ni following the procedure developed by Lindsay & Norvell (1978).

$CaCl_2$ Extraction

Soil samples were also extracted for 1 M $CaCl_2$ solution following the method described by Young et al. (2000).

STATISTICAL TREATMENT OF DATA

The data were statistically analyzed using variance analysis (ANOVA) in an asymmetrical three factorial design set-up to evaluate the contribution to the total variance of metal source, moisture levels and incubation period. The statistical significance was tested by F-test at $P= 0.05$.

RESULTS AND DISCUSSION

SPECIATION OF SLUDGE AND ENRICHED SLUDGE

Properties of Sludge Used in the Study (Table 2.3)

Table 2.3: Properties of Sludge

Samples	Ni (mg kg^{-1})	Cu (mg kg^{-1})	pH	Organic Carbon (OC) %
Sludge	184.28±0.19	871.85±3.06	6.51±0.14	1.713±0.122

Chemical Pools of Heavy Metals in Sludge

Among different chemical pools, the highest content of both the metals in sludge exits in the residual pool. In case of copper, the second main pool was NaOAc extractable pool, indicating tendency of these metals to bind with carbonates present in the sludge materials. Lower concentration of Cu in exchangeable plus water-soluble pools while Ni in NaOAc extractable and exchangeable plus water-soluble pools may be due to higher mean content of the organically bound and residual pools of these in sludge. In case of Ni, the second most abundant pool was organically bound followed by NaOAc extractable, water soluble and reducible pools.

Effect of Metal Addition and Incubation on Chemical Pools of Enriched Sludge

Heavy metal addition and incubation significantly increased the water soluble and exchangeable pool of both metals (Figures 2.1 and 2.2). The effect was more pronounced in case of Ni as compared to Cu. The NaOAc extractable fraction of Ni and Cu in sludge also significantly increased with metal enrichment and incubation. The organically bound pool of Cu significantly increased while that of Ni suffered a decrease. Metal pool of Ni and Cu in Fe-Al oxides significantly increased with metal addition and incubation. The residual pool of both the metals registered a significant decrease. The effect was more significant in case of Cu as compared to Ni. It appeared that bio-oxidation of organic carbon and consequent acidification affected release of residual pool of both metals and organically bound pool of Ni in sludge due to metal enrichment and incubation. The released metals might incorporated into reducible or Fe-Mn oxide bound pool in case of Ni and Cu, into organically bound pool in case of Cu, into NaOAc extractable pool in case of Ni and Cu and invariably increased the water soluble and exchangeable pool of both the tested heavy metals.

Effect of Metal Addition and Incubation Period on CaCl-$_2$ and DTPA Extractable Metal Content of Sludge

Copper and nickel addition and incubation significantly increased 1M $CaCl_2$ extractable content (water soluble and exchangeable) and 0.005M DTPA (pH 7.3) extractable Cu and Ni content in sludge. The effect was more pronounced in case of Cu as compared to Ni (Figures 2.1 and 2.2). DTPA partly extract metals from most of chemical pools except residual fraction.

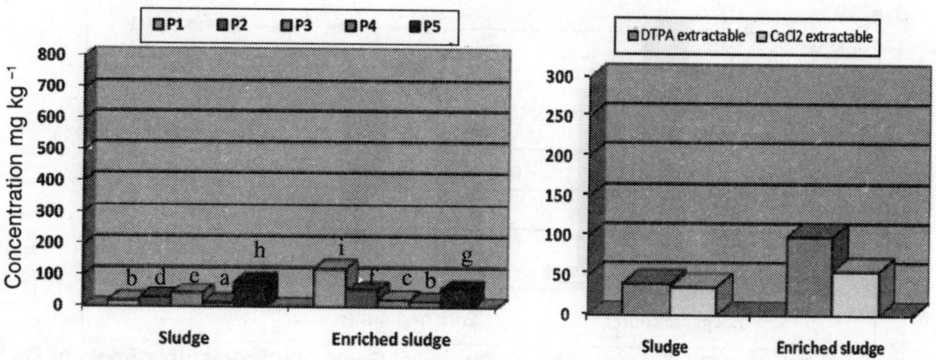

Fig. 2.2: Changes in Chemical Pools (P_1, P_2, P_3, P_4, P_5) and DTPA and 1M $CaCl_2$ Extractable Ni

EFFECT OF METAL SOURCES, MOISTURE LEVELS AND INCUBATION PERIOD ON CHEMICAL POOLS AND DTPA & $CACL_2$ EXTRACTABLE CONTENT OF NICKEL AND COPPER

Copper

The changes in the mean content of different chemical pools of Cu the soil amended with inorganic or enriched sludge under oxic or anoxic environments are presented in Figure 2.3 to Figure 2.5.

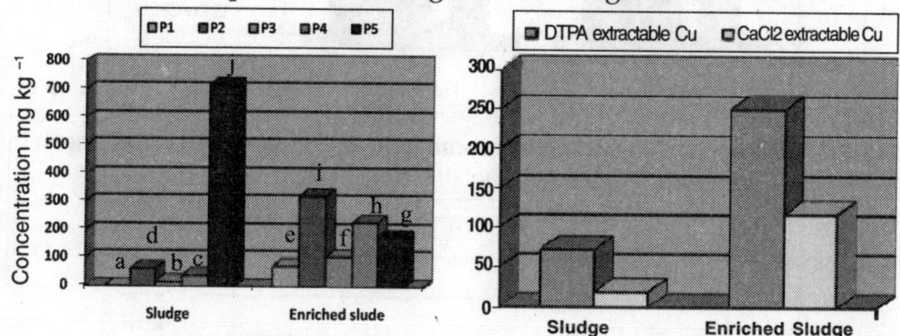

Fig. 2.3: Changes in Chemical Pools (P_1, P_2, P_3, P_4, P_5) and DTPA and 1M $CaCl_2$ Extractable Cu (Similar Alphabets are not Significantly Different at pd$\leq$0.5)

Chemical Pools

Water Soluble and Exchangeable (Cu-P_1) Pool

Inorganic source maintained higher Cu-P_1 mean content as compared to the enriched sludge. The mean content of Cu-P_1 pool was higher under oxic environment as compared to the anoxic environment. The content of Cu-P_1 pool decreased with incubation period. (Figures 2.4 to 2.6).

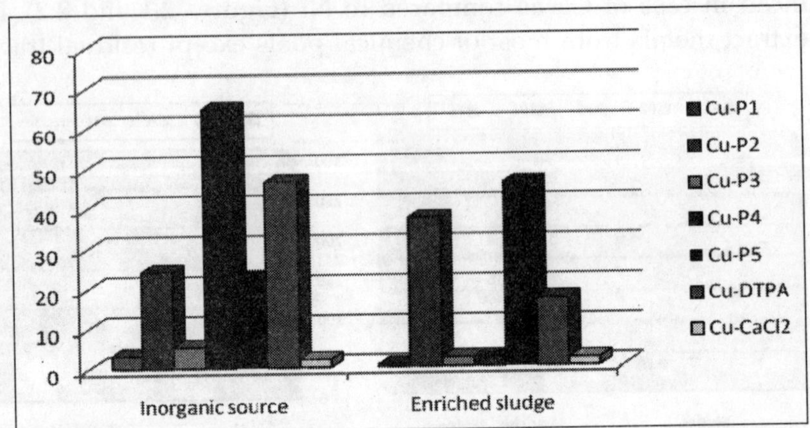

Fig. 2.4: Effect of Source on Different Chemical Pools and Extractable Pools of Cu

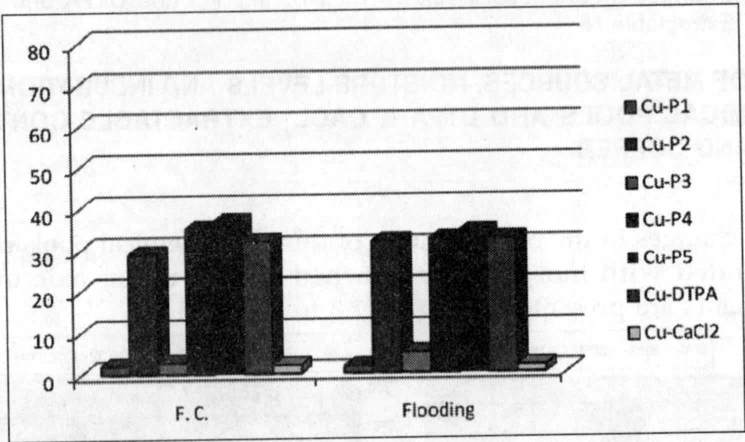

Fig. 2.5: Effect of Moisture Environment (Oxic or Anoxic) on Different Chemical Pools and Extractable Pools of Cu

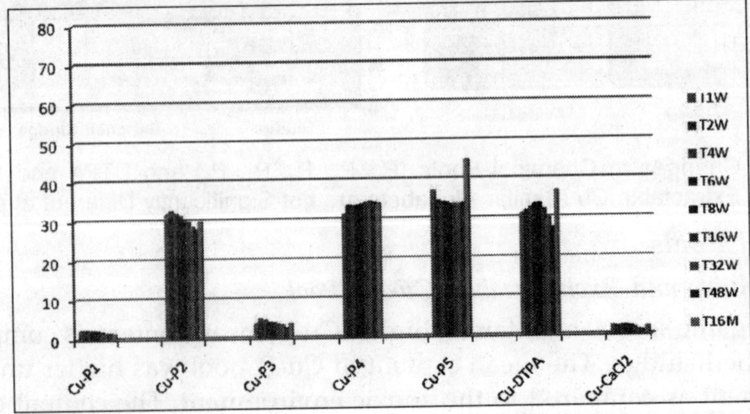

Fig. 2.6: Effect of Time Interval on Different Chemical Pools and Extractable Pools of Cu in Alkaline Soil

In inorganic source amended soils, under oxic environment the highest mean content of Cu-P_1 pool was observed at 1W (4.56 μg g^{-1}). Under anoxic environment, the highest concentration of Cu-P_1 pool was detected at 1W (3.74 μg g^{-1}). With enriched sludge, the highest mean content of Cu-P_1 pool was recorded at 4W (1.15 μg g^{-1}) under oxic environment. Under anoxic environment, the highest mean content of Cu-P_1 pool was recorded at 48W (0.63 μg g^{-1}) (Table 2.4).

Table 2.4: Concentration of Water Soluble and Exchangeable Pool of Cu (Cu-P_1)

Time Interval	Inorganic Source			Organic source			Mean		
	Oxic	Anoxic	Av	Oxic	Anoxic	Av	Oxic	Anoxic	Av
T_{1W}	4.56	3.74	4.15	0.37	0.59	0.48	2.46	2.02	2.24
T_{2W}	4.41	3.45	3.93	0.65	0.51	0.58	2.53	1.99	2.26
T_{4W}	3.82	3.47	3.64	1.15	0.59	0.87	2.32	2.03	2.17
T_{6W}	3.70	3.62	3.66	0.82	0.41	0.62	2.26	2.01	2.14
T_{8W}	3.66	3.18	3.42	0.82	0.28	0.55	2.22	1.73	1.98
T_{16W}	3.65	2.73	3.19	0.75	0.46	0.60	2.12	1.59	1.86
T_{32W}	2.76	2.60	2.68	0.78	0.50	0.64	1.67	1.55	1.61
T_{48W}	2.61	2.27	2.44	0.59	0.63	0.61	1.59	1.45	1.52
T_{16M}	2.48	1.75	2.12	0.57	0.39	0.48	1.60	1.07	1.34
Av.	3.52	2.88	3.25	0.72	0.48	0.60	2.09	1.72	
S.e.m.	0.03	0.03	0.06	0.04	0.09	0.09	0.12		
L.S.D.	0.09	0.09	0.18	0.12	0.26	0.26	0.36		

Carbonate Bound (Cu-P_2) pool

The mean concentration of Cu-P_2 pool was higher under anoxic environment. Enriched sludge maintained higher mean concentration of Cu-P_2 pool as compared to the inorganic source. The mean content of Cu-P_2 pool declined with incubation period (Figures 2.4 to 2.6). With inorganic source under oxic and anoxic environments, the highest mean concentration of Cu-P_2 pool was recorded at 1W. With enriched sludge, the highest mean content of Cu-P_2 pool was recorded at 2W under oxic environment (40.42 μg g^{-1}) and anoxic environment (38.55 μg g^{-1}) (Table 2.5).

Organically Bound (Cu-P_3) Pool

The mean concentration of Cu-P_3 pool was found to be higher under anoxic environment as compared to oxic environment. Inorganic source maintained higher concentration of Cu-P_3 pool as compared to enriched sludge. Cu-P_3 pool declined with incubation period (Figures 2.4 to 2.6).

Table 2.5: NaOAc Extractable Pool of Cu (Cu-P_2)

Time Interval	Inorganic Source			Organic Source			Mean		
	Oxic	Anoxic	Av	Oxic	Anoxic	Av	Oxic	Anoxic	Av
T_{1W}	23.45	30.74	27.10	38.37	35.74	37.05	30.91	32.71	31.81
T_{2W}	22.63	29.68	26.15	40.42	38.55	39.49	31.52	33.63	32.58
T_{4W}	21.38	28.67	25.03	39.81	38.46	39.13	30.20	33.58	31.89
T_{6W}	21.28	28.71	24.99	39.02	37.63	38.33	29.82	32.86	31.34
T_{8W}	20.77	28.10	24.43	38.36	36.47	37.42	29.05	31.94	30.50
T_{16W}	20.49	27.40	23.95	37.72	36.56	37.14	28.52	30.95	29.73
T_{32W}	19.22	26.70	22.96	37.33	35.20	36.27	27.30	29.88	28.59
T_{48W}	18.63	26.33	22.48	36.54	33.42	34.98	27.00	28.90	27.95
T_{16M}	17.34	25.50	21.42	35.38	32.30	33.84	27.72	31.84	29.78
Av.	20.58	27.64	24.28	38.11	36.04	37.07	29.12	31.81	
S.e.m.	0.03	0.03	0.06	0.04	0.09	0.09	0.12		
L.S.D.	0.09	0.09	0.18	0.12	0.26	0.26	0.37		

With inorganic source, under oxic environment, the highest mean concentration of Cu-P_3 pool was found at 1W (3.28 µg g^{-1}) while in inorganically polluted soils, the highest mean concentration of Cu-P_3 pool was noted at 6W (9.98 µg g^{-1}). In enriched sludge amended soil, under oxic environment, the highest mean content of Cu-P_3 pool was detected at 2W (5.27 µg g^{-1}) with enriched sludge, it was observed at 48W (2.60 µg g^{-1}) (Table 2.6).

Table 2.6: Organically Bound Pool of Cu (Cu-P_2)

Time Interval	Inorganic Source			Organic Source			Mean		
	Oxic	Anoxic	Av	Oxic	Anoxic	Av	Oxic	Anoxic	Av
T_{1W}	3.28	7.75	5.52	2.17	0.81	1.49	2.73	4.75	3.74
T_{2W}	3.17	8.70	5.93	5.27	1.27	3.27	4.22	5.63	4.92
T_{4W}	2.90	9.41	6.16	4.73	1.39	3.06	3.48	5.69	4.58
T_{6W}	2.56	9.98	6.27	4.06	0.74	2.40	2.98	5.09	4.03
T_{8W}	2.83	9.44	6.13	3.40	1.08	2.24	2.81	4.96	3.89
T_{16W}	2.04	8.85	5.44	3.50	1.36	2.43	2.24	4.95	3.59
T_{32W}	1.68	8.43	5.05	2.79	1.47	2.13	1.66	4.81	3.24
T_{48W}	1.89	7.09	4.49	2.44	2.53	2.48	1.77	3.09	2.43
T_{16M}	1.62	5.41	3.52	1.64	0.76	1.20	2.48	4.84	3.66
Av.	2.44	8.41	5.39	3.33	1.27	2.30	2.71	4.87	
S.e.m.	0.02	0.02	0.04	0.03	0.06	0.06	0.09		
L.S.D.	0.06	0.06	0.13	0.09	0.19	0.19	0.26		

Reducible ($Cu\text{-}P_4$) Pool

The mean content of $Cu\text{-}P_4$ pool was higher under oxic environment than anoxic environment. The mean concentration of $Cu\text{-}P_4$ pool was higher with enriched sludge than inorganic salt. The concentration of $Cu\text{-}F_4$ fraction increased with time with some intermediate fluctuations and the highest value was noted at the end of incubation period i.e. 16 months (Figures 2.4 to 2.6). Except in sludge amended soil, the highest mean concentration of $Cu\text{-}P_4$ pool was observed at the end of incubation. With the time of incubation, the mean content of $Cu\text{-}P_4$ increases (Table 2.7).

Table 2.7: Reducible Pool of Cu ($Cu\text{-}P_4$)

Time Interval	Inorganic Source			Organic Source			Mean		
	Oxic	Anoxic	Av	Oxic	Anoxic	Av	Oxic	Anoxic	Av
T_{1W}	62.64	57.37	60.00	2.17	0.81	1.49	32.41	30.24	31.32
T_{2W}	65.66	59.66	62.66	5.27	1.27	3.27	35.46	31.44	33.45
T_{4W}	66.21	60.41	63.31	4.73	1.39	3.06	35.13	31.51	33.32
T_{6W}	66.95	60.71	63.83	4.06	0.74	2.40	35.17	31.69	33.43
T_{8W}	67.46	61.62	64.54	3.40	1.08	2.24	35.12	32.72	33.92
T_{16W}	67.94	62.64	65.29	3.50	1.36	2.43	35.19	33.43	34.31
T_{32W}	68.57	64.36	66.47	2.79	1.47	2.13	35.11	34.02	34.56
T_{48W}	68.56	65.50	67.03	2.44	2.53	2.48	35.10	33.68	34.39
T_{16M}	69.41	66.60	68.01	1.64	0.76	1.20	36.37	31.98	34.18
Av.	67.04	62.69	64.57	3.33	1.27	2.30	35.01	32.30	
S.e.m.	0.03	0.03	0.06	0.04	0.08	0.08	0.11		
L.S.D.	0.08	0.08	0.17	0.11	0.23	0.23	0.33		

Residual ($Cu\text{-}P_5$) Pool

The mean concentration of $Cu\text{-}P_5$ pool was higher under oxic environment as compared to anoxic environment. The mean concentration of this fraction was also higher with enriched sludge than inorganic salt. The mean concentration of this fraction increased (Figures 2.4 to 2.6).

With inorganic source, the highest concentration of $Cu\text{-}P_5$ pool was noted at 16 M under both oxic environment (30.49 µg g^{-1}) and anoxic environments (20.78 µg g^{-1}). With enriched sludge, the highest mean concentration of $Cu\text{-}P_5$ pool was detected at 1W under Oxic environment (50.49 µg g^{-1}) and anoxic environments (51.44 µg g^{-1}) (Table 2.8).

Table 2.8: Residual Pool of Cu (Cu-P_5)

Time Interval	Inorganic Source			Organic Source			Mean		
	Oxic	Anoxic	Av	Oxic	Anoxic	Av	Oxic	Anoxic	Av
T_{1W}	26.73	20.27	23.50	50.49	51.80	51.15	38.61	35.57	37.09
T_{2W}	25.58	19.35	22.47	43.23	51.24	47.24	34.41	34.74	34.57
T_{4W}	25.64	18.42	22.03	43.53	50.80	47.16	33.92	34.51	34.22
T_{6W}	25.46	16.56	21.01	42.20	50.58	46.39	33.60	34.53	34.07
T_{8W}	25.50	18.23	21.86	41.71	49.36	45.53	33.67	33.54	33.60
T_{16W}	26.66	18.48	22.57	41.54	48.81	45.18	33.43	34.27	33.85
T_{32W}	26.77	17.71	22.24	40.67	48.03	44.35	34.04	33.59	33.81
T_{48W}	28.58	19.74	24.16	40.09	47.43	43.76	35.00	33.07	34.03
T_{16M}	30.49	20.78	25.64	39.51	45.36	42.43	55.98	34.05	45.02
Av.	26.82	18.84	22.83	42.55	49.27	45.91	34.69	34.05	
S.e.m.	0.03	0.03	0.06	0.04	0.09	0.07	0.12		
L.S.D.	0.08	0.08	0.18	0.12	0.25	0.25	0.36		

Different Extracts

DTPA Extractable Cu in Soils (Cu-DTPA)

The mean concentration of Cu-DTPA pool was higher under anoxic as compared to oxic environment. The mean content of Cu-DTPA was the highest in enriched sludge amended soils as compared to the soils enriched with inorganic salts as a source of metal. The mean concentration of Cu-DTPA was the highest at 6W of incubation and declined at later incubation periods (Figures 2.4 to 2.6).

In inorganic salt amended soils, under oxic environment, the mean concentration of Cu-DTPA was highest at 6W (53.59 μg g^{-1}) while under anoxic environment, the highest mean concentration of Cu-DTPA was recorded at 8W (47.63μg g^{-1}). In sludge enriched soils, under oxic environment, the highest mean content of Cu-DTPA was recorded at 6W (16.71μg g^{-1}) and under anoxic environment, the peak concentration of this form was noted at 8W (25.45μg g^{-1}) (Table 2.9).

1M $CaCl_2$ extractable Cu in soils (Cu-$CaCl_2$)

Under oxic environment, the mean concentration of Cu-$CaCl_2$ was higher as compared to anoxic environment. The mean concentration of Cu-$CaCl_2$ was also higher with inorganic source as compared to enriched sludge. The mean concentration of Cu-$CaCl_2$ form reached highest concentration at 6W and declined in the later stages of incubation (Figure 2.4 to 2.6). When inorganic salt was the source of metal, under oxic environment, the highest mean concentration of Cu-$CaCl_2$ form was recorded at 8W (2.59μg g^{-1}). Under anoxic environment, the highest mean concentration was recorded at 2W (3.79μg g^{-1}). With enriched sludge, the highest mean concentration of Cu-$CaCl_2$ extractable form was noted at 32W (3.96μg g^{-1}) and with enriched sludge, under anoxic environment, it was found to be the highest at 4W (1.64 μg g^{-1}) (Table 2.10).

Table 2.9: DTPA Extractable Pool of Cu (Cu-DTPA)

Time Interval	Inorganic Source			Organic Source			Mean		
	Oxic	Anoxic	Av	Oxic	Anoxic	Av	Oxic	Anoxic	Av
T_{1W}	48.37	44.30	46.33	13.71	19.83	16.77	31.04	31.28	31.16
T_{2W}	47.56	42.74	45.15	13.45	18.76	16.10	30.50	33.20	31.85
T_{4W}	47.31	42.84	45.07	12.68	18.63	15.65	32.01	33.13	32.57
T6W	53.59	43.68	48.64	16.71	19.74	18.23	33.68	33.18	33.43
T_{8W}	51.62	47.63	49.63	15.74	25.45	20.60	31.68	35.56	33.62
T_{16W}	49.86	46.62	48.24	14.83	23.69	19.26	31.11	33.22	32.17
T_{32W}	49.61	45.67	47.64	13.51	21.50	17.50	29.02	30.75	29.88
T_{48W}	47.47	42.75	45.11	12.61	18.75	15.68	27.09	27.97	27.53
T_{16M}	43.61	40.62	42.12	10.56	15.32	12.94	41.59	32.14	36.86
Av.	69.41	44.10	46.44	13.76	20.19	16.97	31.97	32.27	
S.e.m.	0.03	0.03	0.06	0.04	0.08	0.08	0.11		
L.S.D.	0.08	0.08	0.17	0.11	0.23	0.23	0.33		

Table 2.10: $CaCl_2$ Extractable Pool of Cu (Cu-$CaCl_2$)

Time Interval	Inorganic Source			Organic Source			Mean		
	Oxic	Anoxic	Av	Oxic	Anoxic	Av	Oxic	Anoxic	Av
T_{1W}	1.05	3.67	2.36	2.63	1.33	1.98	1.84	2.56	2.20
T_{2W}	1.63	3.79	2.71	1.91	1.53	1.72	1.77	2.18	1.98
T_{4W}	1.60	3.40	2.50	2.73	1.64	2.19	2.25	2.24	2.25
T_{6W}	1.80	2.93	2.37	2.90	1.13	2.02	2.94	1.57	2.25
T_{8W}	2.59	2.83	2.71	3.29	0.87	2.08	2.73	1.47	2.10
T_{16W}	1.51	2.01	1.76	3.26	0.67	1.97	2.38	1.07	1.73
T_{32W}	1.10	2.08	1.59	3.96	0.69	2.32	1.27	1.11	1.19
T_{48W}	0.88	1.46	1.17	3.67	0.76	2.22	1.17	0.96	1.06
T_{16M}	0.68	1.09	0.88	1.66	0.83	1.25	2.16	1.82	1.99
Av.	1.43	2.58	2.00	2.89	1.05	1.97	2.06	1.66	
S.e.m.	0.02	0.02	0.04	0.03	0.06	0.06	0.88		
L.S.D.	0.06	0.06	0.13	0.09	0.18	0.18	0.26		

Therefore, bioavailability of Cu was much higher with inorganic source as compared to enriched sludge and it was enhanced under anoxic environment during the later stage of incubation possibly due to slower microbial activity and less incorporation of released metal in residual fraction under flooding water regime.

Nickel

Chemical Pools

The changes in the concentrations of different chemical pools of Ni in different soils polluted by inorganic or enriched organic sludge under oxic or anoxic environment are presented in Figures 2.7 to 2.9 (Tables 2.11-2.17).

Table 2.11: Concentration of Water Soluble and Exchangeable Pool of Ni (Ni-P_1)

Time Interval	Inorganic Source			Organic Source			Mean		
	Oxic	Anoxic	Av	Oxic	Anoxic	Av	Oxic	Anoxic	Av
T_{1W}	16.43	6.55	11.49	2.80	1.55	2.17	9.62	4.05	6.83
T_{2W}	15.34	5.82	10.58	2.83	1.73	2.28	9.08	3.78	6.43
T_{4W}	14.84	5.96	10.40	2.43	1.74	2.08	8.64	9.85	6.24
T_{6W}	14.46	5.97	10.08	2.16	1.60	1.88	8.31	3.65	5.98
T_{8W}	14.11	5.43	9.77	2.01	1.46	1.74	8.06	3.44	5.75
T_{16W}	13.63	4.58	9.10	1.76	1.42	1.59	7.70	3.00	5.35
T_{32W}	13.97	4.52	9.24	1.43	1.00	1.22	7.70	2.76	5.23
T_{48W}	12.62	3.92	9.24	2.18	1.41	1.79	7.40	2.67	5.03
T_{16M}	12.60	3.48	8.27	1.76	1.19	1.47	7.18	2.33	4.76
Av.	14.22	5.11	9.66	2.15	1.46	1.80	8.19	3.28	
S.e.m.	0.032	0.032	0.068	0.045	0.096	0.096	0.136		
L.S.D.	0.091	0.091	0.194	0.124	0.274	0.274	0.388		

Table 2.12: NaOAc Extractable Pool of Ni (Ni-P_2)

Time Interval	Inorganic Source			Organic Source			Mean		
	Oxic	Anoxic	Av	Oxic	Anoxic	Av	Oxic	Anoxic	Av
T_{1W}	2.26	2.38	2.31	3.65	2.56	3.11	2.95	2.47	2.71
T_{2W}	3.58	4.67	4.13	3.67	2.54	3.10	3.62	3.60	3.61
T_{4W}	4.62	4.83	4.73	4.36	3.88	4.12	4.49	4.36	4.43
T_{6W}	4.27	5.40	4.84	5.32	3.50	4.41	4.79	4.45	4.62
T_{8W}	3.87	5.77	4.82	5.43	3.46	4.45	4.65	4.62	4.63
T_{16W}	3.47	4.64	4.05	5.32	3.55	4.44	4.39	4.10	4.25
T_{32W}	2.87	4.55	3.71	4.79	2.76	3.78	3.83	3.66	3.74
T_{48W}	2.16	3.63	2.90	3.70	1.85	2.78	2.93	2.74	2.84
T_{16M}	1.37	2.44	1.91	2.44	1.88	2.71	2.46	2.16	2.31
Av.	3.16	4.26	3.71	4.26	2.89	3.65	3.79	3.57	
S.e.m.	0.037	0.037	0.078	0.052	0.111	0.111	0.157		
L.S.D.	0.105	0.105	0.224	0.149	0.316	0.316	0.447		

Table 2.13: Organically Bound Pool of Ni (Ni-P_3)

Time Interval	Inorganic Source			Organic Source			Mean		
	Oxic	Anoxic	Av	Oxic	Anoxic	Av	Oxic	Anoxic	Av
T_{1W}	0.66	1.62	1.14	2.61	0.73	1.67	1.64	1.17	1.40
T_{2W}	0.90	2.55	1.72	2.54	0.91	1.72	1.72	1.73	1.72
T_{4W}	0.88	2.62	1.75	2.70	0.88	1.79	1.79	1.75	1.77
T_{6W}	0.86	2.52	1.69	2.47	1.38	1.93	1.67	1.95	1.81
T_{8W}	1.04	3.73	2.38	3.60	1.41	2.50	2.32	2.57	2.44
T_{16W}	1.46	3.37	2.41	3.43	0.77	2.10	2.44	2.07	2.26
T_{32W}	1.37	2.79	2.08	4.42	0.91	2.66	2.89	1.85	2.37
T_{48W}	1.53	2.60	2.07	4.82	0.91	2.86	3.17	1.76	2.46
T_{16M}	1.09	2.44	1.77	4.25	0.89	2.57	2.67	1.67	2.17
Av.	1.09	2.69	1.89	3.43	0.98	2.20	2.26	1.83	
S.e.m.	0.034	0.035	0.073	0.049	0.104	0.104	0.147		
L.S.D.	0.099	0.099	0.209	0.140	0.296	0.296	0.419		

Table 2.14: Reducible Pool of Ni (Ni-P-$_4$)

Time Interval	Inorganic Source			Organic Source			Mean		
	Oxic	Anoxic	Av	Oxic	Anoxic	Av	Oxic	Anoxic	Av
T_{1W}	3.83	6.32	5.08	2.32	0.53	1.42	3.07	4.115	3.595
T_{2W}	4.55	7.70	6.13	2.84	1.56	2.20	3.69	3.545	3.620
T_{4W}	4.48	7.55	6.02	2.04	1.04	1.54	3.26	3.285	3.405
T_{6W}	4.76	6.66	5.71	2.57	0.86	1.71	3.66	4.250	3.945
T_{8W}	4.60	5.53	5.07	2.68	0.81	1.74	3.64	3.265	3.543
T_{16W}	5.00	7.64	6.32	2.61	0.74	1.68	3.80	2.410	3.375
T_{32W}	5.32	5.72	5.52	2.64	0.71	1.68	3.98	2.445	3.348
T_{48W}	5.47	4.08	4.78	3.36	0.81	2.09	4.42	3.875	4.138
T_{16M}	5.77	6.84	6.31	3.03	0.91	1.97	4.40	3.667	3.719
Av.	4.86	6.45	5.66	2.68	0.88	1.78	3.77	3.429	
S.e.m.	0.039	0.039	0.082	0.054	0.116	0.116	0.163		
L.S.D.	0.11	0.11	0.23	0.16	0.33	0.33	0.47		

Table 2.15: Residual Pool of Ni (Ni-P_5)

Time Interval	Inorganic Source			Organic Source			Mean		
	Oxic	Anoxic	Av	Oxic	Anoxic	Av	Oxic	Anoxic	Av
T_{1W}	65.53	62.32	63.93	77.63	82.57	80.10	71.58	72.44	72.01
T_{2W}	65.53	58.30	61.92	75.63	81.33	78.48	70.58	69.82	70.20
T_{4W}	63.61	58.78	61.20	75.71	79.65	77.68	69.66	69.22	69.44
T_{6W}	64.58	58.32	61.45	74.40	80.42	77.41	69.49	69.40	69.43
T_{8W}	64.83	58.32	61.87	73.85	80.55	77.20	69.34	69.73	69.53
T_{16W}	65.55	58.91	62.06	74.38	80.56	77.47	69.96	69.57	69.77
T_{32W}	65.52	58.57	63.53	74.18	81.64	77.91	69.85	71.59	70.72
T_{48W}	67.32	61.53	66.42	73.48	82.42	77.95	70.40	73.97	72.18
T_{16M}	68.74	65.51	67.13	74.69	82.48	78.59	71.71	73.37	72.54
Av.	65.69	60.72	63.21	74.88	81.29	78.09	70.29	71.01	
S.e.m.	0.033	0.033	0.070	0.047	0.099	0.099	0.139		
L.S.D.	0.09	0.09	0.20	0.13	0.28	0.28	0.40		

Table 2.16: DTPA Extractable Pool of Ni (Ni-DTPA)

Time Interval	Inorganic Source			Organic Source			Mean		
	Oxic	Anoxic	Av	Oxic	Anoxic	Av	Oxic	Anoxic	Av
T_{1W}	14.48	8.48	11.48	3.67	2.61	3.14	9.08	5.55	7.31
T_{2W}	19.46	9.66	14.56	2.91	1.95	2.43	11.18	5.81	8.50
T_{4W}	18.68	8.67	13.68	2.51	2.03	2.27	10.60	5.35	7.98
T_{6W}	18.59	11.74	15.17	2.46	1.84	2.15	10.53	6.79	8.66
T_{8W}	16.66	10.70	13.68	2.28	1.74	2.01	9.47	6.22	7.84
T_{16W}	15.83	9.69	12.76	1.72	1.75	1.73	8.77	5.72	7.25
T_{32W}	14.58	9.42	12.00	1.81	1.73	1.77	8.20	5.57	6.88
T_{48W}	11.67	8.79	10.23	1.74	1.66	1.70	6.71	5.22	5.96
T_{16M}	9.66	6.70	8.18	1.71	1.33	1.52	5.68	4.02	4.85
Av.	15.51	9.32	12.41	2.31	1.85	2.08	8.91	5.58	
S.e.m.	0.032	0.03	0.07	0.046	0.097	0.10	0.137		
L.S.D.	0.092	0.092	0.195	0.129	0.275	0.275	0.389		

Table 2.17: $CaCl_2$ Extractable Pool of Ni (Ni-$CaCl_2$)

Time Interval	Inorganic Source			Organic Source			Mean		
	Oxic	Anoxic	Av	Oxic	Anoxic	Av	Oxic	Anoxic	Av
T_{1W}	17.54	26.68	22.11	8.65	22.47	15.56	13.10	24.57	18.83
T_{2W}	16.67	26.62	21.65	7.42	20.52	13.97	12.04	23.57	17.81
T_{4W}	16.00	25.85	20.93	6.77	20.44	13.60	11.38	23.14	17.26
T_{6W}	15.58	25.25	20.41	6.56	20.52	13.54	11.07	22.88	16.98
T_{8W}	15.53	24.80	20.16	5.59	19.60	12.59	10.56	22.19	16.38
T_{16W}	14.86	22.49	18.68	5.35	18.42	11.88	10.11	20.45	15.28
T_{32W}	13.58	22.63	18.11	4.62	18.30	11.46	9.10	20.46	14.78
T_{48W}	12.83	21.71	17.27	4.35	16.54	10.45	8.59	19.13	13.86
T_{16M}	11.61	20.65	16.13	3.74	15.62	9.68	7.67	18.14	12.09
Av.	14.91	24.07	19.49	5.90	19.16	12.53	10.40	21.62	
S.e.m.	0.032	0.032	0.068	0.046	0.097	0.097	0.137		
L.S.D.	0.09	0.09	0.19	0.13	0.28	0.28	0.39		

Water Soluble and Exchangeable (Ni-P_1) Pool

The mean concentration of Ni-P_1 pool was higher under oxic environment than anoxic environment. Ni-P_1 pool was higher in inorganically polluted soil as compared to organically polluted one. The mean concentration of Ni-P_1 pool decreased with incubation period (Figures 2.7 to 2.9).

In inorganic salt amended soils under oxic and anoxic environments, the highest mean concentration of Ni-P_1 pool was observed at 1W (16.43µg g^{-1} and 6.55µg g^{-1} respectively). With enriched sludge, under oxic environment, the highest mean concentration of Ni-P_1 pool was noted at 2W (2.83µg g^{-1}) while under anoxic environment, it was observed at 4W (1.74µg g^{-1}) (Table 2.11).

NaOAc Extractable (Ni-P_2) Pool

The mean concentration of Ni-P_2 pool was found to be higher under oxic environment as compared to anoxic environment. Enriched sludge maintained higher mean concentration of Ni-P_2 pool as compared to inorganic salts and the mean concentration of Ni-P_2 pool increased with incubation time attaining the highest mean concentration around 6 to 8W (Figures 2.7 to 2.9).

With inorganic source, under oxic environment, the highest concentration of Ni-P_2 pool was noticed at 6W (4.62µg g^{-1}) while under anoxic environment, highest mean concentration of Ni-P_2 pool was recorded at 8W (5.77µg g^{-1}). With sludge under oxic environment, the highest mean concentration of Ni-P_2 pool was observed at 8W (5.43 µg g^{-1}) while under anoxic environment, it was observed at 4W (3.88µg g^{-1}) (Table 2.12).

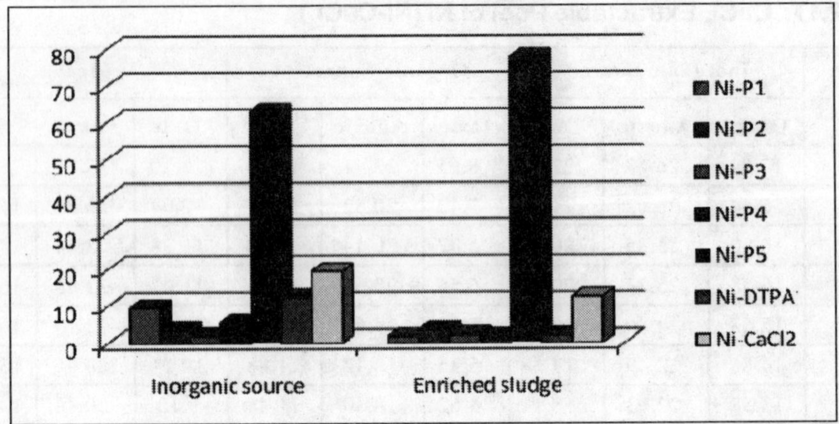

Fig. 2.7: Effect of Source on Different Chemical Pools and DTPA & $CaCl_2$ Extractable Pools of Ni

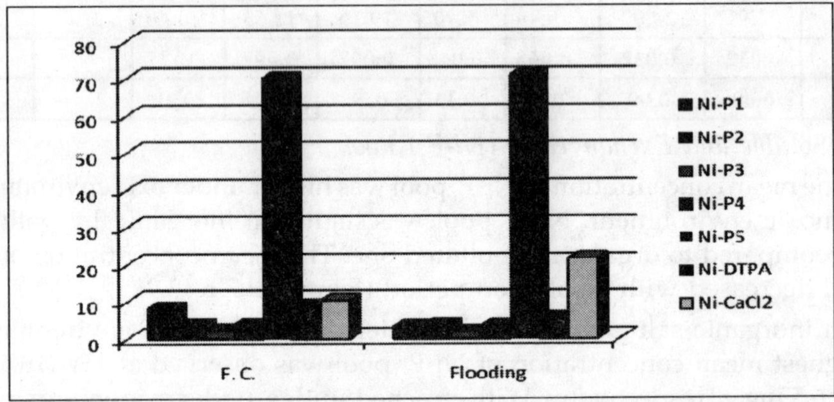

Fig. 2.8: Effect of Moisture Levels on Different Chemical Pools and DTPA & $CaCl_2$ Extractable Pools of Ni

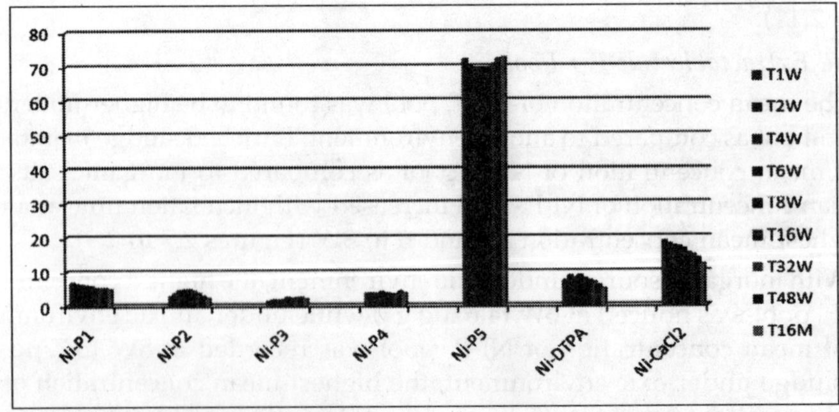

Fig. 2.9: Effect of Incubation Period on Different Chemical Pools and Extractable Pools of Ni

Organically Bound (Oxidizable) (Ni-P_3) Pool

The mean concentration of Ni-P_3 pool was found to be higher under oxic environment as compared to anoxic environment. Sludge maintained higher mean concentration of Ni-P_3 pool as compared to inorganic salts. The mean concentration of this pool increased with the incubation period (Figures 2.7 to 2.9).

When inorganic salts were the source of amendment, under oxic environment, the highest concentration of Ni-P_3 pool was recorded at 48W (1.53µg g^{-1}) while under anoxic environment, this content was found to be the highest at 8W (3.73µg g^{-1}). With sludge, under oxic environment, the highest mean concentration of Ni-P_3 pool was observed at 48W (4.82µg g^{-1}) and under anoxic environment, the highest mean concentration of Ni-P_3 pool was noted at 8W (1.41µg g^{-1}) (Table 2.13).

Iron and Mn oxide bound (Ni-P_4) Pool

The mean concentration of Ni-P_4 pool was higher under anoxic environment as compared to oxic environment. The mean concentration this pool was higher with sludge as compared to inorganic salts. The mean concentration of Ni-P_4 pool significantly increased with incubation period (Figures 2.6-2.8). Irrespective of moisture levels and source, the highest concentration of Ni-P_4 pool was recorded at the end of incubation (48W to16M) period (Table 2.12).

Residual (Ni-P_5) Pool

The mean concentration of Ni-P_5 pool was higher under anoxic environment as compared to oxic environment. The mean concentration of Ni-P_5 pool was also higher with sludge than inorganic salts. The mean concentration of Ni-P_5 pool was increased with incubation period (Figures 2.7 to 2.9).

With inorganic salt, under oxic as well as anoxic environments, the highest mean concentration of Ni-P_5 pool was noted at 16M (68.74µg g^{-1} and 65.51µg g^{-1} respectively). With sludge, under both oxic and anoxic environments, the highest concentration of Ni-P_5 pool was noted at 1W (77.63µg g^{-1} and 82.57µg g^{-1} respectively) (Table 2.14).

Different Extracts

DTPA Extractable Ni in Soils (Ni-DTPA)

The mean concentration of Ni-DTPA was higher under oxic environment than anoxic environment. Inorganic source maintained mean higher concentration of Ni-DTPA as compared to sludge. The mean concentration of Ni-DTPA decreased with incubation (Figures 2.7 to 2.9).

With inorganic salt as source of nickel, under oxic environment, the highest concentration of Ni-DTPA form was observed at 2W (19.46µg g^{-1})

while under anoxic environment, the highest mean concentration of Ni-DTPA was observed at 6W (11.74μg g^{-1}). With enriched sludge, under oxic and anoxic environments, the highest mean concentration of Ni-DTPA form was noted at 1W (3.67μg g^{-1} and 2.61 μg g^{-1} respectively) (Table 2.16).

1M $CaCl_2$ Extractable Ni in Soils (Ni-$CaCl_2$)

The mean concentration of Ni-$CaCl_2$ was higher under anoxic environment as compared to oxic environment. The mean concentration of Ni-$CaCl_2$ was higher with inorganic salts than enriched sludge. The mean concentration of Ni-$CaCl_2$ decreased with incubation period (Figures 2.7 to 2.9).

Irrespective of the metal source and moisture levels, the highest concentration of Ni-$CaCl_2$ form was noted at 1W (17.54μg g^{-1}, 26.68μg g^{-1}, 8.65μg g^{-1} and 22.47μg g^{-1}) (Table 2.17).

Thus, bioavailability of Ni was observed to be higher with inorganic source than organic source and enhanced under oxic environment and decreased during later stages of incubation.

DISCUSSION

The experimental results on metal addition and incubation study of samples sample were similar to the results observed by Kandpal et al. (2004) as metal spiking and incubation increased P_1, P_2 and P_4 pools of Cu and Ni, P_3 fraction of Cu and decreased P_3 pool of Ni and P_5 pool of both the metals. Our results suggested that availability of Cu and Ni decreased under anoxic environment especially in sludge amended soils. Dry yield of spinach was recorded higher in sludge amended soils as compared to inorganic salt polluted soils (Tewari et al., 2006) as availability of metals (metal toxicity) decreased in sludge amended soils. Singh & Nongkynrih (1999) explained that on flooding, pH values of soils increased which cause a decrease in the solubility of the native soil copper. Submergence had been reported to decrease availability of Cu in soils due to the precipitation of Cu as sulfide under reducing condition (Dutta et al., 1989). Transformation of added heavy metals in soils under flooded condition was studied by Misra et al. (1990) and observed that anoxic environment decreased metal availability in polluted soils. During the eight annual applications of Cu-sulfate and Cu-enriched manure to field-soils, copper was observed to bind with the organic and oxide associated fractions (Payne et al., 1988). In our study also the Cu was bound to residual and organically bound pool. According to Han & Banin (1999) during prolonged incubation at the field capacity moisture, added Cu and Ni were transformed into the ERO, OM and RO fractions. On the other hand, during prolonged incubation at saturated conditions, Cu and Ni were mainly transferred to the RO and OM fractions (Han & Banin, 1997). Tewari et al. (2009) observed that added Cu was transformed to Fe-Mn oxide fraction (more stable) at the end of 16 month incubation under oxic and anoxic environment. Han & Banin (2000) studied long-term transformation pathways, kinetics and liability of Cd, Cu, Co, Ni, Zn, Mn, Fe and V in two arid-zone soils under a saturated water regime. During 16 month of incubation, Ni was observed to be transformed into Fe-Mn oxide fraction (Tewari et al., 2010). The distribution of Ni in native soil was dependent on soil properties. Low pH favoured the soluble plus exchangeable fraction, while higher pH favoured Fe/Mn oxides, clay-Fe/Mn oxide and residual fractions (Tu, 1996). Added Cu to paddy soil under 75% field capacity, wetting-drying cycle and flooding moisture regimes was observed to transformed from the exchangeable fraction to more stable fractions such as Fe-Mn oxide and organic matter bound (Zheng and Zhang, 2011).

CONCLUSION

From our results, it appeared that due to metal enrichment and incubation, bio-oxidation of organic carbon and consequent acidification affected released residual pool of both metals (Cu and Ni) and organically bound pool of Ni in enriched sludge. The released metals might be incorporated into reducible or Fe-Mn oxide bound pool in case of Ni and Cu, into organically bound pool in case of Cu, into NaOAc extractable pool in case of Ni and Cu and invariably increased the water soluble and exchangeable form of both the tested heavy metals. DTPA and $CaCl_2$ extraction of Cu & Ni suggested that the bioavailability of these metals was higher with inorganic source under oxic environment and decreased with the incubation time. Thus, excessive Cu and Ni addition through inorganic source especially under oxic environment should be avoided to check accumulation of both the metals in food chain.

REFERENCES

Ahnstrom, Z.S. and Parker, D.R. (1999): Development and Assessment of a Sequential Extraction Procedure for the Fractionation of Soil Cadmium, *Soil Science Society of American Journal*, 63: 1650-1658.

Bower, C.A., Reitemeter, R.F. and Fireman, M. (1952): Exchangeable Cation Analysis of Saline and Alkali Soils, *Soil Science*, 73(4): 251-262.

Cheraghi, M., Lorestani, B. and Yousefi, N. (2009): Effect of Waste Water on Heavy Metal Accumulation in Hamedan Province Vegetables, *International Journal of Botany*, 5(2): 190-193.

Dudka, S. and Chlopecka, A. (1990): Effect of Solid-phase Speciation on Metal Mobility and Phytoavailability in Sludge Amended Soil, *Water, Air and Soil Pollution*, 51: 153-160.

Dutta, D., Mandal, B. and Mandal, L. N. (1989): Decrease in Availability of Zinc and Copper in Acidic to Near Neutral Soils on Submergence, *Soil Science*, 147: 187-195.

Emmerich, W.E., Lund, L.J., Page, A.L. and Chang, A.C. (1984): Accumulation of Heavy Metals in Sewage Sludge-treated Soils, *Journal of Environmental Quality*, 11: 174-178.

Han, F.X. and Banin, A. (1997): Long Term Transformation and Redistribution of Potentially Toxic Heavy Metals in Arid Zone Soil: I. Under Saturated Conditions, *Water, Air and Soil Pollution,* 95 (1-4): 399-423.

Han, F.X. and Banin, A. (2000): Long Term Transformations of Cadmium, Copper, Nickel, Zinc, Vanadium, Manganese and Iron in Arid Zone Soils Under Saturated Condition., *Communication to Soil Science and Plant Analysis*, 31(7-8): 943-957.

Han, Feng Xiang and Banin, Amos. (1999): Long-term Transformation and Redistribution of Potentially Toxic Heavy Metals in Arid Zone Soils: II. Incubation at the Field Capacity Moisture Content, *Water, Air and Soil Pollution*, 114(3-4): 221-250.

Jackson, M.L. (1958): Soil Chemical Analysis. Prentice Hall Inc., New Jersey, USA, pp. 38-226.

Jain, A.P. and Pant, G. B. (1994): Solid Waste Management in India. Affordable Water. Supply And Sanitation. 20th WEDC Conference Colombo, Sri Lanka. pp. 177-182.

Kandpal, Geeta, Ram, Bali, Srivastava, P.C. and Singh, S.K. (2004): Effect of Metal Spiking on Different Chemical Pools and Chemically Extractable Fractions of Heavy Metals in Sewage Sludge, *Journal of Hazardous Materials*, 106B: 133-137.

McGrath, S.P. and Cegarra, J. (1992): Chemical Extractability of Heavy Metals during and After Long Term Application of Sewage Sludge to Soil. *Journal of Soil Science*, 43: 313-321.

Misra, A.K., Sarkunan, V., Das, Mira and Nayar, P.K. (1990): Transformation of Added Heavy Metals in Soils Under Flooded Condition, *Journal of the Indian Society of Soil Science*, 38(3): 416-418.

Page, A.L., Miller, R.H. and Kenney, D.R. (1982): Methods of Soil Analysis-Part 2(Ed) No. 9, Agronomy Series ASA-SSSA Publisher, Madison, Wisconsin, U.S.A.

Payne, G.G., Martens, D.C., Winarko, C. and Perera, N.F. (1988): Form and Availability of Copper and Zinc Following Long-term Copper Sulfate and Zinc Sulfate Applications, *Journal of Environmental Quality*, 17(4): 707-711.

Payne, G.G., Martens, D.C., Winarko, C. and Perera, N.F. (1988): Form and Availability.

Purves, D. (1985): Trace-Element Contamination of the Environment, Elsevier, Amsterdam.

Sharma, S.D. and Pande, K.S. (1998): Pollution Studies on Ramganga River at Moradabad-physico-chemical Characteristics and Toxic Metals, *Pollution Research*, 17(2): 201-209.

Silviera, D.J. and Sommers, L.E. (1977): Extractability of Copper, Zinc, Cadmium and Lead in Soils Incubated with Sewage Sludge, *Journal of Environmental Quality*, 6(1): 47-52.

Singh, A.K. and Nongkynrih, P. (1999): Distribution and Transformation of Copper in Wetland Soils and its Availability to Rice Plant, *Journal of Indian Society of Soil Science*, 47(3): 452-457.

Sposito, G., Levesque, C.S., Le Claire, J.P. and Chang, A.C. (1983): Trace Metal Chemistry in Arid-zone Field Soils Amended with Sewage Sludge: III. Effect of Time on the Extraction of Trace Metals. *Soil Science Society of American Journal*, 47: 898-902.

Tewari, Geeta, Srivastava, P.C., Ram, Bali and Tewari, Lalit. (2006): Chemical Fractions and Bioavailability of Heavy Metals in Polluted Soils. *In*: Hudson, Robert C. (ed.), Hazardous Materials in the Soil and Atmosphere: Treatment, Removal and Analysis, Nova Science Publishers. New York, pp. 89-115.

Tewari, Geeta, Tewari, Lalit, Srivastava, P. C. and Ram Bali. (2010): Nickel Chemical Transformation in Polluted Soils as Affected by Metal Sources and Moisture Regime, *Chemical Speciation and Bioavailability*, 22(3): 141-155.

Tewari, Geeta, Tewari, Lalit, Srivastava, P.C. and Ram, Bali. (2009): Chemical Transformation of Copper in Some Sludge Amended Soils, *Archives of Agronomy and Soil Science*, 55(4): 415-427.

Tu, C. (1996): Distribution and Transformation of Native and Added Ni Fractions in Purple Soils from Sichuan Province, *Pedosphere*, 6: 183-192.

W.L. Lindsay, W.L. and Norvell, W.A. (1969): Development of a DTPA Micronutrient Soil Test, Agronomy Abstract, p. 84.

Walkley, A. and Black, I.A. (1934): An Examination of the Degtjareff Method for Determining Organic Carbon in Soils: Effect of Variations in Digestion Conditions and of Inorganic Soil Constituents, *Soil Science*, 63: 251-263.

Young, S.D., Tye, A., Carstensen, A., Resende, L. and Crout, N. (2000): Methods for Determining Labile Cadmium and Zinc in Soil, *European Journal of Soil Science*, 51: 129-136.

Zheng, Shunan and Zhang, Mingkui. (2011): Effect of Moisture Regime on the Redistribution of Heavy Metals in Paddy Soil, *Journal of Environmental Sciences*, 23(3): 434-443.

Pages: 36-47

SOIL CONTAMINATION AND CONSERVATION

Edited by: **Dr. Ezeaku Peter Ikemefuna; Dr. Pawan Kumar 'Bharti'**

ISBN: 978-93-5056-737-1

Edition: **2015**

Published by: **Discovery Publishing House Pvt. Ltd., New Delhi (India)**

Phytoremediation Against Soil Cadmium Contamination by Some Weeds

Priya Bajaj* and **B. Tabassum**

ABSTRACT

Cadmium (Cd) has been in industrial use for a long period of time. Its serious toxicity moved into scientific focus during the middle of the last century. In this review, we discuss various methods regarding the removal of this metal from contaminated soil. In the present study we have tried to analyze the phytoremediating efficiency of *Catharanthus roseus* and *Mentha piperita* with respect to heavy metal cadmium. These plants were grown in soil treated with measured cadmium concentration. Further, cadmium concentration was measured in different plant parts after 20, 40 and 60 days of experiment. The result showed that roots absorb maximum cadmium from soil which is further transported to stem and leaves and accumulated therein. It was also found that *Cathaarnthus roseus* absorbs more cadmium than *Mentha piperita.*

Key words: Cadmium, *Cathaarnthus roseus, Mentha piperita,* Phytoremediation.

Toxicology Laboratory, Department of Zoology, Govt. Raza PG College, Rampur (UP) - 244 901, India.

INTRODUCTION

Heavy metals are currently of much environmental concern. Heavy metals are those metallic elements, which have their atomic weight more than 20 or in other words, with a density higher than 5 g/cm^3. There are 90 naturally occurring elements that are heavy metals, but not all of them are biologically significant. Based on their solubility under physiological conditions, 17 heavy metals may be available for living cells and of importance for organisms and ecosystems (Weast, 1984). Among these metals, Iron, Molybdenum and Manganese are important as micronutrients. Zinc, Nickel, Copper, Vanadium, Cobalt, Tungsten and Chromium are elements with high or low importance as trace elements. Whereas, Cadmium, Arsenic, Mercury, Silver and Lead have no known function as nutrients in the living system and are toxic at very low concentrations (Goldbold and Huttermann, 1985; Breckle, 1991; Nies, 1999; Sogut et al., 2005; Baek et al., 2006). However, elevated concentrations of both essential and nonessential metals can result in growth inhibition and toxicity symptoms (Akinola and Ekiyoyo, 2006).

Geological and anthropogenic activities are potential sources of heavy metal contamination (Dembitsky, 2003). Sources of anthropogenic metal contamination include industrial effluents, fuel production, mining, smelting processes, military operations, utilization of agricultural chemicals, small-scale industries (including battery production, metal products, metal smelting and cable coating industries), brick kilns and coal combustion. One of the prominent sources contributing to increased load of soil contamination is disposal of municipal wastage. These wastes are either dumped on roadsides or used as landfills, while sewage is used for irrigation. These wastes, although useful as a source of nutrients, are also sources of carcinogens and toxic metals. Other sources can include unsafe or excess application of pesticides, fungicides and fertilizers (Zhen-Guo *et al.*, 2002).

Additional potential sources of heavy metals include irrigation water contaminated by sewage and industrial effluent leading to contaminated soils and vegetables *(Bridge, 2004)*. The mobilization of heavy metals by man (through mining from ores and processing for different applications) has led to the contamination of different environmental segments by these elements. They are harmful to humans, animals and tend to bioaccumulate in the food chain. By contaminating food chain, these elements pose a risk to environmental and human health.

As a result of their release and presence in the ecosystems, these pollutants are accumulated by living organisms in their bodies and subsequently biomagnified as they pass from one trophic level to the next. Since man also is at the top of food chain, he is vulnerable to heavy metal pollution. According to (Nriagu, 1996) about 90% of the anthropogenic emissions of heavy metals have occurred since 1900 AD; it is now well recognized that human activities lead to a substantial accumulation of heavy metals in soils on a global scale (e.g. 5.6 – 38 × 106 kg Cadmium/year). These toxic substances are released into the environment and contribute to a variety of toxic effects on living organisms in food chain by bioaccumulation and bio-magnification (Manohar *et al.*, 2006).

Heavy metals, such as arsenic, cadmium, copper, lead; chromium, zinc and nickel are important environmental pollutants, particularly in areas with high anthropogenic pressure (USEPA, 1997). Higher levels of heavy metals disturb the normal physiology and biochemistry of living systems. Activities such as mining, smelting of ores, industrial emissions and application of insecticides and fertilizers have all contributed to elevated levels of heavy metals in the environment. Additional potential sources of heavy metals include irrigation water contaminated with sewage and industrial effluents leading to contamination of soil and water.

Cadmium is one such metal known for its high toxicity at low concentrations and prolonged persistence in the environment. It is widely distributed in the Earth's crust (0.1-0.5 µg/g), the atmosphere (1-5 ng/m^3), marine sediment (~1 µg/g) and sea water (~0.1 µg/L). Cadmium is much less mobile in soils than in air and water. The input of cadmium to the soils is from both natural and anthropogenic sources. Natural sources include underlying bedrock or transported parent material such as alluvium. The cadmium in soils occur at very low levels, but it is added to the soils by other products such as, fertilizers, phospho-gypsum, certain zinc additives, biosolids (sewage sludge), manures and other wastes. It is regularly found in ores together with zinc, copper and lead. Therefore volcanic activity is one major natural reason for a temporary increase in environmental cadmium concentrations. Besides this, increased environmental levels of cadmium occur following the natural weathering of minerals, forest fires and volcanoes.

Larger amounts of cadmium are released following human activities. These include the application of phosphate fertilizers, fossil fuel combustion, the production of iron, steel and non-ferrous metals, cement production and waste incineration. Cadmium is widely used in industrial processes like as an anticorrosive agent, as a stabilizer in PVC products, as a colour pigment, a neutron-absorber in nuclear power plants, and in the fabrication of nickel-cadmium batteries. Phosphate fertilizers load a big amount of cadmium to the environment. Although some cadmium-containing products can be recycled, a large share of the general cadmium pollution is caused by dumping and incinerating cadmium-polluted waste. The anthropogenic sources of cadmium contribute to human exposure to a greater extent due to production, use and disposal of cadmium products and the incineration of cadmium-containing products (Chaney etal., 1997).

Since cadmium is prevalent in all the three main environmental compartments- air, water and soil, the majority of cadmium exposure arises from air and soil, by atmospheric deposition and by the ingestion of vegetables such as lettuce, spinach, celery and cabbage that accumulate cadmium. The main route of exposure to cadmium is inhalation or ingestion via food and drinking water, dermal absorption is rare. Ground water is an important source of water, as the surface water is getting scarcer day-by-day. Discharge of municipal wastewater and industrial effluents either onto land or surface water bodies, may percolate through soil and may affect ground water resources. Agricultural usage is also another route through which metallic ions could percolate to the ground water source. Natural weathering of rocks and stones incorporated with anthropogenic activities like waste disposal, use of chemical fertilizers, pesticide and industrial effluents has increased the density of heavy metals in soil ultimately in groundwater.

Cadmium present in utensils, pottery and trays can be leached out into foods, particularly in foods, which are acidic in nature (fruit juice) due to the presence of organic acids. The additives are added to food to enhance the flavor, taste and to maintain quality but these additives may also contain traces of heavy metals including cadmium. The contaminant include toxic elements like mercury, lead, cadmium, arsenic etc. found in raw food, before processing remain in the food until consumption The food crops grown in industrially polluted soil and soil mixed with from sewage sludge or irrigated with polluted waters may contain increased content ratio of cadmium. The incident of cadmium poisoning resulted from the escape of mining wastes over a period of more than 20 years into the river stream of Jintsu in Japan. The river water irrigated soil and crops cultivated were the reason for outbreak of the disease itai itai.

Currently, conventional remediation methods of heavy metal contaminated soils are expensive and environmentally destructive. Major component of inorganic contaminates are heavy metals (Alloway, 1990) they present a different problem than organic contaminants. Soil microorganisms can degrade organic contaminants, while metals need immobilization or physical removal. Thus, metals render the land unsuitable for plant growth and destroy the biodiversity. Cadmium extraction using physiochemical methods is usually expensive and often suitable only for small areas (Patel et al, 2005), so there is need for the less- expensive cleanup technologies.. Biological methods are suggested as a cheap and efficient alternative for eliminating pollution and recovering heavy metals from soil solutions (Hanif et al, 2009).One of the biological methods is Phyteromediation, emerging as a cost-effective alternative.

Phytoremediation is the direct use of living green plants for in situ, or in place, removal, degradation, or containment of contaminants in soils, sludges, sediments, surface water and groundwater. It mitigates pollutant concentration in contaminated soils, water or air with plants able to contain, degrade, or eliminate metals, pesticides, solvents, explosives, crude oil and its derivatives, and various other contaminants from the media that contain them. Phytoremediation of soil metals has been successfully carried out at military sites, agricultural fields, industrial sites and mine tailings. Application of phytoremediation for the clean-up of industrial waste dump sites contaminated with toxic metals is another important area that has blossomed in recent years. Phytoremediation is an environmentally sound technology for pollution prevention, control and remediation. More importantly, the process is *in situ* thus avoids dramatic landscape disruption and preserves the ecosystem.

Depending on species, metal tolerance of plants involved in phytoremediation may result from two basic strategies- metal exclusion and metal accumulation (Baker, 1981). The exclusion strategy comprise the avoidance of metal uptake and restriction of metal transport to the shoot (De Vos *et al.*,1991), while the accumulation strategy comprises of import of heavy metals through root epidermal cells and their accumulation in the vacuoles and further transport to different parts of the plant body. As a plant-based technology, the success of phytoremediation is inherently dependent upon proper plant selection. Plants used for phytoremediation must be fast growing, containing deep root (about pollutants which are transferred to the depth), easily reproducing and have the ability to accumulate large quantities of environmentally important metal contaminants in their tissues (Cunningham and Ow, 1997; Fischerova *et al*, 2005).

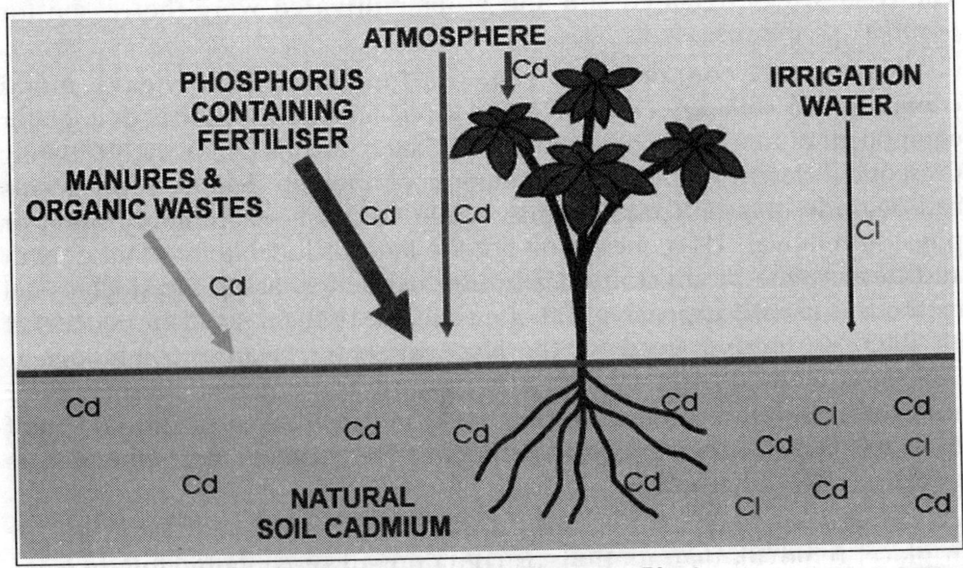

Potential Uptake of Cadmium by Plants

Several researchers have screened fast-growing, high-biomass accumulating plants, including agronomic crops, for their ability to tolerate and accumulate metals in their shoots (Banuelos *et al*, 1997). In the present study we have tried to analyze the phytoremediating efficiency of two plants occurring very commonly in all type of climates, *viz. Catharanthus roseus* and *Mentha piperita* with respect to heavy metal cadmium.

Periwinkle *Catharanthus roseus* (L.) [= Syn. *Vinca rosea* (L.)] is a perennial herb belonging to the family Apocynaceae. It is pantropical in distribution and is found throughout India on wastelands and sandy tracts, especially in the coastal areas and is often grown in gardens for its pink and white flowers that bloom throughout the year. It has erect stem with flexible branches bearing leaves that are simple axillary and terminal clusters. Fruit is a cylindrical follicle with many black seeds. The commercial crop is a mixture of populations having wide morphological and chemical variations with various range of heritability (Kulkerni *et al.*, 1984) due to fair amount of outcrossing existing in the species (Krishnan *et al.*, 1979). The genus Catharanthus has now gained considerable reputation in the therapeutic world for its wide assemblage of over 100 alkaloids including vincristin, vinblastin, ajmaline, ajmalicine and serpentine which are extremely important. Since stress condition provide suitable environment for synthesis and accumulation of secondary metabolites, Catharanthus was chosen to study its phytoremediation efficiency with respect to alkaloid production.

Mentha piperita is the mint plant belonging to the family Lamiaceae (Labiateae) and native of the Mediterranean region, now grown all over the world for the production of menthol from its essential oil which is used in pharmaceutical, perfumery and food industries (Scora & Chang 1997). India is a Major producer of mint with an annual production of about 5000 tones. The bulk of this production comes from Badaun, Bareilly, Bilaspur, Moradabad and Rampur districts of Uttar Pradesh, North India (Tabassum and Bajaj, 2012). It is a perennial, gramineous, stable and aromatic herbaceous plant (Jackson *et al.*, 2004). It grows up to 1 meter (3 feet) high and has slightly hairy serrated leaves with pinkish-mauve flowers arranged in a long conical shape. The plant consists of shoots, having over ground main stems with big leaves and small flowers, stolons, with crawling succulent stems and underground rhizomes. It has underground runners by which it easily propagates. It grows better in acid sandy soils and prefers medium light and soil with high moisture. The essence of this plant, also, is used in producing cosmetics, painkillers for treating fever, headache, cold etc. and in food industry it is used as flavoring for food and confectionaries.

MATERIALS AND METHODS

Collection and Growing of Plants: The plants under investigation viz. *Catharanthus roseus*, *Mentha piperita* and *Curcuma aromatica* were collected from the experimental botanical garden, Govt. Raza PG College, Rampur. The plants were grown in pots filled with ten kilograms of garden soil in laboratory under standard conditions of temperature, humidity and light/ dark cycles. The seedlings were collected from the uncontaminated soils. All the selected seedlings were of uniform size and free of any disease symptoms. With these plants further experiments were performed.

Soil sample preparation: Soil sample was prepared according to the instruction manual. 5 g soil sample was taken and air-dried properly. The dried soil was then ground and sieved. 5 g soil sample (sieved) was collected in an Erlen Meyer flask and 20 ml of extracting solution (0.5N HCl + 0.025N H2SO4) was added. This was shaken for 15 minutes on a mechanical shaker. Then the extract was filtered through whatman no. 42 filter paper into 50 ml volumetric flask. The final volume was made up to 50 ml with extracting solution. This solution was used for estimation of heavy metals present in the soil.

Preparation of Heavy metal solution: The heavy metals were dissolved in distilled water to prepare stock solution of 1000 ppm for each metal. The calibration curves for each heavy metal were also prepared. A blank reading was also taken to incorporate necessary correction factor. The heavy metal solution of 5mg/L was prepared from the stock and administered to the plants and care was taken to avoid leaching of water from the pots. The metal uptake was estimated once in 20 days.

Experimental design: In this study, The heavy metals selected for the study is Cadmium. The uptake was estimated for every 20 days for a total period of 60 days, in total plant. Four treatments sets for each species were estimated during the experiment:

- *Set I:* Control (blank set)
- *Set II:* Cadmium treated (20 days)
- *Set III:* Cadmium treated (40 days)
- *Set IV:* Cadmium treated (60 days)

The plants of all the four sets were fed with cadmium chloride solution of designated concentration on alternate days.

Assay of Plant Samples: The sample plants were removed from the pots and washed under a stream of water and then with distilled water. The collected plants were air dried, then placed in a dehydrator for 2-3 days and then oven dried for four hours at 100 °c. The dried samples of the plant were powdered and stored in polyethylene bags. The powdered samples were subjected to acid digestion. 1gm of the powdered plant material were weighed in separate digestion flasks and digested with HNO_3 and HCl in the ratio of 3:1. The digestion on hot plate at 110°c for 3-4 hours or continued till a clean solution was obtained. After filtering with Whatman No. 42 filter paper the filtrate was analyzed for the metal contents in AAS (Subhashini *et al.*, 2013).

RESULTS

Tables 3.1 and 3.2 show the concentration of cadmium in different plant parts viz. leaf, stem and roots along with total accumulation of both studied species, *Catharanthus roseus* and *Mentha piperita* during the designated experimental periods.

Table 3.1: Accumulation of Cadmium (mg/kg) in Different Plant Parts of *Catharanthus roseus*

Plant Parts	Control	Experimental Period			Total Accumulation
		20th day	40th day	60th day	
Leaf	0.22	0.69	40.16	40.38	40.16
Stem	0.30	1.14	2.10	3.35	3.05
Root	0.39	6.26	6.73	20.29	19.9
Total Accumulation	0.91	8.09	48.99	64.02	63.11

Table 3.2: Accumulation of Cadmium (mg/kg) in different plant parts of *Mentha piperita*

Plant Parts	Control	Experimental Period			Total Accumulation
		20th day	40th day	60th day	
Leaf	0.18	0.56	38.00	39.24	39.16
Stem	0.23	1.02	1.87	2.98	2.85
Root	0.31	5.89	6.02	18.63	19.79
Total Accumulation	0.80	7.73	46.89	61.98	60.84

Results shows that maximum cadmium was accumulated in roots on 20th day of experiment, which was translocated to leaves those showing maximum cadmium concentration on 60th day of experiment. There was rather a minor difference in cadmium concentration on 40th and 60th day of experiment. Further, *Catharanthus roseus* was found to be comparatively better in accumulation of cadmium, proving its large scale application in affected lands.

DISCUSSION

Land and water are precious natural resources on which rely the sustainability of agriculture and the civilization of mankind. Unfortunately, they have been subjected to maximum exploitation and severely degraded or polluted due to anthropogenic activities. The pollution includes point sources such as emission, effluents and solid discharge from industries, vehicle exhaustion and metals from smelting and mining, and nonpoint sources such as soluble salts (natural and artificial), use of insecticides/

pesticides, disposal of industrial and municipal wastes in agriculture, and excessive use of fertilizers (McGrath *et al.*, 2001; Nriagu and Pacyna, 1988; Schalscha and Ahumada, 1998). Each source of contamination has its own damaging effects to plants, animals and ultimately to human health, but those that add heavy metals to soils and waters are of serious concern due to their persistence in the environment and carcinogenicity to human beings. They cannot be destroyed biologically but are only transformed from one oxidation state or organic complex to another (Garbisu and Alkorta, 2001; Gisbert *et al.*, 2003). Therefore, heavy metal pollution poses a great potential threat to the environment and human health. Soil and water pollution is a severe problem in countries like India, Pakistan and Bangladesh, where small industrial units are pouring their untreated effluents in the surface drains, which spread over near agricultural fields. In these countries raw sewage is often used for producing vegetables near big cities.

In order to maintain good quality of soils and waters and keep them free from contamination, continuous efforts have been made to develop technologies that are easy to use, sustainable and economically feasible. Physicochemical approaches have been widely used for remedying polluted soil and water, especially at a small scale. However, they experience more difficulties for a large scale of remediation because of high costs and side effects. The use of plant species for cleaning polluted soils and waters named as phytoremediation has gained increasing attention since last decade, as an emerging cheaper technology.

Phytoremediation an environmentally sound technology for pollution prevention, control and remediation. Phytoremediation, a fast-emerging new technology for removal of toxic heavy metals, is cost-effective, non-intrusive and aesthetically pleasing. It exploits the ability of selected plants to remediate pollutants from contaminated sites.

Cadmium is an especially mobile element in the soil and is taken up by plants primarily through the roots. The major factors governing cadmium speciation, adsorption and distribution in soils are pH, soluble organic matter content, hydrous metal oxide content, clay content and type, presence of organic and inorganic ligands, and competition from other metal ions. Most of the studies on plant species are mainly based on the interpretation of the analysis of metal concentrations in their plant parts (Nand Kumar etal., 1995 and Huang etal., 1997).

Plants have inter-linked physiological and molecular mechanisms of tolerance to heavy metals. The major processes involved in hyperaccumulation of trace metals from the soil to the shoots by hyperaccumulators include (Yang *et al.*, 2005):

(a) bioactivation of metals in the rhizosphere through root-microbe interaction;

(b) enhanced uptake by metal transporters in the plasma membranes;

(c) detoxification of metals by distributing to the apoplasts like binding to cell walls and chelation of metals in the cytoplasm with various ligands, such as phytochelatins, metallothioneins, metal-binding proteins;

(d) sequestration of metals into the vacuole by tonoplast-located transporters.

Deep rooting plants could change the valance state of heavy metals, which might be much less soluble and therefore, less bioavailable (James, 2001).

Regarding the results of this study it is concluded that *Catharanthus roseus* and *Mentha piperita* was among those plants with metal extracting capacity. These plants are used to eliminate heavy metals from soil through gathering such metals in their aerial parts. (Sabastini *et al.* 2004). The results of the current study are in accordance with those of Sarawet and Rai in 2009. These researchers have shown that those plants with root Bioconcentration factor of more than one, are suitable for fixing Cadmium.

Generally, plants with minor Bioconcentration factor tend to absorb on soil particles and plants with major Bioconcentration factor are less inclined to absorb on soil particles. Therefore, the group of elements that tend to combine with soil, are less freely available and are observed insignificantly and slightly in plants (Karbasi and Bayati, 2007).

The plant species under study seems to have higher uptake of Cd due to specific rooting strategy and a high uptake rate resulting from the existence in this population of Cd-specific transport channels or carriers in the root membrane

CONCLUSION

The results showed that the two plant species *viz. catharanthus roseus & Mentha piperita* has the ability of Phyteromediation and amendment of soils polluted with cadmium due to being fast growing, having high biomass and powerful root in addition to having bioconcentration factor of the root above one in range of different densities of cadmium and high harvest index. It is also concluded that aerial parts of *Catharanthus roseus* and *Mentha piperita* have the capacity of transferring absorbed cadmium from root. Improvement of these plants by genetic engineering, i.e., by modifying characteristics like metal uptake, transport and accumulation and plant's tolerance to metals, opens up new possibilities of phytoremediation.

REFERENCES

1. Akinola, M.O. and Ekiyoyo T.A. (2006): Accumulation of Lead, Cadmium and Chromium in Some Plants Cultivated Along the Bank of River Ribila at Odo-nla Area of Ikirodu, Lagos state. *Nigeria. J. Environ. Biol.,*27: 597-599.
2. Alloway, B.J. (1990): *Heavy Metals in Soils* (ed Alloway B. J.), Blackie, Glasgow.
3. Baek, Kyung-Hwa, Joo-Yun Chang, Yoon-Young Chang, Bum-Han Bae, Jaisoo Kim and In-Sook Lee (2006): Phytoremediation of Soil Contaminated with Cadmium and/ or 2, 4, 6-Trinitrotoluene. *J. Environ. Biol.,* 27: 311-316.
4. Baker, A.J.M. (1981): Accumulators and Excluders - Strategies in the Response of Plants to Heavy Metals. *J. Plant Nutrition.*, 3: 645-654.
5. Banuelos, G.S., Ajaw H.A., Mackey B., Wu L., Cook C., Akohoue S., and Zambruzuski S. (1997): Evaluation of Different Plant Species Used for Phytoremediation of High Soil Selenium. *J. Environ. Qual.* 26: 639-646.
6. Breckle, C.W. (1991): Growth Under Heavy Metals. In: Plant Roots: The Hidden Half (Eds.: Y. Waisel, A. Eshel and U. Kafkafi). New York, NY: Marcel Decker. pp. 351-373.
7. Bridge G., (2004): Contested Terrain: Mining and the Environment. *Annu. Rev. Environ. Resour.* 29: 205-259.
8. Chaney, R.L., Malik M., Li Y.M., Brown S.L., Angle J.S. and Baker A.J.M. (1997): Phytoremediation of Soil Metals. *Current Opinion in Biotech.,* 8: 279-284.
9. Cunningham S.D. and Ow D.W. (1996): Promises and Prospects of Phytoremediation. *Plant Physiol.,* 110: 715-719.
10. De Vos, C.H.R., Schat H., De Waal M.A.M., Vooijs R. and Ernst-WHO (1991): Increased Resistance to Copper-induced Damage of the Root Cell Plasmalemma in Copper Tolerant Silene cucubalus. *Physiologia Plantarum,* 82: 523-528.
11. Dembitsky V. (2003): Natural Occurrence of Arseno Compounds in Plants, Lichens, Fungi, Algal Species, and Microorganisms. *Plant Sci.* 165: 1177-1192.
12. Fischerova Z, Tlustos P, Szakova J and Sichorova K. (2005): A Comparison of Phytoremediation Capacity of Selected Plant Species for given Trace Elements. *Environmental Pollution,* 144: 93-100.
13. Garbisu C and Alkorta I (2001): Phytoextraction: A Cost Effective Plant-based Technology for the Removal of Metals from the Environment. *Biores Technol.* 77(3): 229-236.
14. Gisbert C, Ros R, de Haro A, Walker D J, Pilar Bernal M, Serrano R, and Avino JN (2003): A Plant Genetically Modified that Accumulates Pb is Especially Promising for Phytoremediation. *Biochem Biophys Res Commun.* 303(2): 440-445.
15. Goldbold, D.L. and Huttermann A. (1985): Effect of Zinc, Cadmium and Mercury on Root Elongation of Abies (Karst.) Seedlings and the Significance of these Metals to Forest Die-back. *Environ. Pollut.*, 38: 375-381.
16. Huang, J.W., J. Chen, W.R. Berti, and Cunningham S.D. (1997): Phytoremediation of Lead Contaminated Soils: Role of Synthetic Chelates in Lead Phytoextraction. *Environ. Sci. Technol.* 31 (3): 800-805.
17. Jackson D and Bergeron K (2004): Spearmint (Mentha spicata). Medicinal Herb Uses and Pictures Gallery. 1-3.
18. James, B.R. (2001): Remediation-by-reduction Strategies for Chromate-contaminated Soils. *Environ. Geochem. Health,* 23: 175-189.

19. Karbasi A and Bayati A. (2007): Environmental Geochemistry, *Kavosh Ghalam*, P: 58.
20. Krishnan, R., Naragud V.R. and Vasanta K.T. (1979): Evidences for out Breeding in Catharanthus roseus. *Curr. Sci.,* 48: 80-81.
21. Kulkerni, R.N., Dimri B.P., Rajgopal K., Suresh N. and Chandrasekhar R.S. (1984): Variability for Quantitative Characters in Periwinkle. *Indian Drugs*, 22: 61-64.
22. Manohar S, Jadia C D and Fulekar M H. (2006): Impact of Ganesh Idol Immersion on Water Quality. *Indian J. Environ. Prot.,* 27(3): 216-220.
23. McGrath S P, Zhao F J and Lombi E. (2001): Plant and Rhizosphere Process Involved in Phytoremediation of Metal-contaminated Soils. *Plant Soil.*, 232(1/2): 207-214.
24. Nanda Kumar, P.B. Dushenkov A., V., Motto H., and Raskin I. (1995): Phytoextraction: The Use of Plants to Remove Heavy Metals from Soils. *Environ. Sci. Technol.* 29(5): 1232-1238.
25. Nies, D.H. (1999): Microbial Heavy Metal Resistance. *Appl. Microbiol. Biotechnol.,* 51: 730-750.
26. Nriagu J O and Pacyna J M. (1988): Quantitative Assessment of Worldwide Contamination of Air Water and Soils by Trace Metals. *Nature.*, 333(6169): 134-139.
27. Nriagu J O. (1996): Toxic Metal Pollution in Africa. *Science.* 223: 272.
28. Saraswet S and Rai J P N (2009): Phytoextraction Potential of Six Plant Species Grown in Multimetal Contaminated Soil. *Chemistry and Ecology*, 25 (1): 1-11.
29. Schalscha E and Ahumada I. (1998): Heavy Metals in Rivers and Soils of Central Chile. *Water Sci Technol.*, 37(8): 251-255.
30. Scora R.W. and Chang A.C. (1997): Essential Oil Quality and Heavy Metal Concentrations of Peppermint Grown on a Municipal Sludge-amended soil. *J. Environ. Qual.*, 26: 975-979.
31. Sebastini L, Scebba F and Tognetti R. (2004): Heavy Metal Accumulation and Growth Responses in Poplar Clones Eridano (Populus deltoids × maximowiczii) and I-214 (P. × euramericana) exposed to industrial waste. *Environmental and Experimental Botany*, 52: 79- 88.
32. Sogut, Zerrin, B. Zeynop Z., Reyhan E. and Yavuz Sucu M. (2005): Phytoremediation of landfill leachate using Pennisetum clandestinum. *J. Environ. Biol.,* 26: 13-20.
33. Subhashini, V and Swamy A.V.V.S. (2013): *American International Journal of Research in Formal, Applied & Natural Sciences*, 3(1): 119-122.
34. Tabassum B and Bajaj P (2012). Mentha Piperita Prevents Cadmium Induced Renal Dysfunctioning in Albino rats. *Int. J. Biotech Biosci*, 2 (4): 322-325.
35. United States Environmental Protection Agency (USEPA) (1997): *Recent Developments for In Situ Treatment of Metal Contaminated Soils.* Washington, DC: Technology Innovation Office.
36. Weast, R.C. (1984): CRC Hand Book of Chemistry and Physics, 64th Edn. Boca Raton, CRC Press.
37. Yang X, Feng Y, He Z and Stoffella P J. (2005): Molecular Mechanisms of Heavy Metal Hyperaccumulation and Phytoremediation. *J Trace Elem Med Biol.* 18(4):339-53.
38. Zhen-Guo S, Xian-Dong L, Chun-Chun W, Huai-Man Ch and Hong Ch. (2002): Lead Phytoextraction from Contaminated Soil with High Biomass Plant Species. *J. Environ. Qual.* 31: 1893-1900.

Pages: 48-57

SOIL CONTAMINATION AND CONSERVATION
Edited by: **Dr. Ezeaku Peter Ikemefuna; Dr. Pawan Kumar 'Bharti'**
ISBN: 978-93-5056-737-1
Edition: **2015**
Published by: **Discovery Publishing House Pvt. Ltd., New Delhi (India)**

Changes in Soil Physicochemical Properties due to Forest Destruction

Aftab Hasan

ABSTRACT

Soil represent a short to long term carbon storage medium, which comes after the death of plant and stored in soil as soil organic carbon (SOC). It can act as a mean to measure the adverse effect of global climatic change. Present study is designed to measure the effect of land-use change on SOC pool and different physical parameters in Delhi ridge forest ecosystem. Soil samples were collected and estimated for soil pH, soil moisture (%) and bulk density. Soil organic carbon was found significantly higher at natural site compared to managed site at Northern ridge. Air temperature and Relative humidity were also significantly higher at managed site compared to natural site. The study conclude that deforestation is mainly responsible to increase atmospheric CO2 concentration.

Key words: SOC, Deforestation, Managed sites, Climate change.

Department of Botany, University of Delhi, New Delhi - 110 007, India.

INTRODUCTION

The soil carbon pool is the major reservoir where long term storage of atmospheric carbon is targeted. Soil represent a short to long term carbon storage medium, and contain more carbon then all terrestrial vegetation and atmosphere combined.The issue of climate change and its impact on the natural ecosystems has got the attention of many scientists (Patil *et al.*, 2011).In order to understand the global climate change and its adverse effects, it is important to understand the various processes which lead to the storage of the carbon in the soils (Paustian *et al.*, 1998). Carbon sequestration in soils occurs through plant production. Plants fix atmospheric carbon dioxide into complex organic compound in leaves. After the plant dies, dead plant material is partially decomposed by microorganisms and stored in soil as soil organic carbon (SOC). These SOC can persist in soils for hundred or even thousands of years.

Soil contains a large amount of carbon and acts as a reservoir or sink. Carbon (C) stored in soil is an important part of the terrestrial carbon pool (Lal and Kimble 1997) and soils of the world are potentially viable sinks for atmospheric carbon, it reduces atmospheric carbon dioxide and stores it (Lal*et al.*, 1995; Bajracharya *et al.*, 1998; Singh and Lal 2001). There are different carbon pool, the oceanic C pool is the largest one, in which 38.000 Petagrams (1Pg= 10^{15}) C is stored (Lal, 2003). Soil represents the largest amount of stored terrestrial C. The global soil C pool is estimated to be 2300 Pg, which is 3 times more than atmospheric C (770 Pg) and 3.8 times the size of vegetation pools(610 Pg) (Lal, 2001). The upper most meter of the soil contains SOC pool of approximately 1.500 Pg C and further 1-2 m has SOC pool of 900 Pg C (Jobbagyand Jackson, 2000; Batjes, 2002).The *"global soil organic carbon map"* shows that significant amounts of soil organic carbon (SOC) are found in temperate zones. Soil carbon density increases with increasing rainfall and decreasing temperature (Post *et al.*, 1982).Soils of arid semi-arid regions (Yermosols and Xerosols) contain small amounts of organic C as plant growth is limited and the annual input of C is low because of limited plant growth. Soil C stocks is influenced by a number of management practices (Batjes and Sombroek, 1997), deforestation, afforestation, biomass burning and cultivation are some of the activities that affect global SOC pools (Lal *et al.*, 1995). The result of management and different land use systems to increase or decrease SOC are limited by socioeconomic issues (Lal *et al.*, 1995).

India is a developing country and from the beginning of the industrial period, there are many changes in the climate of India due to the emission of GHGs. So it is important to understand current state of soil carbon pools of India and the different environmental factors interacting with it.). Tropical forest play an important role in global carbon cycle in terms of carbon stored.India constitutes 2.4% of the world land area and about 2% of the world forests,in India60.83 million ha (Mha), 20.66% of the geographical area of country (329 Mha) is covered by forest (FSI, 2003).

Delhi is one of the most populated cities in India where GHGs and other environmental pollutantsis a major problem due to increased vehicular exhaust, urbanization and industrial and domestic exhausts. So it is important to understand the factors which can reduce the amount of different GHGs. Delhi Ridge forest ecosystem is one of the key system which is helping the city in mitigating with environmental stresses. It is also known as GREEN LUNGS of Delhi which help in reducing the concentration of atmospheric $CO_{2.}$ But presently, Delhi ridge forest cover is not capable of reducing the greenhouse gases in the city because of regular sprawl of jungle and deforestation for construction and other kind of land uses over the time. As a consequence of deforestation and other anthropogenic activities, the vegetation cover has reduced and the C inputs to soil also decreased as C inputs to the soil is directly related to litter inputs by vegetation. Hence, it is important to estimate dynamics of ridge forest Carbon stocks. The objectives of the present study were:

- To determine physical parameters in Delhi ridge forest ecosystem.
- To study SOC pool in Delhi ridge forest ecosystem.
- To study the effect of land-use change on SOC pool and different physical parameters.

MATERIAL AND METHODS

1. Site description

The study was carried out inDelhi the capital city of India. Delhi is located between 28° - 24′ and 28° - 54′ North latitude and 76° - 20′ and 77° - 50′ East longitude. It covers an area about 1463 km^2. Delhi has Semi-arid climate characterised by hot summers and average rainfall.

We conducted our study in Delhi ridge forest ecosystem between October 2012 and July 2013. Delhi ridge is the northern most extension of Aravali mountain range which is one of the most ancient mountain chains of the world. For the present study we selected Northern ridge forest which was further divided into natural and managed site based on the degree of disturbance.

2. Soil sampling

The seasonal micro-environmental variables such as air temperature, soil moisture, relative humidity and light intensity were recorded between 11 AM and 2 PM during each season. Five random soil replicates were collected from both natural and managed sites of ridge forest. Soil samples were collected from three different depths (0-10 cm; 10-20 cm and 20-30 cm) using a soil augar. Soil samples were collected in polybags and brought to laboratory for further analysis. Soil replicates of each depth mixed thoroughly to prepare a composite sample. After removing stones, pebbles and large pieces of plant material, soils were air-dried and sieved (2 mm) for use in nutrient analysis.

Table 4.1: Geographical Coordinates of Soil Sampling site at Kamla Nehru Northern Ridge Forest

Sl. No.	Natural Site	Elevation (m.a.s.l)	Managed Site	Elevation (m.a.s.l)
1.	N 28°41'6.46" E 77°12'54.78"	232	N 28°41'2.39" E 77°13'5.52"	227
2.	N 28°41'13.37" E 77°12'57.02"	234	N 28°41'6.46" E 77°13'0.31"	229
3.	N 28°41'20.08" E 77°12'56.96"	227	N 28°41'8.36" E 77°13'7.06"	227
4.	N 28°41'20.55" E 77°13'5.67"	232	N 28°41'15.27" E 77°13'5.56"	231
5.	N 28°41'26.04" E 77°13'8.84"	225	N 28°40'52.43" E 77°13'4.21"	226

3. Analytical procedure

Soil pH, soil moisture (%), bulk density was estimated following Allen *et al.* (1974). SOC was measured through combustion process (Liqui II TOC Elementar Analyser). Observed data was statistically analysed by one way ANOVA (Statistica version 6, StatSoft.Inc.2001, USA).

RESULTS

Air temperature was significantly higher at managed site compared to natural site(F= 10.24, *p*= <0.05). Relative humidity (%) and light intensities was also higher at managed sites compared to natural sites (F= 92.65, *p*= <0.01). Soil organic carbon was significantly higher (F= 140.51, *p*= < 0.01) at natural site compared to managed site at Northern ridge. Depth wise variation in SOC was also significant (*p* = <0.01) at both natural and managed site. SOC was highest at top soil layer (0-10 cm) which gradually decreased toward the depth and lowest SOC was measured at 20-30 cm soil depth at both sites.

Soil moisture showed a significant change with land use change at Northern ridge. Higher soil moisture % at managed site was the result of watering process which was conducted at managed sitemost of the time during studied periods. Soil moisture was higher at top soil depths and decreased toward the depth.

(a)

(b)

Fig. 4.1 (a, b): Natural sites

(c)

(d)

Fig. 4.1 (c, d): Managed or Disturbed sites

Soil pH significantly increased with management practice (F= 106, p = <0.001). It showed a significant spatial variation among three depths at both natural (F= 38.4, p= <0.01) and managed sites (F=30.8, p= <0.01). Lowest soil pH was observed for top soil depth (0-10 cm) which increased significantly with depth and highest was measured for 20-30 cm depth at both site of Northern ridge.

Land use change affects the bulk density. It was significantly higher at managed site (F= 120.14, p= <0.01). BD increased with increasing depth at both the sites (p= <0.05).

Table 4.2: Showing Different Parameters at Study Site

Parameters	Natural Site			Managed Site		
	0-10 cm	10-20 cm	20-30 cm	0-10 cm	10-20 cm	20-30 cm
SOC Mg ha^{-1}	23.19	14.73[a]	8.86[a]	12.9	8.92[a]	6.27[a]
Soil moisture (%)	7.62	6.45[a]	5.32[a]	18.15	14.52[a]	14.13[b]
Bulk density gm cm^{-3}	1.02	1.08[b]	1.15[a]	1.13	1.18[b]	1.23[b]
Soil pH	7.27	7.41[a]	7.5[b]	7.49	7.58[b]	7.72[a]
Air temperature° C		34.2			35.6	
Humidity (%)		53			57	
LUX		3197			14210	

a significant variation at p = < 0.01

b significant variation at p = < 0.05

DISCUSSION

1. Soil organic carbon

Forests have a significant higher amount of SOC stocks than any other land-use types. Canopy cover is responsible for increasing SOC. Land-use change altered the inputs of organic matter thus affecting SOC stores.Higher concentration of SOC at top soil layer is mainly due to the fallen leaves and branches on the first horizon. SOC content varied depth wise, having the highest value in surface soil at both the land-uses. SOC decreased as the soil depth increased because of reduced soil organic matter at deeper layers (Jobbagy and Jackson, 2001; Chowdhury et al 2007; Albaladejo, 2012).

2. Soil pH

In our work soil pH is significant negatively correlated with soil organic carbon (p = < 0.01). It indicates that increased SOC decreases the soil pH. Low SOC in the disturbed stands may be attributed higher pH at managed sites.Soil pH significantly increased with increasing soil depths across all the sites which were due to less SOC at deeper soil layers (Koul, 2008; Toni *et al.*, 2009).

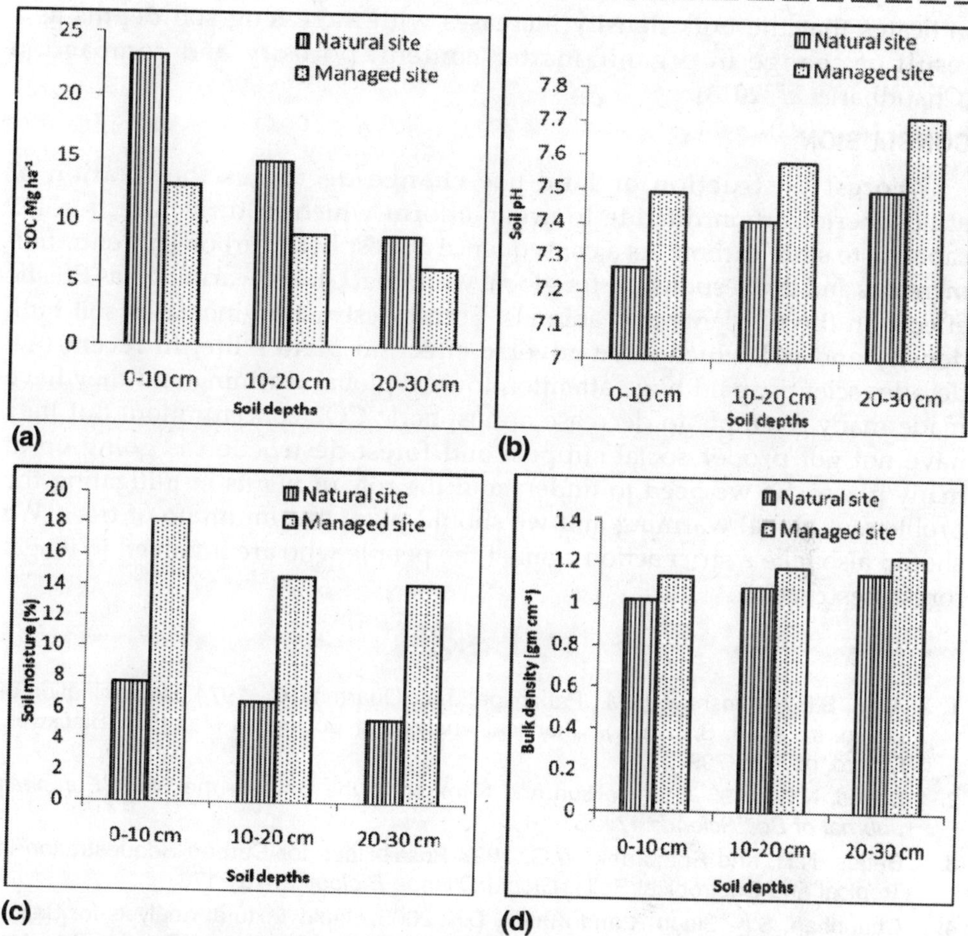

Fig. 4.2: Graphical presentation of: (a) SOC, (b) Soil pH, (c) Soil moisture and (d) Soil bulk density

3. Soil moisture (%)

The soil moisture content was higher at the managed site of both the ridges because of regular watering (morning and evening).Soil moisture content significantly decreased toward the depth at all the sites. The high moisture content at surface soil layers is because the higher organic matter content improves the soil moisture storage capacity of the soils (Jiang 1997; Larney*et al.* 1998; Teresaecheverria and Martinez 2001; Zhao *et al.* 2006).

4. Soil bulk density

Lower bulk density at natural was due to the presence of more no of trees. Higher tree density increases soil organic matter which in turns is responsible for more porosity(Halvorson *et al.* 2002; Kaul, 2008).Present study indicates that the bulk density increases with increasing soil depths as a result of change in organic matter content, porosity and compaction (Chaudhari*et al.* 2013).

CONCLUSION

Forest destruction or land-use change decreases the fixation of atmospheric carbon dioxide to organic form which in turns affects soil's capacity to store carbon. As a consequence atmospheric carbon concentration increases and it is responsible for global warming. Global warming has drastic effects on life of plants and animals. Forest destruction increases soil bulk density and pH which have adverse effect on plant's life. In recent few decades scientist paid huge attention toward global warming and they have made many attempts to decrease atmospheric CO2 concentration. But they have not got proper social support and forest destruction is going on at many places. So we need to understand the role of plants in mitigating the problem of global warming and we should plant maximum no of trees. We should also take a strict action against the people who are involved in illegal forest destruction.

REFERENCES

1. Allen, S.E., Grimshaw, H.M., Parkinson, J.A., Quarmby, C., 1974. Determination of Lignin. In: Allen,. S.E. (Ed.), Chemical Analysis of Ecological Materials. Blackwell, Oxford, pp. 785-799.
2. Batjes, N.H. 1996 Total Carbon and Nitrogen in the Soils or the World.*European Journal of Soil Science* 47: 151-163.
3. Batjes, N.H. and Sombroek, W.G. 1997 Possibilities for Carbon Sequestration in Tropical and Subtropical Soils. *Global Change Biology* 3: 161-173.
4. Chaudhari, S.K, Singh R and Kundu, D.K. 2008. Rapid Textural Analysis for Saline and Alkaline Soils with different Physical and Chemical Properties. *Soil Sci. Soc. Am. J.* 72 431-41.
5. Halvorson Ardell D., Brian J., Wienhold and Black A.L., 2002. Tillage, Nitrogen, and Cropping System Effects on Soil Carbon Sequestration. *Soil Science Society of America Journal* 66: 906-912.
6. Jobbagy EG, Jackson RB. 2000. The Vertical Distribution of Soil Organic Carbon and its Relation to Climate and Vegetation. *Ecological Application* 10: 423-436.
7. Jobbagy, E.G and Jackson, R.B. 2001. The Distribution of Soil Nutrients with Depth: Global Patterns and Imprint of Plants Biogeochemistry 53: 51-77.
8. Kaul M, Dadhwal VK and Mohren GMJ. 2009. Land Use Change and Net C Flux in Indian Forests. *For EcolManag* 258(2): 100-108.
9. Lal R, Kimble J, and Stewart B.A. 1995.World Soils as a Source or Sink for Radiatively-active Gases. In: Lal R, and Stewart BA (eds.) Soil Management and Greenhouse Effect, pp 1-8 Lewis Publishers, Boca Raton, FL, USA 80.Lal R and Kimble JM 1997. Conservation Tillage for Soil Carbon sequestration. *Nutr Cycl Agroecosyst* 49: 243-253.

10. Lal, R., Kimble, J.M., Follet, R.F. and Cole, C.V. 1998. The Potential of US Cropland to Sequester Carbon and Mitigate the Greenhouse Effect.Ann Arbor Press, Chelsea, MI, 128pp.
11. Lal, R., 2001. Desertification Control to Sequester Carbon and Reduce Net Emissions in the United States. *Arid lands Newsletter*, No. 49, May/June 2001.
12. Lal, R. 2003. Soil Erosion and the Global Carbon Budget. *Environment International* 29(4): 437-450.
13. Patil, P., Singh, S. and Dadhwal, V.K., 2012.Above Ground Forest Phytomass Assessment in Southern Gujarat. *J. Indian Society of Remote Sensing* 40(1): pp. 37-46.
14. Paustian, K., Andren, O., Janzen, H., Lal, R., Smith, P., Tian, G., Tiessen, H., Noordwijk, M., and Woomer, P.1997. Agricultural Soils as a Sink to Mitigate CO2 Emissions. *Soil Use and Management*: 13(4): 230-244.
15. Post WM, Emanuel WR, Zinke PJ and Stangenberger AG. 1982. Soil Carbon Pools and World Life Zones. *Nature* 298: 156-159.
16. Singh, J.S., Raghubhanshi, A.S., Singh, R.S. and Srivastava, S.C., Microbial Biomass Acts as a Source of Plant Nutrients in Dry Tropical Forest and Savanna. *Nature*: 1989, 338, 499-500.
17. Toni, L.R.M. et al. 2004. Nutrient and Bulk Density Characteristics of Soil Profiles in Six Land Use Systems Along Topo-sequences in Inland Valley Watersheds of Ashanti Region. Ghana. *Soil Science and Plant Nutrition*, Tokyo, Volume 50, No. 5, pp. 649-664.
18. Zhao, H.L., He, Y.H., Zhou, R.L., Su, Y.Z., Li, Y.Q and Drake, S. 2009. Effects of Desertification on Soil Organic C and N Content in Sandy Farmland and Grassland of Inner Mongolia. *Catena* 77: 187-191.

Pages: 58-63

SOIL CONTAMINATION AND CONSERVATION
Edited by: Dr. Ezeaku Peter Ikemefuna; Dr. Pawan Kumar 'Bharti'
ISBN: 978-93-5056-737-1
Edition: 2015
Published by: Discovery Publishing House Pvt. Ltd., New Delhi (India)

Phytoremediation of Heavy Metal Polluted Soils and Water *Progresses and Perspectives*

B. Tabassum[*], **Priya Bajaj**[*] and **Alina Javed**[**]

ABSTRACT

Environmental pollution affects the quality of pedosphere, hydrosphere, atmosphere, lithosphere and biosphere. Great efforts have been made in the last two decades to reduce pollution sources and remedy the polluted soil and water resources. Phytoremediation, being more cost-effective and fewer side effects than physical and chemical approaches, has gained increasing popularity in both academic and practical circles. More than 400 plant species have been identified to have potential for soil and water remediation.

"What we plant in the soil of contemplation, we shall reap in the harvest of action."

Key words: Heavy-metals, Phytoremediation, Pollution

* Toxicology Laboratory, Department of Zoology, Govt. Raza PG College, Rampur (UP) - 244 901, India.

** Department of Biotechnology, Jamia Millia Islamia, New Delhi.

INTRODUCTION

Land and water are precious natural resources on which rely the sustainability of agriculture and the civilization of mankind. The pollution includes point sources such as emission, effluents and solid discharge from industries, vehicle exhaustion and metals from smelting and mining, and nonpoint sources such as soluble salts (natural and artificial), use of insecticides/pesticides, disposal of industrial and municipal wastes in agriculture, and excessive use of fertilizers. Each source of contamination has its own damaging effects to plants, animals and ultimately to human health, but those that add heavy metals to soils and waters are of serious concern due to their persistence in the environment and carcinogenicity to human beings. They cannot be destroyed biologically but are only transformed from one oxidation state or organic complex to another. Therefore, heavy metal pollution poses a great potential threat to the environment and human health.

In order to maintain good quality of soils and waters and keep them free from contamination, continuous efforts have been made to develop technologies that are easy to use, sustainable and economically feasible. The use of plant species for cleaning polluted soils and waters named as phytoremediation has gained increasing attention since last decade, as an emerging cheaper technology.

TECHNOLOGIES FOR THE RECLAMATION OF POLLUTED SOILS

The cleaning of contaminated soils from heavy metals is the most difficult task, particularly on a large scale. The soil is composed of organic and inorganic solid constituents, water and mixture of different gases present in various proportions.

Different approaches have been used or developed to mitigate/reclaim the heavy metal polluted soils and waters including the landfill/damping sites. These may be broadly classified into physicochemical and biological approaches.

The physicochemical approach includes excavation and burial of the soil at a hazardous waste site, fixation/inactivation (chemical processing of the soil to immobilize the metals), leaching by using acid solutions or proprietary leachants to desorb and leach the metals from soil followed by the return of clean soil residue to the site, precipitation or flocculation followed by sedimentation, ion exchange, reverse osmosis and microfiltration. The physicochemical approaches are generally costly and have side effects.

Biological approaches of remediation include:

1. Use of microorganisms to detoxify the metals by valence transformation, extracellular chemical precipitation, or volatilization.

2. Use of special type of plants to decontaminate soil or water by inactivating metals in the rhizosphere or translocating them in the aerial parts. This approach is called phytoremediation, which is considered as a new and highly promising technology for the reclamation of polluted sites and cheaper than physicochemical approaches.

WHAT IS PHYTOREMEDIATION?

Phytoremediation, also referred as botanical bioremediation involves the use of green plants to decontaminate soils, water and air. It is an emerging technology that can be applied to both organic and inorganic pollutants present in the soil, water or air. There are different categories of phytoremediation, including phytoextraction, phytofiltration, phytostabilization, phytovolatization and phytodegradation, depending on the mechanisms of remediation.

- **Phytoextraction** involves the use of plants to remove contaminants from soil. The metal ion accumulated in the aerial parts that can be removed to dispose or burnt to recover metals.
- **Phytofiltration** involves the plant roots or seedling for removal of metals from aqueous wastes.
- **Phytostabilization** involves the absorbance of the pollutants from the soil by plant roots and keep them in the rhizosphere, rendering them harmless by preventing them from leaching.
- **Phytovolatization** involves the use of plants to volatilize pollutants from their foliage such as Se and Hg.
- **Phytodegradation** means the use of plants and associated microorganisms to degrade organic pollutants.

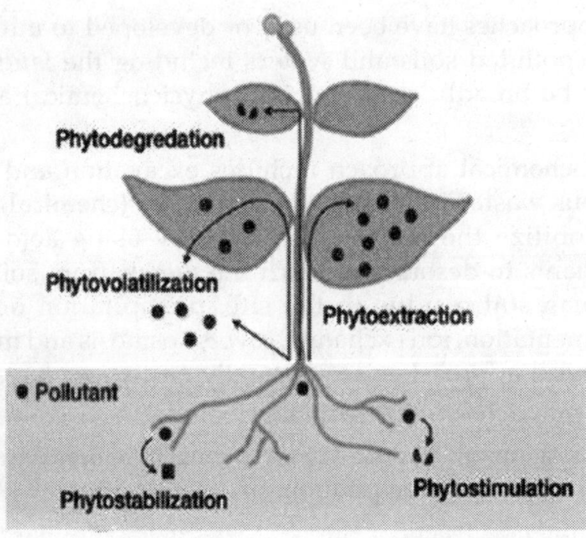

PLANT SPECIES FOR PHYTOREMEDIATION

The hyperaccumulators that have been most extensively studied by scientific community include *Thlaspi* sp., *Arabidopsis* sp., *Sedum alfredii* sp. *Thlaspi* sp. are known to hyperaccumulate more than one metal, i.e., *T. caerulescens* for Cd, Ni, Pb and Zn, *T. goesingense* for Ni and Zn, *T. ochroleucum* for Ni and Zn, and *T. rotundifolium* for Ni, Pb and Zn). Among the genus *Thlaspi*, the hyperaccumulator plant *Thlaspi caerulescens* received much attention and has been extensively studied as potential candidates for Cd and Zn contaminated soils.). *T. caerulescens* has higher uptake of Cd due to specific rooting strategy and a high uptake rate resulting from the existence in this population of Cd-specific transport channels or carriers in the root membrane.

PHYTOREMEDIATION OF POLLUTED WATER

Rhizofiltration is the removal of pollutants from the contaminated waters by accumulation into plant biomass. Several aquatic species have been identified and tested for the phytoremediation of heavy metals from the polluted water. These include sharp dock (*Polygonum amphibium* L.), duck weed (*Lemna minor* L.), water hyacinth (*Eichhornia crassipes*), water lettuce (*P. stratiotes*), water dropwort [*Oenathe javanica* (BL) DC], calamus (*Lepironia articulate*), pennywort (*Hydrocotyle umbellate* L.).The roots of Indian mustard are found to be effective in the removal of Cd, Cr, Cu, Ni, Pb and Zn, and sunflower can remove Pb, U, Cs-137 and Sr-90 from hydroponic solutions.

The potential of duck weed was investigated by Zayed et al.(1998) for the removal of Cd, Cr, Cu, Ni, Pb and Se from nutrient-added solution and the results indicate that duck weed is a good accumulator for Cd, Se and Cu, a moderate accumulator for Cr, but a poor accumulator of Ni and Pb. Water hyacinth possesses a well-developed fibrous root system and large biomass and has been successfully used in wastewater treatment systems to improve water quality by reducing the levels of organic and inorganic nutrients. This plant can also reduce the concentrations of heavy metals in acid mine water while exhibiting few signs of toxicity. Water hyacinth accumulates trace elements such as Ag, Pb, Cd, etc.

Among the ferns, *Pteris vitta* commonly known as Brake fern has been identified as As hyperacccumulator for As contaminated soils and waters.

ENHANCEMENT OF PHYTOREMEDIATION BY CHEMICAL AND BIOLOGICAL APPROACHES

In order to cope with heavy metal contaminated soils, various phytoremediation approaches (phytostabilization, phytoimmobilization and phytoextraction) can be applied. However, the choice will depend on many factors, such as plant tolerance to pollutants, soil physicochemical properties, agronomic characteristics of the plant species, climatic conditions (rainfall, temperature), and additional technologies available for the recovery of metals from the harvested plant biomass. It appears that both chemical and biological approaches are passing through their infancy and need more efforts for their effective use in the future.

The solubility of heavy metals in the polluted soils can be increased by using organic and inorganic agents, thus enhancing the phytoextraction capabilities of many plant species. Enhancement materials include ethylene diamine tetraacetic acid (EDTA), citric acid, elemental sulfur or ammonium sulfate. Uranium, cadmium and zinc concentrations in plant biomass were increased by the application of citric acid, elemental sulfur or ammonium sulfate, respectively). In addition to the chelating material, the plant roots excrete metal-mobilizing substances called phytosiderophores.

Amendable to a variety of organic and inorganic compounds Restricted to sites with shallow contamination within rooting zone of remediative plants In Situ/Ex Situ Application May take up to several years to remediate a contaminated site In Situ applications decrease the amount of soil disturbance compared to conventional methods Restricted to sites with low contaminant concentrations Reduces the amount of waste to be landfilled (up to 95%) Harvested plant biomass from phytoextraction may be classified as a RCRA hazardous waste In Situ applications decrease spread of contaminant via air and water Climatic conditions Does not require expensive equipment or highly specialized personnel.

CONCLUSION AND PERSPECTIVES

The contamination of heavy metals to the environment, i.e., soil, water, plant and air is of great concern due to its potential impact on human and animal health. Cheaper and effective technologies are needed to protect the precious natural resources and biological lives. Substantial efforts have been made in identifying plant species and their mechanisms of uptake and hyperaccumulation of heavy metals in the last decade. Variations exist for hyperaccumulation of different metals among various plant species and within populations. In order to develop new crop species/plants having capabilities of metal extraction from the polluted environment, traditional breeding techniques, hybrid generation through protoplast fusions, and production of mutagens through radiation and chemicals are all in progress. With the development of biotechnology, the capabilities of hyperaccumulators may be greatly enhanced through specific metal gene identification and its transfer in certain promising species. This can play a significant role in the extraction of heavy metals from the polluted soils. Nevertheless, the recent advances in plant biotechnology have created a new hope for the development of hyperaccumulating species.To date the available methods for the recovery of heavy metals from plant biomass of hyperaccumulators are still limited. Traditional disposal approaches such as burning and ashing are not applicable to volatile metals; therefore, investigations are needed to develop new methods for effective recovery of metals from the hyperaccumulator plant biomass.

"Water and air, the two essential fluids on which all life depends, have become global garbage cans."

REFERENCES

1. Ahmad SS, Reshi ZA, Shah MA, Rashid I, Ara R, Andrabi SM. Phytoremediation Potential of Phragmites Australis in Hokersar Wetland – A Ramsar Site of Kashmir Himalaya.
2. David E. Salt, Michael Blaylock, Nanda P.B.A. Kumar, Viatcheslav Dushenkov, Burt D. Ensley, Ilan Chet & Ilya Raskin. Phytoremediation: A Novel Strategy for the Removal of Toxic Metals from the Environment Using Plants.
3. E. Lombi, F.J. Zhao, S.J. Dunham and S.P. McGrath. Phytoremediation of Heavy Metal–Contaminated Soils. Efficiency of Constructed Wetlands in Decontamination of Water Polluted by Heavy Metals. Shuiping Chenga, Wolfgang Grossea, Friedhelm Karrenbrockb, Manfred Thoennessen.
4. Huguenot D, Bois P, Cornu JY, Jezequel K, Lollier M, Lebeau T. Remediation of Sediment and Water Contaminated by Copper in Small-scaled Constructed Wetlands: Effect of Bioaugmentation and Phytoextraction.
5. Li Z, Xiao H, Cheng S, Zhang L, Xiel X, Wu Z. A Comparison on the Phytoremediation Ability of Triazophos by Different Macrophytes.
6. Q. Wang†, Y. Cui and Y. Dong Phytoremediation of Polluted Waters Potentials and Prospects of Wetland Plants.
7. Sridhar Susarlaa, Victor F. Medinab, Steven C. McCutcheonc. Phytoremediation: An Ecological Solution to Organic Chemical Contamination.

***Pages:* 64-111**

SOIL CONTAMINATION AND CONSERVATION
***Edited by:* Dr. Ezeaku Peter Ikemefuna; Dr. Pawan Kumar 'Bharti'**
ISBN: 978-93-5056-737-1
***Edition:* 2015**
***Published by:* Discovery Publishing House Pvt. Ltd., New Delhi (India)**

Heavy Metals in Soil and Aquatic Environment and Their Toxicity

Pawan Kumar 'Bharti'

ABSTRACT

Heavy metals become toxic when they are not metabolized by the body and accumulate in the soft tissues. Heavy metals may enter the human body through food, water, air, or absorption through the skin when they come in contact with humans in agriculture and in manufacturing, pharmaceutical, industrial, or residential settings. Industrial exposure accounts for a common route of exposure for adults. Ingestion is the most common route of exposure in children.

The study reflects the impact assessment of industrial effluents on quality characteristics of groundwater, surface water, agriculture soil and crop plants tissues in Panipat region of Haryana state (India).

The chapter mainly deals with heavy metal toxicity and pollution aspects of industrial effluents drained by dyes houses and textile industries, which play a

Society for Environment, Health, Awareness of Nutrition & Toxicology (SEHAT) 1775, Sohan Ganj, Near Clock Tower, Delhi - 7, India.

significant role in degrading the water quality of surface and groundwater and ultimately effected the entire surrounding environment. Further, the chapter has emphasized on the distributional pathway of heavy metals from industrial effluents to ground water as well as agricultural soil system and plant tissues. The accumulation of heavy metals as transfer and enrichment factor also described and calculated the metal accumulation factor among all trophic levels.

The aim of this study was to assess the extent of heavy metal contamination of vegetation due to irrigation with contaminated ground water affected by textile industrial effluents, on agricultural land. Samples of ground water, surface water, soils and crop plants have been analyzed for seven heavy metals, viz. Mn, Ni, Fe, Cu, Cd, Pb and Zn, using atomic absorption spectrophotometry. The results show the presence of some of the heavy metals in agricultural soil, comparatively to ground water. Metal transfer factors from effluent to ground water, from ground water to irrigated agricultural soil and from soil to vegetation were calculated for heavy metals. Comparing the results of heavy metals in water, soil and vegetation with their respective levels, it is observed that impact of ground water on vegetation was found to be more than the soil.

The present study deals with the distribution of heavy metals in textile industrial effluents, surface water, ground water, irrigated agricultural soil and in crop plant tissues. Ground water quality was monitored in industrial area regarding water supply, human consumption and irrigation, which may caused the human and livestock health hazards and reduce agricultural plant productivity.

Key words: Heavy metals, Toxicity, Industrial effluents, Ground water, Agriculture soil, Accumulation.

INTRODUCTION

Environmental Pollution an undesirable and unwanted change in physical, chemical and biological characteristics of air, water and soil which is harmful for living organisms both animal and plants Pollution can take the form of chemical substances or energy, such as noise, heat or light. Pollutants, the elements of pollution, can be either foreign substances/energies or naturally occurring contaminants.

Environmental pollution is the result of rapid industrialization and technological advancement and unprecedented increase in population. The increased technological advancement, urbanization, industrial revolution, the intensive use of raw material and agricultural technology have, no doubt, improved our life styles, which could not be imagined a decade ago, but these advancements have simultaneously polluted the natural environment. Pollution is reduction in the quality of the environment by introduction of impurities. Smoke and dust pollute air; junks etc pollute land and industrial wastes, municipal sewage and domestic waste cause water pollution. Most of the industries discharged their waste directly (without any treatment) into the stream, lakes, oceans as well as in the open land and that contaminate the ground water (Bharti, 2007). There are number of pollutants like fertilizers, pesticides, heavy metals which seriously affect human like by entering into the system directly or indirectly through food material. Pollution of environment with heavy metals is a serious problem. Besides causing specific toxicity symptoms, these metals may also contribute to global warming by destroying the atmosphere ozone layer like atmosphere methane, nitrous oxide and sulphur dioxide because of potentially harmful effects on human and animal health, few toxic metals (lead, cadmium, mercury, arsenic, and chromium).it is major concern to ecologist or researcher, because air or water pollution of local or distant origin may contribute significantly to the load of metals on natural ecosystem (Mani *et al.*, 2005).

Heavy metals are usually present in trace amounts in naturally waters but many of them are toxic even at very low concentration. Metals such as arsenic, lead, cadmium, nickel, mercury, chromium, cobalt, zinc and selenium are highly toxic even in minor quantity. Increasing quantity of heavy metals in our resources is currently an area of greater concern especially since a large number of industries are discharging their metal containing effluents in to fresh water without any adequate treatment

Environmental contamination and exposure to heavy metals such as mercury, cadmium and lead is a serious growing problem throughout the world. Human exposure to heavy metals has risen dramatically in the last 50 years as a result of an exponential increase in the use of heavy metals in industrial processes and products.

Heavy metals can directly influence behavior by impairing mental and neurological function, influencing neurotransmitter production and utilization, and altering numerous metabolic body processes. Systems in which toxic metal elements can induce impairment and dysfunction include the blood and cardiovascular, eliminative pathways (colon, liver, kidneys, skin), endocrine (hormonal), energy production pathways, enzymatic, gastrointestinal, immune, nervous (central and peripheral), reproductive, and urinary. The adverse effects of excess accumulation of HM are well documented. Many cases of HM burden are associated with industrial exposure, but our food, drinking water and environment do not appear to be getting any purer (tuberose.com, 2006).

Metals are unique among pollutants that cause adverse health effects in that they occur naturally and, in many instances, are ubiquitous in the environment. Regardless of how metals are used in consumer products or industrial processes, some level of human exposure is, in most instances, inevitable. Furthermore, many are biologically essential but become toxic with increasing dosage. The problem for the toxicologists, therefore, is to be able to recognize the adverse effects. Metals are an important emerging class of human carcinogens. At least five transition metals or metalloids, in one form or another, are accepted as human carcinogens by the international agency on cancer. Several more metals and/or their compounds are suspected to have carcinogenic potential in humans (IARC, 1980).

The toxic heavy metals entering the ecosystem may lead to geo-accumulation, bioaccumulation and biomagnifications. Heavy metals like Fe, Cu, Zn, Ni and other trace elements are important for proper functioning of biological systems and their deficiency or excess could lead to a number of disorders. Food chain contamination by heavy metals has become a burning issue in recent years because of their potential accumulation in bio-systems through contaminated water, soil and air. Therefore, a better understanding of heavy metal sources, their accumulation in the soil and the effect of their presence in water and soil on plant systems seem to be particularly important issues of present-day research on risk assessments (Lokeshwari and Chandrappa, 2006).

In the last three decades, the rapid growth of industrialization, urbanization and development has created negative impacts on each component of the environment viz. lithosphere, atmosphere and hydrosphere. The industrial wastes containing organic pollutants and heavy metals in their effluents have been polluted surface and ground water. In India, the industrial effluents have contributed a major source of pollution (Bharti, 2012).

In most parts of India, textile handloom business including cotton, woolen, dying, printing, weaving, etc. are the main source of economy and employments for a major low income group. Textile industries consume a large quantity of water and generate a huge amount of wastewater, which generally discharged into a common effluent drain of industrial area. The composite effluents from textile industries in Panipat city consisting high concentrations of heavy metals, organic pollutants and toxic colours, which may affect the quality of surface water, soil, ground water and plant tissues of the region.

Toxic pollutants may percolate down via soil profile and reach in ground water, which ultimately cause the health hazards among human being and livestock after consumption as daily drinking requirements. The waste water without any treatment may cause adverse effect on the health of human, domestic animals, wildlife and environment (Sharma *et al.*, 1999). Thus, contaminated ground water has deteriorated immensely the drinking utilities, post agriculture irrigation and impacts on soil systems and crop productivity.

Textile effluent when discharged into the pond and through pond they percolated to the ground water (Malik *et al.*, 2006). When this water is used for irrigation purpose affects our crop health. The textile effluent had consisting high concentration of trace heavy metals and through its accumulation in different trophic levels of ecosystem ultimately cause the health hazards among livestock and human beings (Malik *et al.*, 2004). So, it is very much essential to assess the quality of wastewater before discharging it and to develop an economical method for prevention and control of ground water pollution.

Water is one of the widely distributed and abundant substance found in the nature it covers about 75% of the earth surface therefore earth is sometimes called a "water planet" water is in sea, river, ocean, pond, streams and even in the atmosphere in the form of humidity. Most of the earth surface water is in the sea, the ocean contain about excessive quantities of salts. Fresh water is in lakes, ponds, rivers and streams. Fresh water is also available in the forms of rain, snow, dew etc. We live on the water planet and water has many unique-almost magical properties. A precious film of water-most of it salt water-covers about 71% of the earth's surface. Water, one of the fundamental resources, is also one of the most unusual substances. Although its chemical formula is simple yet the effect of water on environment is more consequential than ever imagined. The Earth's atmosphere contains 0.02 to 4 percent water by volume, depending on the location. In addition to providing sources for precipitation, atmospheric water vapours intercept some of the ultraviolet radiation and intercept heat loss from the earth sand redirect part of it to the Earth.

Water is one of the prime necessities of life. We can hardly live for a few days without water. In human body 70% is water. Blood, cells and bones contain 18%, 75% and 22% water respectively. Even teeth and nails also contain some parts of water. Water has become an essential commodity for the development of industries and agriculture (Kudesia, 1992).

The available natural freshwater resources today are threatened by hazard of pollution; particularly rivers are greatly polluted due to release of untreated effluents and waste material from agriculture practices and industries located around rivers. The poor living conditions of people in settlement around rivers, non availability of treatment from urban areas and negligence of industries for treatment of effluent before release of natural water bodies are the major reason of pollution of Indian rivers and other water bodies like ponds, lakes, etc. Our drinking water are obtained from all sorts of sources, some good, some not well, some bad and some outright dangerous. These are reflected in the health, vitality and longevity of people. Since we gulp water, and it is taken straight into the body its cleanliness is vitally important. It should be free from pathogens, it should not contain excessive amount of salts and toxic elements. Scientifically distilled water is the cleanest, but it is not good drinking water.

Water is the most used for industrial, municipal and agricultural purpose. The quantity and quality of available water are very important for the purpose of textile industries. Each industry has its own water requirements and sometimes adequate supply of water may be very suitable for one industry but the same may be dangerous for other. It is therefore, extremely important to take into account the use of water to be carried out, its suitability based on the result of chemical analysis.

With the fast increasing in our industrial civilization, the demand for water is increasing tremendously day by day. Although water pollution is an age old problem but in this modern age, the problems like population increase, sewage disposal, industrial waste, radioactive waste etc. have polluted our water resources so much so that about 70% rivers and streams not only of India but of all the countries contain polluted waters (Kudesia, 1992). The industrial effluents and trade waste play a significant role in pollution of water. The industries are – pulp and paper, distillery, fertilizer, electroplating, asbestos, silt, alcohol, detergents, steel, tannery, textile, cane sugar, oils, pesticides and herbicides, radioactive wastes, etc.

As far as the textile mills are concerned boiler feed water should be as soft as possible and should contain least amount of nitrate and organic matter in order to prevent encrustations or corrosion of boilerplates. For the purpose of dyeing water should be free from iron and should posses little hardness only. The textile industry has not been one of the major sources of air pollution by the nature of its operations. Its air pollution has been considerably less severe than its water pollution problem. Emissions from textile processes, excluding steam generation, fall into four general categories, namely oil and acid mists, solvent vapours, odours, dust and lint.

Textile industries in general consume large volume of water of high purity. Consequently, these units discharge large quantities of effluent that normally exhibit polluting characteristics. According to review of available literature the quantity of effluent discharged and quantity of consumed water by woollen units and in case of composite cotton textile industries, always remain high.

Synthetic dyes using in textile industrial sectors generally contain some toxic heavy metals according to its colour, which may alter the quality of adjoining surface water, ground water by leaching and persist again soil after irrigation.

Ground water contaminated by textile effluents, has deteriorated immensely the post agriculture irrigation, drinking utilities and impacts on soil and agricultural systems. For prevention of ground water pollution, it is very essential to treat industrial wastewater before discharging in to the surface water, because through the surface water pollutants may reach in ground water by leaching process.

Although many of the metals are essential components of the biological system yet some of these are potentially toxic. The detection and determination of metal ions of biological importance at ultra level in aqueous and biological material provides valuable information concerning their distribution and role in natural systems and finally related to the human health (Mohan and Sharma, 2002). Heavy metals are usually present in trace amounts in naturally waters but many of them are toxic even at very low concentration. Metals such as arsenic, lead, cadmium, nickel, mercury, chromium, cobalt, zinc and selenium are highly toxic even in minor quantity. Increasing quantity of heavy metals in our resources is currently an area of greater concern especially since a large number of industries are discharging their metal containing effluents in to fresh water without any adequate treatment (Canter, 1987).

Heavy metals become toxic when they are not metabolized by the body and accumulate in the soft tissues. Heavy metals may enter the human body through food, water, air, or absorption through the skin when they come in contact with humans in agriculture and in manufacturing, pharmaceutical, industrial, or residential settings. Industrial exposure accounts for a common route of exposure for adults. Ingestion is the most common route of exposure in children. Children may develop toxic levels from the normal hand-to-mouth activity of small children who come in contact with contaminated soil or by actually eating objects that are not food (dirt or paint chips).

Agricultural soils require sufficient irrigation for high production and irrigation water with poor quality can result in a build-up of soil salts and high soil pH. The chief minerals in irrigation water are chloride, sulphate, bicarbonate, sodium, calcium, and magnesium. These minerals contained in the irrigation water can build up in the soil and cause problems. Sodium, bicarbonate, and chloride are the three minerals that contribute most to soil salinity and alkalinity. More frequent irrigations become necessary to keep up with increasing soil salinity levels. Plants are most sensitive to saline soils during germination. Once established, they have the ability to tolerate higher soil salinity levels. Soil acidity affects a plant's ability to absorb nutrients.

The sediments existing as the bottom of the water column play a major role in the pollution scheme of an aquatic system by heavy metals (Forstner, 1985). They reflect the current quality of the water system and can be used in detecting the presence of contaminants that do not remain soluble after discharge into surface water. As a result of complex physical, chemical and biological processes a major fraction of heavy metals (contributed naturally as well as through various anthropogenic activities) is found to be associated with bottom sediments (Baruah *et al.*, 1996). Bed sediments in surface water systems thus act both as a sink and source of metals. Metal accumulation in sediments provides a record of the spatial and temporal history of pollution (Martin and Whitfield, 1983). Hence, sediment monitoring can provide important information on various pollution events.

So, it is essential to assess the status of heavy metals discarding from textile industries for health safety of regional environment as well as people. This will help to generate the baseline data of environment pollution of the region.

HISTORICAL RESUME

Thus textile effluents may affect different parts of environment in various ways. So, the assessment and monitoring textile effluents characteristics, affected surface and ground water, agriculture soil, plants and other suffered biota must be required. A lot of researchers are playing very important role to find out and evaluate the various parameters of various medium at different localities in different times. Textiles industries mostly used Vat and Azo dyes as a constituent for dyeing and discharging the effluent directly into a common composite drain. This drainage system joined the effluent to the pond thus influencing the surface water quality and the land quality of area. After delay of effluent in pond for a prolong time period, leaching of pollutants especially heavy metals will started and contaminate the ground water of this particular area. Use of this contaminated ground water in irrigation purposes may harmful for soils of agriculture fields, productivity of agriculture crop plants, and soil macrobiotic community.

Different workers from India and abroad have discussed various aspects of characteristics of water bodies, affected agricultural soils and bottom sediments from time to time. This review includes some of important contribution made from various parts of the country and abroad, with references to physical, chemical and biological parameters of ground water, surface water, characterization of textile industrial effluents, contaminated agricultural irrigated soil and bottom sediment soils.

Eaton (1950) gave the significance of carbonates in waters mostly used for irrigation purposes in agriculture, because it may maintain the pH of agriculture soil and balanced its texture and fertility. Aggarwal and Mehrotra (1952) surveyed the Soil and soil water in some selected regions of Uttar Pradesh.

Richards (1954) evaluated the quality of saline and alkali soils and gave a technique for the improvement of these sick soil systems in the agricultural sector for good performance of agriculture productivity.

Souther and Alsapaugh (1957) has also made some suggestion for the abatement of pollution in the textile industry e.g. process chemical substitution, closer process control and good housekeeping. Kanwar (1961) assessed the quality of irrigation water as an index of suitability for irrigation purposes. Seeber (1962) highlighted the cation hydrological facies of ground water in the English town Formation in New Jersey. Darra *et al.* (1964) evaluated the water quality of irrigation water used in Rajasthan. Hoston (1965) stated that the water quality index is a rating of water quality parameters by a single numerical expression reflecting the composite influence of water quality parameters (physical, chemical and bacteriological) significant for a specific beneficial use, which is very useful tool asses the overall water quality of water resources.

Saksena *et al.* (1966) evaluated the quality of ground waters for irrigation in Ahor developmental block, Jalore. Bhakuni and Bopardikar (1967) stated the method of recovery Zinc from the spinning bath waste of Viscos reyon factory by using ion exchange method and found it significant useful in metal removal process. Singh and Bhumbla (1968) analyzed the effect of quality of irrigation water on soil properties. Singh *et al.* (1969) reported the salinity problem in high water table areas. Porter (1970) highlighted the changing nature of textile processing and wastewater treatment technology according to time. Walker (1970) described the different metabolism of azo compounds used in textile dyeing unit. Nemerow (1971) described the origin of industrial water pollution, characteristics and treatment of industrial wastewater. Eckenfelder and Bornad (1971) justified the cost of waste treatment and relationship with its application for industrial waste. Singh and Sharma (1971) studied on the effects of saline irrigation waters on physico-chemical properties of some soils of Rajasthan.

Williums (1972) described the characteristics and various properties of Metals. Sharma and Parihar (1973) evaluated the effect of depth and salinity of ground water on evaporation and soil salinization. Considine (1974) described the various activities and functions of different chemicals and their related process. Verma and Mathur (1974) studied the toxicity of industrial wastes to some organisms such as macrobranchium deyanum. Widyanto (1975) conducted a survey on textiles factories and revealed that using the waste water from textile factory a 1:1 dilution of the concentrate may stimulate the growth of water hyacinth after 10 days. Katz (1975) highlighted the effect of heavy metals on aquatic some environmental components and biotic organisms. Dowedy and Larson (1975) reported the availability of some metals in various vegetable crops in a polluted region.

Dulka and Risby (1976) stated ultra trace metals in some environmental and biological systems. Horing (1976) evaluated the characterization and treatment of textile dyeing wastewaters with the help of a designed model. Shivakumar *et al.* (1977) made a graphical approach for toxic trace element pollution in ground water around Patancheru and Bollaram Industrial area, A.P., India.

Judlins and Hornsby (1978) carried out an observation on color removal from textile dye waste using magnesium carbonate. McKay (1979) described the color removal method from textile waste effluents. Todd (1980) described the ground water movement; ground water properties and hydrogeology for explain the behaviour of ground water pollution. Samy and

Gananarethinam (1980) found that industrial effluents were toxic to the aquatic plants like *Eicchornia* even after dilution. Synthetic compounds were found toxic to *Spirodela polyrhiza* and *Lemna aquinoctialis*. Wint (1981) indicated the disposal and handling problem of toxic wastes.

Martin and Cougherty (1982) stated the basic monitoring techniques for detection of heavy metals pollution through the biological agents. Ireland (1983) described the heavy metals uptake and their distribution in tissues of organisms. Numberg (1984) studied on the volumetric approach in trace metal chemistry of natural waters and atmospheric precipitation.

Michaels and Lewis (1985) postulated the sorption and toxicity of azo and triphenyl methane dues to aquatic microbial populations. Vates (1986) made a study on septic tank density and ground water contamination. Rhoades (1987) studied on the use of saline water for irrigation. Nriagu and Pacyna (1988) carried out a study on the quantitative assessment of worldwide contamination of air,. water and soil with trace metals. Zilliox (1989) determined the industrial impacts on the quality of ground water in a large basin as a case of the Rhine aquifer in France and noticed it harmful for public consumption. Mishra et al. (1990) had reported on heavy metals in crop plants of Sanagar more than the permissible limits presence of which may cause the adverse effect on the plant/human health and may cause high mortality of fish population in affected aquatic environment.

Minhas and Gupta (1992) indicated the effects of poor irrigation water quality on agriculture soils and also in crops of the fields. They defined the infiltration problem and identification and management of poor water quality. Kumar *et al.* (1992) studied the relationship between Fluoride, total hardness and total alkalinity in the ground water of Bharmar District (Rajsthan). Navarro *et al.* (1993) reported the waste dumping and accumulation of industrial and domestic waste in an industrial area, and impacts of untreated textile waste water respectively. Singh *et al.* (1994) highlighted the degradation of water and soil quality of Parwanoo area with respect to heavy metals.

Sharma *et al.* (1995) assessed the quality of ground water in municipal and fringe areas near Gwalior. Sharma and Patel (1996) determined copper in water of Raipur with the help of spectrophotometer. Khurshid and Shabeer (1997) observed water quality degradation due to heavy metal pollution. Olaniya *et al.* (1998) studied ground water pollution due to refuse leachate. Garg *et al.* (1998) observed fluoride in underground water of Hissar, Haryana. Mohan *et al.* (1998) observed heavy metals (Fe, Pb, Ca & Zn). Kashem and Singh (1999) had also found the decreasing concentration of Cu, Mn, Pb and Zn with increasing distance from disposal point.

Stetzenbach *et al.* (1999) evaluated the heavy metals in ground water and used multivariate statistical analysis. Sharma *et al.* (1999) and Sastry and Rathee (1999) had reported the impact of industrial effluents on fresh water system. Rao and Rao (1999) identified the path lines of pollutants migration in ground water of the Visakhpatanam urban area of south India using *MODFLOW* and *FLOWPATH* computer models. Particles path lines in the ground water indicated a predominant north east and south-west migration of ground water pollution in the area. Pujari and Sinha (1999) studied on the water and soil quality of some villages of Attabira area irrigated by bargarg main canal originated from Hirakund reservoir of Orissa.

Tyagi and Budhi (2000) postulated the degradation of ground water quality due to heavy metals in industrial area of India. Al-Degs, et al. (2000) described the effect of carbon surface chemistry on the removal of reactive dyes from textile effluent and observed a method for decolorization of wastewater of textile industry having reactive dyes with azo bond and associated chromophores. Reddy and Linn (2000) used catalysts against nitrate pollution in ground water and observed it significantly suitable for abatement of ground water pollution.

Sheth and Patel (2001) studied on characterization, treatment and comparative cost analysis of textile processing wastewater of Vatva industrial complex. Kumar *et al.* (2001) studied on the impact of textile industry on ground water quality of Sanagar, Jaipur. Thorat and Pathade (2001) described the characterization, processes, pollution and the treatment of wastewater generated from each step of textile industry. They identified the main sources of waste water generated in textile industry and give a flowchart for the neutralization of alkaline waste and their chemical and biological treatments. Aurangabadkar *et al.* (2001) studied on ground water quality at Chennai. Srinivas *et al.* (2002) pointed out the ground water pollution due to the industrial effluents in Kothur industrial area, Mahaboonagar, A.P. Siddiqui and Pathani (2002) made some studies on heavy metals in surface and ground water of Jalandhar and Ludhiana districts of Haryana state. Vishwanath and Ananthmurthy (2002) assessed the ground water quality around a solid waste dumping site and concluded that ground water contains high electric conductivity; TDS, hardness and fluorides but the nitrates and chlorides were within the permissible limits of potable drinking water standards.

Annadurai et al. (2002) used the cellulose based wastes for adsorpation of dyes from aqueous solutions, because dyes from the dye manufacturing industry, textile industry, pulp and paper industry are highly colored. The discharge of colored water into streams not only affects their aesthetic nature but also interferes with the transmission of sunlight into streams and therefore reduces photosynthesis action. Yadav *et al.*, (2002) highlighted the post irrigation impact of domestic sewage effluent on composition of soils, crops and ground water in Kurukshetra district. Mohan and Sharma (2002) and Yadav *et al.* (2003) determined the ground water quality of different places of Rajasthan. Mohanasundaram (2003) suggested the affordable and effective

Textile processing effluent treatment plants. They make a baseline diagram and flowchart for explaining all the function and process of this treatment plant in a very easy way.

Ameta *et al.*, (2003) observed that there was a prominent growth and increased sugar and protein percentage and chlorophyll content in onion grown in photocatalytically treated effluent. Based on the above results, photocatalytic treatment of wastewater can be considered as an effective method, which will help in reusing the effluent from dye industry for irrigation purposes. Shrivastava *et al.*, (2003) collected some soil samples were from surface of the soil from different agriculture fields in the Khandesh region where wheat, jawar, cotton, sugar cane and groundnut crops were cultivated. Tapi River sediment samples were also collected from five different stations which were 7-8 km away from each other. The concentrations of heavy metals have been determined by ICP-AES and physico-chemical characteristics have been detected by following standard methods. Royee and Prakasham (2003) analysed the water characteristics of dug and tube wells of Kollam municipality. Khan *et al.* (2003) harvested some *Solanum melongena* plant in a laboratory experiment using five different levels of textile waste water. After the crop harvesting the soil was found to contain 1.417 mg/g of Zn, 1.003 mg/g of Cu, 0.378 mg/g of Ni, 0.378 mg/g of Cd, 0.773 mg/g of Cr, 1.139 mg/g of Pb and 0.427 mg/g of Co in the soil of pots treated with highest ratio of distilled water and waste water. Yadav and Sumanlata (2003) indicated the pollution in ground water in Bahadurgarh block of districts Jhajjar, Haryana Mor *et al.* (2003) assessed the quality of ground water of Jind city in Haryana state. Mishra and Sahoo (2003) evaluated the ground water quality in and around Deogarh.

Lee *et al.* (2004) used nitrogen for colour and COD removal by fungi in textile effluent. Bousselmi *et al.* (2004) studied textile wastewater treatment by solar catalysis from a plant in Tunisia. Krull & Dopkens (2004) recycled the dye house effluents by biological and chemical treatment in Germany. Bae *et al.* (2004) used Fenton process for textile dyeing wastewater treatment in Korea.

Malik *et al.* (2004) demonstrated the accumulation of heavy metals in crop plants through irrigation of contaminated ground water in panipat region. Textile effluent when discharged into the pond and through pond they percolated to the ground water. When this water is used for irrigation purpose affects our crop health. The different crop plant samples collected from agricultural field adjoining of textile industrial effluent flowing channels contained in situ these heavy metals e.g. Lead (Pb), Copper (Cu), Manganese (Mn), Nickle (Ni), Iron (Fe), Cadmium (Cd) and Zinc (Zn). The bioremediation processes are urgently required to combat ground water pollution. Mahesha and Prasad (2004) elaborated the physico-chemical characteristics of bore well water.

Yu *et al.* (2005) studied color, dye and DOC removal, and acid generation during Fenton oxidation of dyes. The removal of color, dye and dissolved organic carbon by Fenton discoloration was investigated using the synthetic dye wastewater containing various dyes (reactive blue 19, Erichrome Black-T or Fast Green FCF). The result indicated that a discoloration of dyes was very rapid but mineralization of dyes was insignificant based on the removal of dissolved organic carbon.

Sevimli *et al.* (2005) carried out the work on investigating the effect of some operational parameters on the de-colorization of textile effluent and dye solution by ozonation. Dhar *et al.* (2005) studied the effect of acid activated sawdust on the removal of different dissolved tannery dyes (Acid dye) from aqueous solution. The effectiveness of acid activated sawdust in absorbing D-Brown EGP and Lurazol Brown PM dyes from aqueous solution was studied as a function of agitation time and initial dye concentration. Saw dust is an excellent low cost adsorbent of coloured organic anions and may have significant potential as a colour removal from tannery wastewater.

Aboulhassan *et al.* (2005) suggested the treatment process of textile wastewater using a natural flocculants. Chao *et al.* (2005) reported the heavy metal contaminated site in Taiwan and described the status and distribution of heavy metals in environment.

It is necessary to reduce the levels of toxic metals from industrial effluents before discharging into surface waters. The general methods of treating wastewater containing metals are coagulation, ion exchange, reverse osmosis and adsorption. Adsorption is a highly effective physico-chemical treatment for removing heavy metals for effluents. Due to high cost of activated carbon, efforts are being directed towards finding low cost adsorbents. Recently much interest has been shown for removal of heavy metals using a large number of low cost materials. Coal fly ash, the solid waste of power plants is one of the cheapest and non-conventional adsorbents De (2005). He demonstrated a technique of adsorption of cadmium and zinc on coal fly ash.

Bhat and Kulkarni (2005) studied on Chemical Oxygen Demand reduction of dye industry effluent having COD in excess of 100000 mg/l and are extremely difficult to treat and pose severe pollution problems if discharged directly to treatment plants. They used rice husk, saw dust and charcoal as adsorbents for the reduction of COD load of dye waste. It was found that activated charcoal is suitable adsorbent under specified condition. Also, cheaply available adsorbent such as saw dust and rice husk also show some good results.

Saed *et al.* (2005) prepared a novel adsorbent from sugarcane bagasse for removing dye from water. The adsorption process was carried out in a batch process with different concentrations of the dye concentrations of the dye solution, different adsorbent doses, adsorbent with different particle size at different pH values and contact times. Sheth and Desai (2005) developed the Bench Scale Completely Mixed Activated Sludge Reactor Model in the laboratory and observed the changes in various treatment parameters and terminate the experiments when reactor has reached to a steady state. Using the concept of the Monod expression by a graphical method all the bio-kinetic parameters for textile wastewater was determined.

Dwivedi *et al.* (2005) indicated the contamination of groundwater due to the artificial ground water recharging. According to them it is important for the authorities to gain scientific knowledge of artificial recharging in order to adequately protect the groundwater aquifers. There are certain grounds, which should be analyzed and review before taking the decision of artificial recharging, such as quality of source water available for recharging; underground storage space available; transmission characteristics, best possible applicable method (injection/infiltration), cost of construction, regulation and the recurring charges, public perception, maintenance problem, etc. Kumar *et al.* (2005) described the status of water resources of India. They highlights the hydrological cycle, monsoon and precipitation, surface and ground water resources, water requirements in domestic use, irrigation, hydroelectric power, industrial requirement and ground water management in India. Dutta (2005) highlighted the ethics of ground water for its sustainability and the vulnerability and depletion of ground water due to rapid growth of population, urbanization, industrialization and competition for economic development. He also stated the ground water contamination, concepts of ground water management, strategies for the ground water protection and suggested use of contaminated groundwater.

Malik *et al.* (2006) reported the impact of textile effluents on surface water quality of Panipat industrial area. They noticed the adverse changes in the water quality of pond water which consist a huge amount of textile effluents and sewage waste water of industrial area on Jatal road near dye houses of Binjhole village. Pond water quality was found so poor that all the biotic community even macrophytes, plankton, nekton and benthos can't survive in pond water. Palanivelu *et al.* (2006) evidenced the poor ground water quality in areas like Kottivakkam beach, Kuppam Oorurokot Kuppam (seashore), Raja Rangasamy Avenue (Thiruvanmaiyur), Foreshore estate, Dhidir nagar, Nochikuppam, Anna MGR memorial, which lie in close proximity to the sea and where sea water inundated during the tsunami. Zheng *et al.*, (2006) assessed the heavy metals pollution of agricultural soil in Guanzhong District of China.

Lokeshwari and Chandrappa (2006) evaluated the impact of heavy metals contamination of a Lake on soil and cultivated vegetation near Bangalore. They found the presence of some heavy metals in rice and vegetables, beyond the limit of Indian Standrads. Metal transfer factors from soil to vegetation are found significant for Zn, Cu, Pb and Cd. Compareing the results of heavy metals in water, soil and vegetation with their respective natural levels; it was observed that impact of lake water on vegetation was found to be more than the soil. Hedge *et al.* (2006) demonstrated the provenance of heavy minerals with special reference to ilmenite of the Honnevar beach in central west coast of India. They observed some trace heavy elements like Co, Cr, V and Ni in the sandy soil of the beach. Singh (2006) indicated the contamination of ground water of Ganges-Brahmaputra river basin in north east India and found the ground water unfit for direct human consumption.

Malik *et al.* (2007) quantified the migration of heavy metals in the ground water regime of Panipat industrial area on the behalf of different spatial variations the heavy metals were found in maximum quantities at point source of pollution, while it was observed comparatively less at 1 km ahead from pollution source and so on. High concentrations of cadmium, lead and copper were found in most samples of ground water in point source of textile industrial area, while rest metal concentrations were found within the level of drinking water quality criteria. Malik and Bharti (2007) studied on the agricultural soil quality near an industrial area.

Rizk, *et al.*, (2007) identified the sources of dissolved solids and water in Wadi Al Bih aquifer, Ras Al Khaimah Emirate in United Arab Emirates. Vijith and Satheesh (2007) completed the Geographical Information System based assessment of spatiotemporal characteristics of groundwater quality of upland sub-watersheds of Meenachil River, parts of Western Ghats, Kottayam District of Kerala, India.

Va´zquez, *et al.* (2007) monitored the heavy metal pollution in San Antonio Bay, Rý´o Negro, Argentina. Obiri (2007) determined the heavy metals in water from boreholes in Dumasi in the Wassa West District of Western Region of Republic of Ghana. Huang *et al.* (2007) indicated the speciation and mobility of heavy metals in mud in coastal reclamation areas in Shenzhen in China. Walker *et al.* (2007) identified the influence of heavy metals and mineral nutrient supply on *Bituminaria bituminosa*. Gharaibeh *et al.* (2007) found the impact of field application of treated wastewater on hydraulic properties of vertisols.

Golia *et al.* (2007): measured the accumulation of metals on tobacco leaves (primings) grown in an agricultural area in relation to soil. Trevors and Saier (2007) described the regulation of pollution in various environmental components viz. water, air and soil. Fransson (2007) studied on to verify the methods for estimating transmissivity distributions along boreholes. Mico *et al.*, (2007) described the comparison of two digestion methods for the analysis of heavy metals by flame atomic absorption spectroscopy. Padmavathiamma and Li (2007) explained the phytoremediation Technology through the hyper-accumulation metals in plants and different aspects of phytoremediation technology and the biological mechanisms underlying phytoremediation.

Malik *et al.*, (2008) pointed out the dispersion of heavy metals in textile effluent and pond environment in Panipat industrial area. Malik *et al.*, (2009) described the role of aquatic macrophytes in the remediation of metal pollutants. Bharti et al., (2010) identified the influence of Heavy Metals on Abundance of Cyanophyceae Members in Three Spring-fed Lake in Kempty, Dehradun. Malik and Bharti (2010) described the environment Pollution in a textile industrial area. Malik and Bharti (2011) studied on spatial distribution of heavy metals in ground water regime of Panipat industrial area, India. Bharti (2012) explained the heavy metals distribution in the Groundwater of Panipat industrial area.

STUDY AREA

Geographically, Haryana is situated between 27° 37′ to 30° 35′ North latitude and between 74° 28′ to 77° 36′ longitude on the globe. Uttar Pradesh borders Haryana on the East, Punjab on the West, Himachal Pradesh on the North, and Delhi and Rajasthan on the South direction. In the geographical conditions, Haryana is agriculture based green state of the India. The state of Haryana came in 1966, when it was curved out of Punjab. Haryana ranks as one of India's most prosperous states among all other states of India.

Panipat is situated on the bank of river Yamuna, it lies between 29′ 09′ 50″ and 29′ 50′ North latitude and 76° 31′ 15″ and 77° 12′ 45″ East longitude with a height of 255 masl. Karnal, Sonipat, Jind, Kaithal districts of Haryana and Uttar Pradesh bordered this district. Population of Panipat city is 261874.

Panipat town is located on the national highway no.1 about 90 km toward north of Delhi has a population of about 0.27 million. Average population density of the urban area of Panipat city is 25,278 per Sq. Km., while the area of town is 10.8 Sq. Km. Panipat was the part of District Karnal till 31 October, 1989 in Haryana state, which was upgraded as a separate District, including Assandh Tehsil of district Karnal. When the District was reformed on 01 January, 1992 Assandh Tehsil was excluded from this District.

Climatic Conditions

Topographically, Ground is flat but gently slopes towards south-east. Water table is 5 m BGL (Ground Level). Panipat city is situated on the bank of Yamuna river, which is flowing through the west portion of the city. Agricultural soil is almost of loamy sand type and sandy type. Regarding the atmosphere and temperature, in summer, more summer and in winter the temp goes up to Minimum 4.4 °C in December, January, However in summer it goes up to 42.4 °C in June.

The samples were collected from the selected sampling sites during the month of April 2005 to March 2007 in morning hours (from 9.00 am to 11.00 am) as follows:

(A) Experimental sampling site:

(i) Water samples:

1. Effluent from textiles outlet [EF]
2. Tube wells/Hand pumps of the area [TW/HP]
3. Surface water from pond [SW/PW]

(ii) Soil samples:

1. Effluent drain sediment [EFS]
2. Pond bottom sediment [PDS]
3. Agricultural soil [AGS]

(B) Control sampling site:

Water and soil samples were collected from two sampling points of control, located 10 km distance in non industrial area.

Parameters have studied:

(a) Physico-chemical parameters of Textile effluents, surface water and ground water:
Temperature, pH, Total solids, Total suspended solids, Total dissolved solids, Electrical conductivity, Dissolved oxygen, Free-CO_2, Biochemical oxygen demand (BOD), Chemical oxygen demand (COD), Total alkalinity, Calcium (Ca^{++}), Magnesium (Mg^{++}), Potassium (K^+), Sodium (Na^+) Chloride (Cl^-)

(b) Physico-chemical parameters of agriculture soils, effluent sediment and pond sediment:
Temperature, Water holding capacity, Bulk density, Soil moisture, pH, Electrical conductivity, Chloride, Potassium (K^+), Sodium (Na^+)

(c) Trace heavy metals in Textile effluent, surface water, ground water, effluent sediment, pond sediment, agriculture soil and crop plants:
Cadmium (Cd), Copper (Cu), Iron (Fe), Manganese (Mn), Nickel (Ni), Lead (Pb), and Zinc (Zn)

MATERIAL AND METHODS

Material

The chemicals, used in the present investigation were procured by E. Merck India, S.D fine chemicals and B.D.H., India of analytical grade. All the glassware used was of corning grade, manufactured by Borosil India Ltd. All the glassware and Jeri canes were cleaned or washed with soda and chromic acid and rinsed with double distilled water 2-3 times. Plastic canes, BOD bottles, Polybags, auger, Water analysing Kit, Thermometer, pH strip, bag, etc. were the materials used during the sampling.

Sampling

Grab sampling was generally applied during the sampling. A grab sample is an ordinary sample, which is taken from a particular place representing the whole water quality. This type of sample is valid only when it is certain that the water quality is not changing in a short time and effluent discharges, if any, are fairly regular. It is advisable to collect and analyze the grab samples separately at various timings, if the water quality is known to change with time. In such cases the schedule of timings shall be dependent on the frequency of discharge or change in water quality. This approach is used in studies to understand diurnal changes in pH, free CO_2, alkalinity, dissolved oxygen, etc. by collecting a 2 or 3 hour sample round the clock. In any kind of water, at least for dissolved oxygen, several grab samples spread over the whole day or even the night shall be important in limnological study, but in the case of ground water, there is not any more diurnal changes in general water quality parameters, so a single grab sample is enough to represent the quality status of ground water.

The sampling of water/soil from stream banks/shallow ground water/pond/drain sediment can be easily carried out using a wide mouthed polythene bottle but a sampler has to be used if the studies are to be undertaken at various strata of water. The sampling of sediments from the bottom of natural water bodies, stabilizing ponds or effluent drains is invariably carried out using special samplers. A large number of water and sediment samplers have been developed over the year with varying degree of sophistication. Most common of them and those, which are readily available in India are Van Dron water sampler, simple laboratory made water sampler, shallow water sampler and Eckmen Dredge sediment sampler.

Eckmen Dredge sediment sampler is a most common type of sampler used for sampling the sediment for physical, chemical and biological analysis. It is made up of a brass or steel box provided at the bottom with two jaws hinged together and to the box. Two hinged lids are provided at the top of the box. It has a fixed sectional area when the jaws are in open position, to sample the soil from a fixed area. The box is lowered in water with jaws in open position. When box reaches the bottom, a messenger is sent with the rope which closes the jaws with the bottom sediment enclosed in the box. The box is then hauled up with the upper lids closing automatically under the pressure of water.

Study point (Textile industrial area/Dye houses) in Panipat city is situated on Jatal road in industrial area near GT Road, quite famous for handloom business. Textile effluents in composite forms were collected from common effluent drain of dye houses and surface water samples were collected from nearest small water bodies, while pond water was collected from a large pond (12 ha) contaminated by textile effluents. The ground water samples were collected from hand pumps/tube wells with the depth of 40ft, 80 ft and deep aquifer (>80 ft) and from discharge point of effluent (A), 1 km away (B) and 2 km away (C) from a large pond (12 ha) of village Binjhole situated nearby, where the effluent drain ends up and percolate down into shallow aquifers. Soil samples were collected from the agricultural fields of the area, sediments soil samples from polluted pond and effluent drain sediment were collected also in polythene bags. Some seasonal plants leaves and roots (5 for each) were also picked up for heavy metals analysis. Total 21 water, 9 soil and 10 plants samples were collected and preserved from industrial area of Panipat. All samples were analyzed by the standard methods (APHA, 1995) and Trivedi and Goel (1984).

Transfer factor between plants and soil, was calculated for each metal according to the following formula

$TF = Ps$ (μg g–1 dry wt)/St (μg g–1 dry wt)

Where,

Ps is the plant metal content originating from the soil and St is the total metal content in the soil. Between soil and water, water and effluent and SW to GW this formula was also applied for transfer coefficient (factor).

Sample Preparation

Water samples (500 ml) were filtered using Whatman no. 41 (0.45 μm pore size) filter paper for estimation of dissolved metal content. Filtrate and as-collected water samples (500 ml each) were preserved with 2 ml nitric acid to prevent the precipitation of metals. Both the samples were concentrated to tenfold on a water bath and subjected to nitric acid digestion using the microwave-assisted technique (APHA, 1995). Soil samples were air-dried and ground into fine powder using pestle and mortar and passed through 1 mm sieve.

Well-mixed samples of 2 g each were taken in 250 ml glass beakers and digested with 8 ml of aqua-regia on a sand bath for 2 h. After evaporation to near dryness, the samples were dissolved with 10 ml of 2% nitric acid, filtered and then diluted to 50 ml with distilled water (Ming and Ma, 2001). Vegetables, fruit, crop and plant samples were thoroughly washed to remove all adhered soil particles. Samples were cut into small pieces, air-dried for 2 days and finally dried at 100 □1□C in a hot-air oven for 3 h. The samples were ground in warm condition and passed through 1 mm sieve. Digestion of these samples (2 g each) was carried out using 10 ml nitric acid, according to the procedure used for soil samples (Lark *et al.*, 2002).

Analysis

Heavy metal analyses were carried out using atomic absorption spectrophotometer ECIL, AAS 4129. The calibration curves were prepared separately for all the metals by running different concentrations of standard solutions. The instrument was set to zero by running the respective reagent blanks. Average values of three replicates were taken for each determination. All the analytical work was executed as per the standard procedures given in APHA (2005), Trivedi and Goel (1984).

Heavy Metals

Following Heavy Metals were selected for the evaluation in water and soil samples:

- Cadmium
- Copper
- Iron
- Lead
- Manganese
- Nickel
- Zinc

Copper (Cu)

Copper in the natural waters also results in higher concentration due to pollution. It is used with sulphate as a pesticides and also separately as an algaecide. Although, it passes as such through the body but there is evidence of accumulation of trace quantities in liver. The limits of it in the standards are not due to its toxic effects but are due to its taste producing capacity.

Preparation of 1000 Cu (μg/ml) standard: Dissolve 1 gm of Cu in 50 ml of 6N of HNO_3 and dilute to 1 L to give 1000 μg/ml Cu.

Cadmium (Cd)

Cadmium is fairy dense silver white malleable and most toxic metal, which melts at 320.9°C. Cadmium is used for dye and paint pigment production, batteries, ceramic industries, wooden industries and plastic production. The Cd found in a sample of Ca is likely in a inorganic form and may be relatively less toxic to plants and animals, while same amount of Cd when present in zinc or phosphates may be highly toxic to plants and animals, especially when there is calcium deficiency in soil or livestock rations.

Preparation of 1000 Cd (μg/ml) standard: Dissolve 1 gm of Cd Metal in 20 ml of 5N HCl containing 0.5 ml of concentrated HNO_3 and dilute to 1 L to give 1000 μg/ml Cd.

Iron (Fe)

Iron is one of the most abundant elements of the rocks and soil, ranking fourth by weight. All kinds of waters including ground water have appreciable quantities of iron. Iron has more solubility at acidic pH, therefore large quantities of iron are leached out from the soils by acidic waters. In the alkaline medium iron remain comparatively low in soluble phase.

Preparation of 1000 Fe (μg/ml) standard, dissolve 1.000 g of iron wire in 50 ml of (1+1) HNO_3 and dilute to 1 liter with de-ionized water to give 1000 μg/ml Fe.

Manganese (Mn)

Although not a toxic metal, Mn imparts objectionable and tenacious stains to laundry plumbing fixtures and clothing. It occurs in domestic waste water, industrial effluents, acid mine drainage and receiving strums and thereby enters water bodies. Mn is relatively non-toxic to animals, but toxic to plants at higher levels.

Preparation of 1000 Mn (µg/ml) standard: Dissolve 1 gm of Mn in 50 ml of 6N of HNO_3 and dilute to 1 L to give 1000 µg/ml Mn.

Nickel (Ni)

At high concentrations, nickel has toxic properties. Aquatic organisms have varying sensitivities to nickel salts depending on the water's pH, hardness, alkalinity and type of nickel compound under consideration. Nickel as a metal is a carcinogen.

Preparation of 1000 Ni (µg/ml) standard: Dissolve 1 gm of Ni metal in 50 ml of 6N of HNO_3 and dilute to 1 L to give 1000 µg/ml Ni.

Lead (Pb)

It is a dense soft metal and is quite resistant to corrosion. It has melting point of 327ºC. Major source of lead is PbS (Galena). Lead is used for pipes, solders, electrodes, batteries, newsprint, and pigments in paints. Lead is also used in insecticides, beverages, ointments and synthetic dyes. The chemical form of lead determines its solubility in water and biological fluids, the extent of its fixation on soil and type of chemical reactions occurring in atmospheric, aquatic as well as soil environment.

Preparation of 1000 Pb (µg/ml) standard: Dissolve 1 gm of Pb metal in 20 ml of 6N of HNO_3 and dilute to 1 L to give 1000 µg/ml Pb.

Zinc (Zn)

Zinc is present in high concentrations in the wastes from pharmaceuticals, paint, galvanizing, cosmetics, dyes and pigments, etc., and their discharge increases its concentration in appreciable amounts in the waters. Zinc is very essential micronutrient in human beings and only at very high concentration it may cause some toxic effects. Zinc salts produce an undesirable taste to the water and causes water to appear milky and on boiling, a greasy surface scum may also form in the water (Mani *et. al.*, 2005).

Preparation of 1000 Zn (µg/ml) standard: Dissolve 1 gm of Zn metal in 40 ml of 5N HCl and dilute to 1 L to give 1000 µg/ml Zn.

Digestion and Dilution

Samples were collected in Borosil BOD bottles and some Jeri canes for laboratory experiments. Some parameters were determined immediately on sampling sites, for rest parameters and heavy metals; samples were stored in refrigerator at 4ºC. Heavy metals may be analyzed in the 6 months period from the preservation date.

Samples were taken in Jeri canes for determination of the parameters like conductivity, total solids, pH (hydrogen ion concentration), COD, free CO_2, total alkalinity, total hardness Ca/Mg, chlorides, lead, manganese, zinc, calcium and magnesium. Caps of cans were closed tightly after filling up of cane.

For dissolved oxygen/biochemical oxygen demand, samples were collected in sterilized 300 ml capacity BOD bottles. The bottles were filled completely with sample water up to the rim and stopper was placed only avoiding any kind of air bubble inside it. DO was immediately fixed by adding 2 ml each of alkaline potassium iodide and manganese sulphate ($MnSO_4$) at sampling spot. While the sample for BOD was incubated for 5 days in BOD incubator at 20°C.

Collected, preserved, diluted water samples were prepared for the evaluation of metal concentrations with the help of AAS 4129.

Metals enter in the surface water ecosystem through the disposing of waste materials and various. For every metal a standard was required and concentration may be detected by AAS. Diluted and completely digested samples were required for metal detection by AAS 4129. Metal elements were determined with the help of Atomic absorption spectrophotometer (Model AAS 4129). Alan Walsh first developed the technique of atomic absorption spectrophotometry in 1955, and since then it has emerged as a powerful tool in quantitative analysis of more than 70 metals. The major advantages of the method are that it is free from any kind of interferences and very small concentrations are possible to be measured (De, 2002). The AAS is based on the principle that atoms of elements, which normally remain in ground state under flame condition, absorb energy when subjected to radiation of specific wavelength. The absorption of radiation is proportional to the concentration of atoms of the element. The absorption of radiation by the atoms is independent of the wavelength of absorption and temperature of the atoms. These to feature provide AAS a distinct advantage over flame spectroscopy.

About AAS

ECIL's Atomic Absorption Spectrophotometer, AAS 4129 is a PC based instrument for absorption and emission analysis. It is used for quantitative elemental analysis mainly like Copper, Iron, Zinc, Lead etc., by measuring the absorbance of a sample atomized in a flame. Some of the metals like Sodium, Potassium, Calcium, and Lithium are analyzed by emission method. PC does the data processing and partial control of the instrument.

The liquid sample is nebulised (reduce to a spray) by the support gas. The fuel gas is mixed and burnt over the burner head. A modulated light from Hollow Cathode lamp of a pre-selected element travels through the flame and enters the monochromator. The monochromator selects the appropriate resonance line of the selected element and directs it on to the PMT. The DC signal generated by the flame emission is rejected by FE compensation circuit and the original signal of the lamp is amplified, phase sensitively rectified averaged by an integrator to obtain sample signal. A computer processes the sample signal for photometric computations (% T, ABS or CONC). Instrument controls like wavelength, lamp current, gain, etc. are achieved and maintained by PC.

The cathode material of Hollow Cathode Lamp corresponds to the element of interest. ECIL's Atomic Absorption Spectrophotometer covers the complete range of Atomic Absorption applications. It incorporates State-of-the-art electronics, safety and operational convenience ensuring reliable and accurate analytical performance.

The data analysis and report making is done by the PC including selection of instrument parameters like wavelength, lamp current selection, and EHT to PMT at various wavelength. The software is user-friendly window based GUI interface using menus, function key, prompts, error messages, enabling ease of operation. Information is presented in easy read menus. In most cases recommended values are filled in.

The instrument was calibrated using regression techniques of linear and quadratic methods against standard solutions and concentration of unknown samples can be quantified. Instrument parameters and calibration parameters can be stored, as applications, which can be retrieved as and when, required. A hard copy of the results can be taken with the aid of a printer connected to one of the parallel ports of the PC.

Standard and Calibration

Whenever, possible metals and metals oxides are to be preferred in the preparation of standards. This enables the analyst to dissolve them that samples and standards will contain identical elements and hence minimizes any chemical or physical interference effects.

Only concentrated standards (above 1000 μg/ml) should be held in storage. Working standards should be diluted from standards stock solutions only when needed. At low concentrations (less than 10 μg/ml) solutions have been found to deteriorate quite quickly because of the absorption on the walls of the container. Similar standard addition solutions can be prepared containing all of the required elements. This will avoid multiple splitting of the sample for individual elements and reduce the amount of time spent in preparing standards.

Before weighting, standards materials should be treated to ensure that they are in a standard state.

- *Metals:* Wash with acetone and ether to remove any oil layers. Remove any oxide coating by abrasion with emery cloth or by acid pickling and drying.

- *Oxides:* Dry at 110° C for two hours. If necessary, heat to evaluated temperatures to remove bound water.
- *Compounds:* Equilibration at constant water content, or drying at 110° C for two hours to remove any water.

Standards of known concentrations were prepared and evaluated the concentration of metal in water/ soil digested sample. Every metal has some specific properties and atomic weight, so for every metal different condition of standard and calibration was applied for every metal (ECIL manual, 2004).

Table 6.1: Standard Criteria for Analyzing Heavy Metals by Atomic Absorption Spectrophotometer (AAS)

Sl. No.	Name	Symbol	Wavelength nm	Flame Gases	Instrument Detection Limits Mg/l	Sensitivity Mg/l	Optimum Concentration range Mg/l
1.	Cadmium	Cd	228.8	A-Ac2	0.002	0.025	0.05-2
2.	Copper	Cu	324.7	A-Ac	0.01	0.1	0.02-10
3.	Lead*	Pb	279.5	A-Ac	0.01	0.05	0.1-10
4.	Manganese	Mn	232.0	A-Ac	0.02	0.15	0.3-10
5.	Nickel	Ni	283.3	A-Ac	0.05	0.5	1-20
6.	Zinc	Zn	213.9	A-Ac	0.005	0.02	0.05-2
7.	Iron	Fe	248.3	A-Ac	0.02	0.12	0.3-10

A-Ac = Air-acetylene,

* The more sensitive 217.0 nm wavelength is recommended for instruments with background correction capabilities (APHA, 2005).

Table 6.2: Periodic Position and Relevant Information of Selected Heavy Metals

Sl. No.	Name	Symbol	Atomic Number	Atomic Weight	Shale Value (mg/kg)
1.	Cadmium	Cd	48	112.411	0.3
2.	Copper	Cu	29	63.546	45
3.	Lead	Pb	82	207.2	20
4.	Manganese	Mn	25	54.93805	850
5.	Nickel	Ni	28	58.6934	68
6.	Zinc	Zn	30	65.39	95
7.	Iron	Fe	26	55.845	47200

Source: IUPAC, 1994.

Toxicity of Heavy Metals

The heightened concern for reduction of environmental pollution that has been occurring over the past 20-25 years has stimulated active continuing research and literature on the toxicology of heavy metals. While the toxic effect of these substances is a widespread concern in the modern industrial context, Man has succeeded in poisoning himself with them repeatedly throughout recorded history. One historian/toxicologist contends that the fall of the Roman Empire was hastened by the chronic lead poisoning experienced by the ruling classes who had water conducted through lead plumbing and drank wine from goblets which had lead/alloy composition. Virtually all metals can produce toxicity when ingested in sufficient quantities, but there are several which are especially important because either they are so pervasive, or produce toxicity at such low concentrations. When speaking of heavy metals we generally mean, lead, mercury, iron, copper, manganese, cadmium, arsenic, nickel, aluminum, silver, and beryllium.

Many effects of Cd action results from interactions of various micro and macro elements as it antagonizes to Cu, Zn and Fe and also interferes with Ca absorption. Cadmium found in a sample of Ca is likely in an inorganic form and may be relatively less toxic to flora and fauna, while same amount of Cd when present in zinc or phosphates may be highly toxic to plants and animals, especially in calcium deficiency in soil. The use of contaminated water into irrigation may be increase the cadmium status in agricultural soil (Mani *et al.*, 2005).

Cadmium derives its toxicological properties from its chemical similarity to zinc an essential micronutrient for plants, animals and humans. Cadmium is biopersistent and, once absorbed by an organism, remains resident for many years (over decades for humans) although it is eventually excreted.

In humans, long-term exposure is associated with renal disfunction. High exposure can lead to obstructive lung disease and has been linked to lung cancer, although data concerning the latter are difficult to interpret due to compounding factors. Cadmium may also produce bone defects (osteomalacia, osteoporosis) in humans and animals. In addition, the metal can be linked to increased blood pressure and effects on the myocardium in animals, although most human data do not support these findings.

The average daily intake for humans is estimated as 0.15µg from air and 1µg from water. Smoking a packet of 20 cigarettes can lead to the inhalation of around 2-4µg of cadmium, but levels may vary widely.

Cadmium is produced as an inevitable by-product of zinc (or occasionally lead) refining, since these metals occur naturally within the raw ore. However, once collected the cadmium is relatively easy to recycle.

The most significant use of cadmium is in nickel/cadmium batteries, as rechargeable or secondary power sources exhibiting high output, long life, low maintenance and high tolerance to physical and electrical stress. Cadmium coatings provide good corrosion resistance, particularly in high stress environments such as marine and aerospace applications where high safety or reliability is required; the coating is preferentially corroded if damaged. Other uses of cadmium are as pigments, stabilisers for PVC, in alloys and electronic compounds. Cadmium is also present as an impurity in several products, including phosphate fertilisers, detergents and refined petroleum products.

In the general, non-smoking population the major exposure pathway is through food, via the addition of cadmium to agricultural soil from various sources (atmospheric deposition and fertiliser application) and uptake by food and fodder crops. Additional exposure to humans arises through cadmium in ambient air and drinking water.

Copper is sometimes found in insufficient quantity in soil (Miller and Turk, 2002) but it may be added in to soil system by some anthropogenic activities. Copper may accumulate in living organisms and their various body parts. High amount if heavy metals like cu and Zn may harm to living organism of existing ecosystem (Aslam *et al.,* 2004).

Iron has more solubility at acidic pH, therefore large quantities of iron are leached out from the soils by acidic waters. In the alkaline medium iron remain comparatively low in soluble phase. Excess calcium can reduced the activity of iron in soil and soil aeration may influence the availability of iron to plants (Miller and Turk, 2002).

Mathess (1974) reported that fresh ground water constitutes 0.00-0.007 ppm cadmium, WHO (1984) recommended Cd concentration should not exceed maximum of 0.01 ppm in raw drinking water supply, 0.5 ppm in irrigation water. USEPA (1990) recommended maximum permissible Cd concentration as 0.04 and 0.02 ppm to protect aquatic life including fish. Hart (1982) reported a concentration range of Pb 0.0003-0.03 ppm in natural fresh water.

Nickel is one of the second trace elements of the present study after cadmium. As it is very toxic to plants and animals in low concentrations and has a tendency to accumulate in body parts. However Ni was presented in very minor concentrations.

The presence of heavy metals in the aquatic environment has been of great concern to scientists and engineers because of their increased discharge, toxic nature, and other adverse effects on receiving waters.

Small amounts of Nickel are needed by the human body to produce red blood cells, however, in excessive amounts, can become mildly toxic. Short-term overexposure to nickel is not known to cause any health problems, but long-term exposure can cause decreased body weight, heart and liver damage, and skin irritation. The EPA does not currently regulate nickel levels in drinking water. Nickel can accumulate in aquatic life, but its presence is not magnified along food chains.

Manganese is frequently associated with iron deposits, and in fact the strata underlying Conception Bay providing the basis for the Wabana mines has a very rich manganese content. This metal is known to block Calcium channels, and with chronic intoxication results in CNS dopamine depletion. This latter condition duplicates almost all the symptomology of Parkinson's Disease, and is treated with some success using typical anti-Parkinson drugs. While the concentration in the surface water does not exceed official public health limits, it is in the high range of acceptable levels. It would be interesting to see if the epidemiology of Parkinsons syndrome in that locality is different from regions in the province with lower manganese concentrations. Manganese excretion can be facilitated by the use of chelator therapy, but it is not as easily managed as lead or mercury, because it is further down the list of chelator affinities.

Copper is an essential substance to human life, but in high doses it can cause anemia, liver and kidney damage, and stomach and intestinal irritation. People with Wilson's disease are at greater risk for health effects from overexposure to copper. Copper normally occurs in drinking water from copper pipes, as well as from additives designed to control algal growth.

Depending on one's location on the face of the planet, the food and water supply as well as the air we breath expose us to lead. Areas of particular risk are places where the drinking water is obtained from geologic strata with significant lead content. Areas which have deposits of gold, zinc, and other economically useful metals, also have lead as an ore contaminant and the "tailings" of the mining and purification of the ore often have a very high lead content. Before the systematic reduction of lead content in regular gasoline, the lead in the atmosphere in high automobile traffic areas was hazardous especially to small children. In old houses in which lead based paints were used there is a risk of toddlers consuming flaking paint chips with high lead content. This was a particular problem in the "slums" of large cities in the US till the ecologic consciousness was raised in the 60's and 70's. There are probably many old houses in Newfoundland with lead paint in their interiors, and there are known to be many communities with significant lead, zinc, and manganese concentrations in the ground water.

In most individuals there is a "lead balance", that is one excretes as much as they take in, and the tissue levels are below the concentrations which result in pathological changes. However an increase in the rate of intake will result in accumulation or a "positive lead balance". Since lead is chemically very similar to calcium, it is handled by the body as if it were calcium. Thus the first place to which it is transported is to the plasma and the membrane sites in soft tissues. It is then distributed to the other sites where calcium plays an important role, most notably in the teeth of developing children and in bone at all ages.

Following ingestion of a large amount of lead, there will be direct tissue interaction. This includes tissue dessication, mucosal tissue damage in the GI tract, and convulsion possibly resulting in death. The most sensitive system is the hematopoietic (blood forming) system, with hypochromic microcytic anemia common. The biosynthesis of hemes in general is deranged by the presence of lead. All actively dividing cells are especially susceptible, hence acute intoxication has major potential for GI and renal mucosal damage. In addition there is a high risk of neurological damage. With acute lead poisoning use of intravenous EDTA is the preferred treatment modality, often supplemented with oral penicillamine, and sometimes with intramuscular injections of dimercaprol.

With a gradual build-up of a positive lead balance there is no sudden onset of symptoms as seen with acute poisoning. The initial symptoms include clumsiness, ataxia, vertigo, irritability and insomnia. In affected children, they are often considered "slow", the real basis for the difficulty is not recognized. As the lead levels rise, hyper-excitability is seen. Confusion, delerium and convulsions may occur in some cases, while in others there is progressive lethargy leading to a comatose state.

One of the earliest diagnostic signs present is the appearance of "lead lines" at the gingival border in the mouth. This occurs because the lead following calcium pathways is secreted with the saliva. It then is involved in a reaction with oral bacteria which produce sulfides. The lead reacts with these compounds to form a purplish, or black lead sulfide deposit which precipitates in the region of highest concentration, the "protected area" at the gingival border. Other metals also produce this phenomenon, but with differing colors for the deposit.

Toxicity from inorganic lead can be treated with chelators, but organic lead compounds such as tetra-ethyl lead produces a similar symptomology, but cannot be treated with these agents because they already have formed strong ligands with their organic constituents. The alkyl lead eventually is converted to inorganic lead, which can be treated with the chelators.

In humans exposure to lead can result in a wide range of biological effects depending on the level and duration of exposure. Various effects occur over a broad range of doses, with the developing foetus and infant being more sensitive than the adult. High levels of exposure may result in toxic biochemical effects in humans which in turn cause problems in the synthesis of haemoglobin, effects on the kidneys, gastrointestinal tract, joints and reproductive system, and acute or chronic damage to the nervous system.

Lead poisoning, which is so severe as to cause evident illness, is now very rare indeed. At intermediate concentrations, however, there is persuasive evidence that lead can have small, subtle, subclinical effects, particularly on neuropsychological developments in children. Some studies suggest that there may be a loss of up to 2 IQ points for a rise in blood leadlevels from 10 to 20μg/dl in young children.

Average daily lead intake for adults in the UK is estimated at 1.6μg from air, 20μg from drinking water and 28μg from food. Although most people receive the bulk of their lead intake from food, in specific populations other sources may be more important, such as water in areas with lead piping and plumbosolvent water, air near point of source emissions, soil, dust, paint flakes in old houses or contaminated land. Lead in the air contributes to lead levels in food through deposition of dust and rain containing the metal, on crops and the soil. For the majority of people in the UK, however, dietary lead exposure is well below the provisional tolerable weekly intake recommended by the UN Food and Agriculture Organisation and the World Health Organisation.

Lead in the environment arises from both natural and anthropogenic sources. Exposure can occur through drinking water, food, air, soil and dust from old paint containing lead. In the general non-smoking, adult population the major exposure pathway is from food and water. Food, air, water and dust/soil are the major potential exposure pathways for infants and young children. For infants up to 4 or 5 months of age, air, milk formulae and water are the significant sources.

Lead is among the most recycled non-ferrous metals and its secondary production has therefore grown steadily in spite of declining lead prices. Its physical and chemical properties are applied in the manufacturing, construction and chemical industries. It is easily shaped and is malleable and ductile. There are eight broad categories of use: batteries, petrol additives (no longer allowed in the EU), rolled and extruded products, alloys, pigments and compounds, cable sheathing, shot and ammunition.

In heavy metals analysis, the total concentrations of the metals are often determined. However, total concentration of trace metals provides no information concerning the fate of the metal in the terms of its interaction with sediments, its mobility, bioavailability, or resultant toxicity. It is now widely accepted that measuring total metal concentrations cannot fully assess the role of aquatic sediments as a sink or as a source of pollutants. In addition, determination of total elements does not given an accurate estimate of the likely environmental impact. Instead, it is desirable to have information on the potential availability of metals (whether toxic or essential) to biota under various environmental conditions. Since the mobility of heavy metals, as well as their bioavailability and related eco-toxicity to plants, critically depends upon chemical forms in which, a metal is present in the sediment, considerable interest exists in trace element speciation (Davidson *et al.*, 1994).

Heavy metals are introduced into aquatic system from various anthropogenic sources. Heavy metals constitute a special group of contaminants of aquatic systems and deserve special attention. Since metals are not removed by natural degradation processes, they may become enriched in sediments over time. Metal contamination of sediments is an issue of growing concerns worldwide. Both natural processes and anthropogenic activities are responsible for introducing metals in to the aquatic system (Bharti, 2007a). Many contaminants discharged into surface waters rapidly become associated with the particulate matter and incorporated in sediments. Metals in aquatic systems become part of the water-sediment system and their distribution is controlled by a dynamic set of physical-chemical interactions and equilibrium, largely governed by pH and type of legends and chelating agents, oxidation state of the mineral components and the redox conditions of the system. Metal contaminated sediments may release heavy metals back to the overlying water column and, thus, pose risk to aquatic life and ecosystems. Due to their particle reactivity, heavy metals tend to accumulate in sediment as a result may persist in the environment long after their primary sources have been removed (Forstner and Wittman, 1981).

Heavy metals have a tendency to accumulate and store in a component or trophic levels. The storage of heavy metals has created harmful effects for biotic components. The heavy metals accumulated in sediment and percolated down in to ground water known as bio-accumulation of metal. From ground water, heavy metals may turn into two ways; one is though irrigation and second is through drinking by human beings. The accumulation of heavy metals through the food chain is called the biomagnifications. The concentrations of metal increased at every next trophic level, whereas metals can cause various harmful effects on irrigated agricultural soil, human beings and livestock by alteration in some biochemical reaction in body cells (De, 2002).

RESULTS AND DISCUSSION

As the major source of heavy metals pollution are dye houses of textile industries in Panipat region (Haryana), India. Metal reach in pond water and percolate down to ground water. Because the ground water is mostly used for irrigation of agricultural fields in most part of Haryana state, so, due to the repeated irrigation practices, agricultural soil quality may be altered. From these contaminate soils some heavy metals may accumulate in the tissues of Agricultural crop vegetations. On all the trophic levels, the heavy metals concentrations variations and transfer factor (coefficient) among all levels will discuss separately in forthcoming paragraphs.

Heavy Metals in Textile Effluents

Average concentrations of heavy metals in textile industrial effluents are depicted in table 6.3. From the results it is found that all the seven metals studied, are present in textile effluents of dye houses collected from common drain. Fe, Zn and Ni were found in low concentrations according to standards limits of effluent discharging (CPCB, 2003) and also of drinking water quality criteria. Copper, iron and manganese concentrations of the present study were supported by some researchers earlier (Yusuf and Sonibare, 2004). Untreated textile effluents consists of high conductance and pollution load than treated one (Garg and Kaushik, 2006). Effluents from industrial estates consists alkaline pH, high TSS load and very high BOD. Heavy metals like Fe, Cu, Mn, etc. remains high in textile effluents due to the dyeing process in which the textile consume some metal containing dyes (Sial *et al.*, 2006).

Table 6.3: Heavy Metals in Effluents, Surface Water, Pond Water and Ground Water

Metals	Effluent				Surface Water				Pond Water				Ground Water			
	Min	Max	Mean	SD	Min	Max	Mean	SD	Min	Max	Mean	SD	Min	Max	Mean	SD
Mn	0.01	0.16	0.09	0.075	0.01	0.09	0.043	0.0416	0.09	0.6	0.397	0.2702	0.07	0.4	0.26	0.1706
Ni	BDL	0.05	0.023	0.025	0.02	0.009	0.013	0.0060	0.008	0.15	0.086	0.0720	0.005	0.12	0.072	0.0596
Fe	0.03	0.3	0.15	0.137	0.13	0.029	0.089	0.0534	1.9	13.2	5.733	6.4671	1.1	5.4	2.767	2.3072
Cu	0.02	0.4	0.183	0.195	0.03	0.29	0.14	0.1345	0.17	0.54	0.363	0.1855	0.12	0.47	0.303	0.1756
Cd	BDL	0.02	0.01	0.01	BDL	0.009	0.003	0.0049	0.001	0.01	0.007	0.0049	0.007	0.01	0.006	0.0046
Pb	0.18	0.59	0.387	0.205	0.14	0.33	0.23	0.0954	0.05	1.9	0.91	0.9318	0.45	1.2	0.74	0.4028
Zn	0.03	0.2	0.113	0.085	0.02	0.18	0.107	0.0808	0.05	0.21	0.129	0.0800	0.03	0.16	0.101	0.0658

Table 6.4: Heavy Metals in Agricultural Soil, Pond Sediment and Drain Sediment

Metals	Agricultural Soil				Pond Sediment				Effluent Drain Sediment			
	Min	Max	Mean	SD	Min	Max	Mean	SD	Min	Max	Mean	SD
Mn	0.02	0.15	0.083	0.0650	0.05	0.17	0.11	0.06	0.33	0.82	0.57	0.2451
Ni	0.04	0.11	0.067	0.0378	0.05	0.13	0.08	0.0436	0.23	0.91	0.57	0.3400
Fe	0.14	0.92	0.483	0.3983	0.19	0.89	0.487	0.3619	0.65	3.54	1.79	1.5385
Cu	0.05	0.42	0.25	0.1868	0.12	0.39	0.267	0.1365	0.19	0.48	0.347	0.1464
Cd	0.001	0.04	0.016	0.0210	0.002	0.05	0.02	0.0261	0.001	0.02	0.01	0.0095
Pb	0.16	0.73	0.367	0.3156	0.15	0.79	0.39	0.3487	0.37	1.2	0.773	0.4155
Zn	0.04	0.23	0.12	0.0985	0.038	0.1	0.136	0.120	0.04	0.18	0.111	0.070

Table 6.5: Vertical Distribution of Heavy Metals in Ground Water at Various Depths

Metal	40 Ft (HP)				80 Ft (HP+TW)				DGW (TW)			
	Min	Max	Mean	SD	Min	Max	Mean	SD	Min	Max	Mean	SD
Mn	0.43	0.61	0.54	0.0964	0.09	0.31	0.203	0.1102	0.02	0.3	0.133	0.1474
Ni	0.009	0.16	0.099	0.0800	0.003	0.11	0.068	0.0569	0.001	0.08	0.037	0.0399
Fe	0.46	4.6	2.12	2.1884	0.38	2.3	1.26	0.9699	0.21	1.2	0.76	0.5041
Cu	0.13	0.57	0.373	0.2236	0.1	0.32	0.223	0.1124	0.09	0.21	0.157	0.0611
Cd	0.0008	0.009	0.0056	0.0043	0.0004	0.006	0.0034	0.0028	BDL	BDL	BDL	–
Pb	0.55	2.1	1.163	0.8240	0.33	0.95	0.703	0.3288	0.13	0.48	0.29	0.1769
Zn	0.06	0.25	0.15	0.0954	0.02	0.18	0.103	0.0802	0.01	0.12	0.07	0.0556

Table 6.6: Horizontal Distribution of Heavy Metals in Shallow Ground Water

Metals	Discharge Point (A)				1 Km away (B)				2 Km away (C)			
	Min	Max	Mean	SD	Min	Max	Mean	SD	Min	Max	Mean	SD
Mn	0.41	0.62	0.517	0.105	0.38	0.57	0.483	0.096	0.27	0.41	0.333	0.071
Ni	0.008	0.17	0.106	0.086	0.007	0.15	0.092	0.075	0.005	0:11	0.041	0.0595
Fe	0.4	4.6	2.133	2.194	0.28	3.2	1.487	1.525	0.17	1.0	0.697	0.458
Cu	0.11	0.58	0.38	0.243	0.09	0.47	0.293	0.191	0.07	0.35	0.233	0.146
Cd	0.006	0.009	0.0077	0.0015	0.005	0.008	0.006	0.0015	0.005	0.006	0.005	0.0006
Pb	0.52	2.2	1.2	0.885	0.49	1.8	1.077	0.665	0.41	1.1	0.8	0.354
Zn	0.05	0.32	0.193	0.136	0.05	0.28	0.173	0.1159	0.03	0.21	0.137	0.095

Table 6.7: Horizontal Distribution of Heavy Metals in Deep Ground Water

Metals	Discharge Point (A)				1 Km Away (B)				2 Km Away (C)			
	Min	Max	Mean	SD	Min	Max	Mean	SD	Min	Max	Mean	SD
Mn	0.03	0.32	0.1467	0.153	0.01	0.29	0.1266	0.1457	0.01	0.17	0.0966	0.0808
Ni	0.003	0.08	0.0443	0.0388	0.005	0.5	0.1783	0.2788	0.003	0.03	0.0176	0.0136
Fe	0.25	1.22	0.8	0.4979	0.31	1.19	0.7933	0.4463	0.19	0.98	0.64	0.4063
Cu	0.1	0.25	0.1867	0.0776	0.08	0.22	0.16	0.0721	0.05	0.17	0.1166	0.0611
Cd	BDL	0.004	0.0013	0.0023	BDL	BDL	BDL	BDL	BDL	BDL	BDL	BDL
Pb	0.26	0.48	0.4033	0.1242	0.21	0.43	0.3166	0.1101	0.13	0.31	0.23	0.0916
Zn	0.07	0.12	0.0967	0.0252	0.03	0.1	0.07	0.0360	0.01	0.08	0.0466	0.0351

Table 6.8 Mean Values of Heavy Metals in Crop Tissues

Metals	Root		Shoot		Correlation
	Mean	SD	Mean	SD	Root Vs Shoot
Mn	0.044	0.0091	0.0222	0.0096	-0.5958
Ni	0.006	0.0135	0.0148	0.0089	0.5725
Fe	0.178	0.0225	0.1546	0.0438	0.6094
Cu	0.012	0.0038	0.0053	0.0042	0.4760
Cd	0.00002	4.47E-05	0.00018	0.0003	-0.3317
Pb	0.025	0.0051	0.009	0.0121	0.9546
Zn	0.164	0.0398	0.2682	0.0140	-0.0330

Table 6.9: Transfer Factor Between Various Components of Industrial Environment (TF from Effluent to Ground Water, from Ground Water to Irrigated Agricultural Soil and from Soil to Vegetation)

	EFF Vs GW	EFF Vs PW	PW Vs GW	GW Vs AGS	AGS Vs GW	AGS Vs CPV
Mn	0.346	0.226	1.525	3.120	0.320	0.396
Ni	0.319	0.271	1.199	1.075	0.930	0.156
Fe	0.054	0.026	2.073	5.724	0.175	0.344
Cu	0.604	0.504	1.198	1.213	0.824	0.034
Cd	1.667	1.499	1.111	0.375	2.666	0.006
Pb	0.522	0.425	1.229	2.018	0.495	0.046
Zn	1.122	0.876	1.280	0.842	1.188	1.800

Table 6.10: Standards Values of Heavy Metals in Ground Water

Metals (ppm)	BIS	USPHS	WHO
Mn	0.10	0.05	0.1
Ni	–	–	0.2
Fe	0.3	0.1	1.0
Cu	0.05	0.05	–
Cd	0.01	0.01	0.01
Pb	0.05	0.1	0.1
Zn	5.0	5.0	5.0

Table 6.11: Standards Values of Heavy Metals in Textile Effluents (CPCB, 2000)

(Inlet Effluent Quality for CETP)	(Concentration in mg/l)
pH	5.5-9.0
Temperature °C	45
Chromium hexavalent as Cr+6	2.0
Chromium total as Cr	2.0
Copper as Cu	3.0
Lead as Pb	1.0
Nickel as Ni	3.0
Zink as Zn	15
Cadmium as Cd	1.0

Heavy Metals in Surface Water

Average concentrations of metals in surface water generally present in the area are presented in table 6.3. From the results, it is found that most of the metals studied, are present in surface water, but in very low concentration, whereas, cadmium was found below detection level in most of the surface water samples. in some samples Cu was found with higher concentrations (0.29 mg l^{-1}) in comparison to textile effluents. Average values of rest metals like Mn, Ni, Fe, Pb, Zn were also found minimum as 0.04, 0.01, 0.09, 0.23 and 0.10 mgl^{-1} respectively in surface water.

Metals in some samples of pond water were found very high concentration in comparison to other surface water of the area. All the seven metals were present in excess amount as comparing with textile effluents too. In pond water, average concentrations for Mn, Ni, Fe, Cu, Cd, Pb and Zn were observed 0.39, 0.08, 5.7, 0.36, 0.006, 0.91 and 0.13 mg l^{-1} respectively. Because all the textile effluents ends up in to a pond via a common drain, thus water quality of pond turns to vast condition due to the frequent discharge of industrial effluents without any adequate treatment (Malik *et al.*, 2006). Some local villagers guess that the same thing is responsible for the degradation of ground water quality of the area. The menace of dye house effluents is going on since a prolong time and will goes to a long period for surrounding.

Heavy Metals in Ground Water

The comparative average concentrations of heavy metals in textile effluents, local surface water, pond water and ground water are given in table 6.3. Results show that the concentrations of some metals like Pb and Fe are present in ground water in excess quantity (0.74 and 2.76 mg l^{-1}). Metals like Mn, Ni, Cu, Cd and Zn were found in ground water as an average of 0.26, 0.07, 0.3, 0.006 and 0.1 mg l^{-1} respectively. In industrial area, metals from surface water may percolate down in to shallow aquifers via soil profile after delaying a long period (Kumar *et al.*, 2001). Leachate effect of heavy metals may results as the excess amount of these metals in the ground water of the region, which may cause health problems to human beings, cattle and plants also (De, 2000)

Vertically, the heavy metals status is similar to horizontal level in ground water regime and concentrations of heavy metals are very close in depth wise and spatial. Vertical distribution of heavy metals in textile industrial area are given in table 6.5 and horizontal distribution of these metals are depicted in table 6.6 and five at deep and shallow water level. It may elaborated the heavy metals concentration in ground water regime, while it may clearly explain the heavy metals status in both vertical and horizontal level. Due to some anthropogenic activities, toxic heavy metals reach in aquifers resources and in deep ground water after a long period of time (Helena *et al.*, 1999).

Heavy Metals Contents in Irrigated Soil

Soil samples of irrigated land used for growing crops and vegetables showed the presence of all seven metals considered in the study. Concentration of Mn, Fe, Zn, Cu, Ni, Cr, Pb and Cd (□g g^{-1}) is depicted in table 6.4. These values are higher in soil samples compared to vegetable samples, except for Zn. The reason might be due to its weak adsorptive nature in the soil1 (Lokeshwari and Chandrappa, 2006). The average total concentration of all metals in soil samples was lower than the pond sediment and effluent sediment soil. In some agricultural soils heavy metals present in trace amount naturally (Nongkynrih *et al.*, 1996).

It was found that the average concentrations of heavy metals in surface soils, i.e. Mn, Ni, Fe, Cu, Cd, Pb and Zn were 0.08, 0.06, 0.48, 0.25, 0.016, 0.36 and 0.12 mg g^{-1} respectively, in which Fe, Pb, Cu were found in excess level due to their cumulative and adsorptive nature in soil after repeated irrigation by contaminated ground water. Cd and Zn were found minimum due to their weak adsorptive nature in soil (Mido and Satake, 2003currsci). Soils near textile industries having comparatively high concentrations of Mn and Zn, while cadmium minimum (Kasem and Singh, 1999). Due to the soil and plant interactions some toxic metals may accumulated in the tissues of crop plants (Henning *et al.*, 2001).

Heavy Metals Contents in Sediments

Agricultural soil is indirectly in touch of point source of metal pollution, but effluent drain and pond sediment is directly attached by heavy metal's source i.e. dyes (e.g. chrome and metal dyes). So, most of the metals having heavy nature, deposited on the bottom sediments of drain and lastly on the pond bottom. In the present study, concentrations of heavy metals were found maximum in sediment of effluent drain and after it in pond sediment, except Zn and Cd due to low adsorptive nature with soil (Lokeshwari and Chandrappa, 2006). The average concentrations of heavy metals like Mn, Ni, Fe, Cu, Cd, Pb and Zn in pond sediment and drain sediment respectively found as 0.11, 0.08, 0.48, 0.26, 0.02, 0.39, 0.14 mg g^{-1} and 0.57, 0.57, 1.79, 0.34, 0.01, 0.77, 0.1 mg g^{-1}, which can easily demonstrate the pollution potential on both sediment medium. Heavy metals settle down in the sediments of water bodies as per their physical and chemical properties with time factor (Nasr *et al.*, 2006). Heavy metals in sediment may influence the adjacent floodplain soils quality (Korfali and Davies, 2004). Some of the load of heavy metals from sediments may migrate to surroundings (Bordas and Bourg, 1998).

Heavy Metals in Crop Plant Vegetations

Most of the laboratory research on biosorption of heavy metals indicates that no single mechanism is responsible for metal uptake. In general, two mechanisms are known to occur, viz. 'adsorption', which refers to binding of materials onto the surface and 'absorption', which implies penetration of metals into the inner matrix (Ramraj et al., 2000currsci). Either one of these or both the mechanisms might take place in the transportation of metals into the body tissues of crop plant vegetations.

Roots and shoots of some vegetables (spinach, radish, cauliflower) and other seasonal crops (Barseem, coriander, wheat) were analysed for total metal content. The order of toxic heavy metal contamination in crop plants is as follows: Zn > Fe, > Mn > Ni > Pb> Cu > Cd. Cadmium was not found in most samples of plant parts. Cd was found in very minor quantity only in barseem shoots (0.7 µg g^{-1}) and wheat shoots (0.2 µg g^{-1}) and cauliflower root (0.1 µg g^{-1}). Accumulation of these heavy metals in vegetables and other crop plants might be due to the use of contaminated ground water for their cultivation. From the results, it is found that the presence of Cd in barseem shoots (0.7 µg g^{-1}) and wheat shoots (0.2 µg g^{-1}) and cauliflower root (0.1 µg g^{-1}) is only in leafy vegetables. The reason for the accumulation is that Cd is relatively easily taken up by food crops and especially by leafy vegetables. Also it may be due to the foliar absorption of atmospheric deposits on plant leaves (Mido and Satake, 2003currsci). Zn is present in appreciable amounts in the vegetables. Barseem, wheat, coriander, cauliflower appear to have higher uptake from the continued irrigated land by contaminated ground water. In case of Pb, maximum concentration is found in cauliflower and barseem compared to other vegetables.

Heavy metal contents in roots and shoots of different crop plants. Heavy metals in plant tissues were found to be lower in comparison to irrigated soil. Fe, Zn, Pb and Mn were found 0.178, 0.164, 0.024, and 0.044 µg g^{-1} maximum in plant roots, while in plants shoots only Zn and Fe were found 0.26 and 0.155 µg g^{-1}. Cd was almost absent in plant tissues, however shoots contain comparatively high concentrations of Cd in few samples (Olaniya et al., 1998curr). The concentrations of Zn and Cd in crops increased with the degree of contamination of the soil. Different vegetable species accumulate different metals depending on environmental conditions, metal species and plant available forms of heavy metals. Studies have shown that uptake and accumulation of metals by different plant species depend on several factors, and various researchers have identified several reasons (Bingham *et al.*, 1975curr; Dowdy et al., 1978currsci). It is found that the average total concentration of metals in plant shoots is higher than the plant roots. Overall results on comparison reveal that metals in water had impact on soil quality and crop plant vegetations also.

Transfer Factor for Heavy Metals

The transfer factors (TF) of different heavy metals from textile effluent to ground water (EFF Vs GW), from textile effluent to pond water (EFF Vs PW), from pond water to ground water (PW Vs GW), from ground water to agricultural soil (GW Vs AGS), from soil to ground water again (AGS Vs GW), from soil to vegetation (AGS Vs CPV), which is one of the key components of human exposure to metals through the food chain. Highest TF values are obtained for Fe (5.72), Mn (3.12), Pb (2.01) from ground water to agricultural soil and Cd from effluent to pond water (1.49) and ground water (1.66). Transfer coefficients from pond water to ground water were found exceed 1 for every metal like Mn (1.52), Ni (1.19), Fe (2.0), Cu (1.19), Cd (1.11), Pb (1.22) and Zn (1.28), while for other environmental components TF values were mostly below 1. So, the migration of heavy metals in Panipat industrial area was found maximum from pond water to ground water (PW Vs GW).

Overall TF values of Zn, Fe, Ni and Mn were found to be minimum and significant overall at every level of industrial area, and it supports the findings that persistence of Cu and Cd is comparatively less while that of Pb is more in ground water and soil systems. Transfer factor from irrigated soils to crop vegetations was not highlighted for any metal during the study. All the TF are depicted in table 6.9 sequentially.

Pathway of Heavy Metals

The present study indicated a pathway of heavy metals discharging from textile industries to ground water by percolation from pond via soil profile and disperses in ground water regime. Soil quality and composition may also alter in irrigated agricultural crop fields and thus metals accumulated in plants body, which may seriously caused health hazards to livestock and ultimately to human beings by direct consumption or by uptake the food products originated by cattle (De, 2002).

Every element has a cyclic pathway in nature, which maintains the quantity of that particular element at various abiotic and biotic components.

But the imbalance of any element may cause some adverse impacts on ecological ecosystem (Sharma, 2002). In the textile industrial area of Panipat, some metals are accumulating at different trophic levels and also in various living and non-living factors since a prolonged time. Finally, after viewing all aspects of the present investigation based figure, which is clearly highlighted an un-recycled pathway of heavy metals in the environment of textile industrial area of Panipat city.

The accumulation of heavy metals in the environment of an industrial area may be highlighted with the help of some environmental bio-indicators, by which some pollution prevention and control measures may be applied for the conservation of ground water resources (Spiegel, 2002).

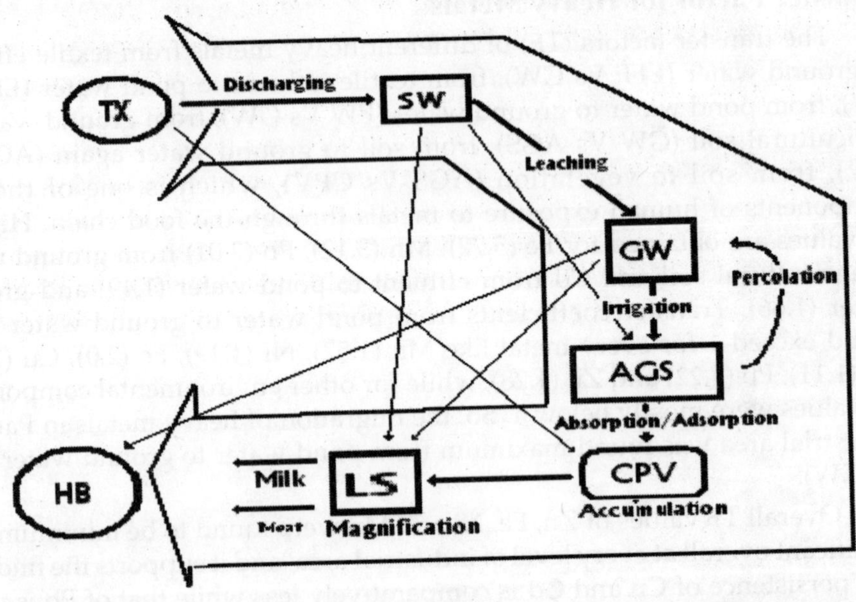

Fig. 6.1: An Un-recycled Pathway of Heavy Metals in Industrial Environment

CONCLUSION

The study reveals that textile effluent is the main source of surface water pollution and furthers the ground water by leaching, which is the major source of water for agriculture irrigation in Haryana state and irrigation with contaminated ground water containing variable amounts of heavy metals leads to increase in concentration of metals in the soil and vegetation. Concentration of metals in vegetation will provide baseline data and there is a need for intensive sampling of the same for quantification of the results. Water, crop plant vegetation and soil quality monitoring, together with the prevention of metals entering the plants, is a prerequisite in order to prevent ground water pollution by textile effluents and to prevent potential health hazards of irrigation with contaminated ground water.

After discussing all environmental conditions, and viewing the figure of un-recycled pathway of heavy metals, it is clear that the textile effluents without any adequate treatment pose negative impacts on surface water, ground water, agricultural soil, crop plant vegetations and ultimately on human being.

REFERENCES

Aboulhassan, M.A.; Souabi, S.; Yaacoubi, A. and Baudu, M. (2005): Treatment of Textile Wastewater Using a Natural Flocculants. *Environmental Technology*. 26: 705-711.

Aggarwal, R.R. and Mehrotra, R.R. (1952): Soil Survey and Soil Water in Uttar Pradesh, *Suptd. Printing and Stationery*, Aallahabad, pp: 361-372.

Ameta Suresh C., Punjabi Pinki Bala, Kothari Shilpa, Sancheti Anjali (2003): Effect of Untreated and Photocatalytically Treated Dyeing Industry Effluent on Growth and Biochemical Parameters of *Allium cepa* (onion), *Polln Res*, 22(3): 389-392.

Annadurai, G.; Juang, R.S. and Lee, D.J. (2002): Use of Cellulose Based Wastes for Adsorption of Dyes from Aqueous Solutions, *J. Haz. Mat.*, B92: 263-274.

APHA (2005): Standard Methods for Examination of Water and Waste Water. *American Public Health Association,* 21th Edition. Inc, New York, 1170.

Aurangabadkar, K.; Swaminathan, K.; Sandhya, S; Uma, T.S.; Jothikumar, N. and Paramasivam, R. (2001): Ground Water Quality Around a Municipality Solid Waste Dumping site at Chennai, *IJEP*, 21(4): 323-327.

Bae, W.; S.H. Lee; and G.B. Ko (2004): Evaluation of Predominant Reaction Mechanisms for the Fenton Process in Textile Dyeing Waste. *Water Sc. and Tech.* 49 (4), pp: 91-96.

Baruah N.K.; Kotoki, P.; Bhattacharya, K.G. and Borah, G.C. (1996): Metal speciation in Jhanjhi River Sediments. *Sci. Total Environ.,* 193: 1-12.

Bhakuni, T.S. and Bopardikar, M.V. (1967): Method of Recovery Zinc from Spinning Bath Waste of Viscos Reyon Factory by Ion Exchange Process, Env. Health, 9(4): 327-338.

Bharti, P.K. (2012): Groundwater Pollution, *Biotech Books*, Delhi, pp: 243 (ISBN: 978-81-7622-242-6).

Bharti, P.K.; Malik, D.S. and Yadav, R. (2010): Influence of Heavy Metals on Abundance of Cyanophyceae Members in Three Spring-fed Lake in Kempty, Dehradun, In: 'Advances in Aquatic Ecology, Vol-III' ed. by V.B. Sakhare, *Daya Publishing House, New Delhi,* (ISBN 978-81-7035-633-2) pp: 107-111.

Bhat, R. and Kulkarni, R. (2005): COD Reduction of Dye Industry Effluent, *J. Ind. Poll. Control*, 21 (1): 147-150.

Bingham, F.T., Page, A.I., Hahler, R.J. and Ganje, T.J. (1975): Growth and Cadmium Accumulation of Plants Grown on Soil Treated with Cadmium Enriched Sewage Sludge. *J. Environ. Qual.*, 4, 207-210.

Bordas, F. and Bourg, A.C.M. (1998): A Critical Evaluation of Sample Pretreatment for Storage of Contaminated Sediments to be Investigated for the Potential Mobility of Their Heavy Metals Load, *Wat. Air and Soil Poll.,* 103: 137-149.

Bousselmi, L.; Gelsson S.V. and H. Schroeder (2004): Textile Wastewater Treatment and Reuse by Solar Catalysis: Results from a Pilot Plant in Tunisia. *Water Sc. & Tech.*, 49(4): 331-337.

Canter, L.W. (1987): Ground Water Quality Protection, *Lewis publications.* Inc., Chelsea, MI, pp: 1-650.

Chao, Keh-Ping; Tsai, Ching-Tsan; Wang, John H.C.; Lin, Shaw-Tao and Chiang, Chow-Feng (2005): Health Risk Assessment of a Heavy Metal Contaminated site in Taiwan. *Jr. Practice Periodical of Hazardous, Toxic, and Radioactive Waste Management,* pp: 167-171.

Considine, D.M. (1974): Chemical and Process Technology Encyclopedia, McGraw Hill Book Co., New York.

CPCB (2003): Ground Water, *Central Pollution Control Board, Parivesh Bhawan,* Delhi, pp: 56.

CPCB (2000): Textile Industry, *Central Pollution Control Board, Parivesh Bhawan*, Delhi, pp: 88.

Darra, B.L.; Mehta, K.M. and Pareek, B.L. (1964): Quality of Irrigation Water in Rajasthan, *J. Indian Soc, Soil Sc.*, 12: 121-130.

De, A. K. (2002): Environmental Chemistry, *New Age International (Ltd) Publishers, New Delhi*, 392.

De, A.K. (2005): Adsorption of Cadmium and Zinc on Coal Fly Ash, *J. Ind. Poll. Control*, 21 (1): 27-30.

Desh, D. (1981): Activated Sludge Treatment of Liquid Waste: A Review, *J. IAWPC Tech.*, Vol. VII, pp: 69-72.

Dhar, N.R.; Khoda, A.K.M.B.; Khan, A.H.; Bala, P. and Karim, M.F. (2005): A Study of Effect of Acid Activated Saw Dust on the Removal of Different Dissolved Tannery Dyes (Acid dye) from Aqueous Solutions. *Journal of Environ. Sciences & Engg.* 47 (2): 103-108.

Dowdy, R.H., Larson, W.E., Titrud, J.M. and Latterel, J.J. (1978): Growth and Metal Uptake of Snap Beans Grown on Sewage Sludge Amended Soil – A Four Year Field Study. *J. Environ. Qual.*, 7, 252-257.

Dowedy, R.H. and Larson, W.E. (1975): The Availability of Sludge Borne Metals in Various Vegetable Crops, *J. Env. Qual.*, 4: 278-282.

Dulka, J.J. and Risby, T.H. (1976): Ultra Trace Metals in Some Environmental and Biological Systems, *Analytical Chemistry*, 48(8): 640-653.

Dutta, P.S. (2005): Ground Water Ethics for its Sustainability, *Current Science*, 89 (5): 812-817.

Dwivedi, A.K.; Shashi and Singh, J. (2005): Water Pollution and Ground Water Recharging, *Current Science*, 91 (4): 407-408.

Eaton, F.M. (1950): Significance of Carbonates in Irrigation Waters, *Soil Sc.*, 39: 123-133.

Eckenfelder, W.W. and Bornad, J.L. (1971): Treatment Cost Relationship for Industrial Waste, *Chemical Engg. Progress*, 67(9): 76.

Forstner, U. (1985): Chemical Forms and Reactivities of Metals in Sediments in Chemical Methods for Assessing Bioavailable Metals in Sludge and Soils, In: Leschber, R., Davies, R.D. and Hermite, L.P. (Eds), *Elsevier, London*, pp: 1-30.

Fransson, Åsa (2007): A Case Study to Verify Methods for Estimating Transmissivity Distributions Along Boreholes, *Hydrogeology Journal*, 15: 307-313, DOI 10.1007/s10040-006-0141-1.

Garg, V.K; Sharma, I.S. and Bishnoi, M.S. (1998): Fluoride in Underground Water of Uklana Town, District Hisar, Haryana. *Poll. Res.* 17(2): 149-152.

Garg, V.K. and Kaushik, P. (2006): Influence of Short-term Irrigation of Textile Mill Wastewater on the Growth of Chickpea Cultivars, *Chemistry and Ecology*, 22(3): 193-200.

Gharaibeh, M.A.; Eltaif, N.I. and Bayan Al-Abdullah (2007): Impact of Field Application of Treated Wastewater on Hydraulic Properties of Vertisols, *Water Air Soil Pollut,* DOI 10.1007/s11270-007-9423-z.

Golia, E.E.; Dimirkou, A. and Mitsios, I.K. (2007): Accumulation of Metals on Tobacco Leaves (Primings) Grown in an Agricultural Area in Relation to Soil, *Bull Environ Contam Toxicol*, DOI 10.1007/s00128-007-9111-0.

Hedge, V.S.; Shalini, G. and Kanchanagouri, D.G. (2006): Provenance of Heavy Minerals with Special Reference to Ilmenite of the Honnevar Beach, Central West Coast of India, *Current Science*, 91 (5): 644-648.

Helena, B.A.; Vega, M.; Barrad, E.; Pardo, R. and Fernandez, L. (1999): A Case of Hydrochemical Characterization of an Alluvial Aquifer Influenced by Human Activities, *Wat. Air Soil Poll.*, 112: 365-387.

Henning, B.J.; Snyman, H.G and Aveling, T.A.S. (2001): Plant-soil Interactions of Sludge Borne Heavy Metals and the Effect on Maize (*Zea mays* L.) Seedlings Growth, *Wat. SA*, 27(1): 71-78.

Horing, R.H. (1976): Characterization and Treatment of Textile Dyeing Wastewaters, In: Proceedings of National Technical Conference, *American Association of Textile Chemists and Colorist*, pp: 100-104.

Hoston, A.K. (1965): An Index Number System for Rating Water Quality, *J. Wat. Poll. Cont. Fed.*, 37(3): 300-306.

http:// www.tuberose.com as accessed on August 2006.

Huang, J.; Huang, R.; Jiao, J.J. and Chen, K. (2007): Speciation and Mobility of Heavy Metals in Mud in Coastal Reclamation Areas in Shenzhen, China, *Environ Geol*, DOI 10.1007/s00254-007-0636-7.

IARC (1980): Monographs on the Carcinogenic Risk to Humans and Their Supplements: Some Metals and Metallic Compounds, International Agency for Research on Cancer, IARC Monographs, Vol. 23.

Ireland, M.P. (1983): Heavy Metals Uptake and Tissue Distribution, In: Earthworm Ecology-from Darwin to Vermiculture (Ed.- Satchell, J.E., Chapman and Hall).

Judlins, J.F. and Hornsby, J.S. (1978): Colour Removal from Textile Dye Waste Using Magnesium Carbonate, *Journal of Water Pollution Control Federation*, 50: 2446-2456.

Kanwar, J.S. (1961): Quality of Irrigation Water as an Index of Suitability for Irrigation Purposes, *Potash Review*, 13: 1-13.

Kashem, M.A. and Singh, B.R. (1999): Heavy Metal Contamination of Soil and Vegetation in the Vicinity of Industries in Bangladesh, *Water, Air and Soil Pollution*, 115: 347-361.

Katz, M. (1975): The Effect of Heavy Metals on Fish and Aquatic Environment. (Ed.- Krenkel, P.A.), Pregamon Press, New York.

Khan T.I., Marwari Richa, Singh N. (2003): Impact of Textile Wastewater on *Solanum melongena* var-FI- Hybrid Kanhaiya in Pot Experiment with Special Emphasis on Analysis of Heavy Metals. *Dimensions Polln*, 2: 108-116.

Khurshid, Zaheeruddin & Mohd. Usman Shabeer (1997): Degradation of Water Quality due to Heavy Metals Pollution in Faridabad District, Haryana, India. *Poll. Res.* 16(1): 41-43.

Korfali, S.I. and Davies, B.D.E. (2004): The Relationship of Metals in River Sediments (Nahribrahim, Lebanon) and Adjacent Floodplain Soils, *J. Sci. Res. Dev.,* 4: 1-22.

Krull, R. and E. Dopkens (2004): Recycling of Dye House Effluents by Biological and Chemical Treatment. *Water Sc. And Tech.* 49(4), pp: 311-317.

Kudesia, V.P. (1992): Water Pollution, *Pragati Prakashan, Meerut*, pp: 407.

Kumar, Rakesh; Singh, R.D. and Sharma, K.D. (2005): Water Resources of India, *Current Science*, 89 (5): 794-811.

Kumar, S.; Bhatacharjee, J.W. and Sharma, R.K. (1992): Relationship Between Fluoride, Total Hardness and Total Alkalinity in the Ground Water of Barmer Dist. (Rajsthan). *Poll. Res.* 11(2): 111-116.

Kumar, S; Kushwaha, R.; Sapra, S. Gupta, A.B. and Bhargava, A. (2001): Impact of Textile Industry on Ground Water Quality of Sanagar, Jaipur, *J. Indian Water Works Association*, 33(4): 321-326.

Lark, B.S., Mahajan, R.K. and Walia, T.P.S. (2002): Determination of Metals of Toxicological Significance in Sewage Irrigated Vegetables by Using Atomic Absorption Spectrometry and Anodic Stripping Voltammetry. *Indian J. Environ. Health*, 44, 164-167.

Lee, K.K.; A.M. Kassim and H.K. Lee (2004): The Object of Nitrogen Supplementation on the Efficiency of Colour and COD Removal by Malaysian White Rot Fungi in Textile Dying Effluent. *Water Sc. and tech.* 50 (50): 73-77.

Lokeshwari, H. and Chandrappa, G.T. (2006): Impact of Heavy Metals Contamination of Bellandur Lake on Soil and Cultivated Vegetation, *Current Science*, 91 (5): 622-627.

Mahesha, N.N. and Prasad, N.R.R. (2004): Physico-chemical Characteristics of Bore Well Water in Arsikara Taluk, Hassan, *IJEP*, 24(12): 897-904.

Malik, D.S.; Bharti, P.K. and Yadav, R.; Kumar, P. and Chauhan, P. (2008): Dispersion of Heavy Metals in Textile Effluent and Pond Environment in Panipat Industrial Area, *Env. Cons. J.* 9 (3): 77-81.

Malik, D.S.; Yadav, R. and Bharti, P.K. (2009): Role of Aquatic Macrophytes in the Remediation of Metal Pollutants, In: Aquatic Ecology, *Narendra Publishing House, New Delhi*, (ISBN-978-81-90-609-15-9), pp: 145-158.

Malik, D.S. and Bharti, P.K. (2007): Soil Quality of Irrigated Agricultural Fields in Textile Industrial Area of Panipat City, *Asian Journal of Experimental sciences,* 21 (2): 445-451.

Malik, D.S. and Bharti, P.K. (2011): Spatial Distribution of Heavy Metals in Ground Water Regime of Panipat Industrial Area, India. In: Water Pollution and Management (Eds. Malik *et al.*) *Biotech Books, New Delhi.* pp: 216-226. (ISBN: 978-81-7622-227-3)

Malik, D.S. and Bharti, Pawan Kr. (2010): Textile Pollution, *Daya Publishing House*, Delhi, pp: 383. (ISBN: 978-81-7035-643-1).

Malik, D.S.; Bharti, P.K. and Sumit Grover (2006): Alteration in Surface Water Quality Near Textile Industries at Panipat (Haryana), *Environment Conservation J.*, 7(2): 65-68.

Malik, D.S.; Bharti, P.K.; Kamboj, N. and Yadav, R. (2007): Quantification of Heavy Metals Migration in Ground Water Regime due to Discharge of Textile Industrial Effluents in Panipat Area, Haryana, *Pollution Research*, 26 (4): 725-727.

Malik, D.S.; Yadav, Rashmi and Bharti, P.K. (2004): Accumulation of Heavy Metals in Crop Plants Through Irrigation of Contaminated Ground Water in Panipat Region. *Environmental Conservation Journal* 5 (1-3): 101-104.

Mani, V.; Kaur, H. and Mohini, M. (2005): Toxic Metals and Environmental Pollution, J. Ind. Poll. Cont., 21(1): 101-107.

Martin, J.M. and Whitfield, M. (1983): The Significance of the River Input of Chemical Elements to the Ocean, In: Wong, C.S.; Boyle, E.; Bruland, K.W.; Burton, J.D. and Goldburg, E.D. (Eds.), Trace Metals in Sea Water, *Plenum Press, New York*, pp: 324-331.

Martin, M.H. and Cougherty, P.J. (1982): Biological Monitoring of Heavy Metals Pollution, Applied Science Publishers, pp: 463.

McKay, G. (1979): Waste Colour Removal from Textile Effluents, *American Dyestuff Reporter*, 68: 29-36.

Michaels, G.B. and Lewis, E.L. (1985): Sorption and Toxicity of Azo and Triphenyl Methane dues to Aquatic Microbial Populations, *Environmental Toxicology and Chemistry*, 4: 45-50.

Mico, C; Recatal, L.; Peris, M. And Sanchez, J. (2007): A Comparison of two Digestion Methods for the Analysis of Heavy Metals by Flame Atomic Absorption Spectroscopy, *Spectroscopy Europe*, 19 (1): 23-26.

Mido, Y. and Satake, M. (2003): Chemicals in the Environment. In *Toxic Metals* (eds. Sethi, M.S. and Iqbal, S.A.), Discovery Publishing House, New Delhi, pp. 45-68.

Ming Chen and Ma, Lena Q. (2001): Comparison of Three Aqua Regia Digestion Methods for Twenty Florida Soils. *Soil Sci. Soc. Am. J.*, 65: 491-499.

Minhas, P.S. and Gupta, R.K. (1992): Quality of Irrigation Water – Assessment and Management, Publication and Information Division, ICAR, *Krishi Anusandhan Bhawan, Pusa, New Delhi*, pp: 123.

Mishra, E; Sharma, D. and Malkania, U. (1990): Fish Mortality as Affected by Liquid Effluents from Raja Textile Ltd., Rampur (U.P.), *Int. J. Ecol. Env. Sc.*, 16 (2-3): 119-123.

Mishra, N.K. and Sahoo, H.K. (2003): Evaluation of Ground Water Quality in and Around Deogarh, *IJEP*, 23 (6): 667-672.

Mohan, Devendra and Yogesh Sharma (2002): Trace Metals in a Few Water Bodies of Pali, Rajsthan, *J. Natcon.* 14 (2): 363-366.

Mohan, R.; Chopra, N. and Chowdhary, G.C. (1998): Heavy Metals (Fe, Pb, Cd, Zn) in the Ground Water of Naini Industrial Area, Dist. Allahabad, U.P. *Poll. Res.* 17(2): 167-168.

Mohanasundaram, S. (2003): Affordable and Effective Textile Processing Effluent Treatment Plants. *South India's Premier Magazine on Environment Sc. and Engg.*, pp. 76-82.

Mor, S.; Bishnoi, M.S. and Bishnoi, N.R. (2003): Assessment of Ground Water Quality of Jind City, *IJEP*, 23(6): 673-679.

Nasr, S.M.; Okbah, M.A. and Kashem, S.M. (2006): Environmental Assessment of Heavy Metal Pollution in Bottom Sediments of Aden Port, Yemen, *Int. J. Oceans and Oceanogra.*, 1(1): 99-109.

Navarro, A. and Font, X. (1993): Discriminating Different Sources of Ground Water Contamination Caused by Industrial Waste in the Besos River Basin, Barcelona, Spain. *J. Applied Biochemistry,* APPGEY, 8: 277.

Neelima Rajvaidya and Dilpi Kumar Markandey (1998): Advanced in Environmental Sciences and Technology. *A.P.H. Publishimg Corporation* New Delhi, 6: 231-249.

Nemerow, N.L. (1971): Industrial Water Pollution: Origins, Characteristics and Treatment, Addision, Wesley Publishing Co.

Nongkynrih, P.D.; Khar, P.S. And Khating, D.T. (1996): Micronutrients Elements in Acid Aflisols of Meghalaya Under Rice Cultivation, *J. Soil Sci.*, 44(3): 455-457.

Nriagu, J.O. and Pacyna, J.M. (1988): Quantitative Assessment of Worldwide Contamination of Air, Water and Soil with Trace Metals, *Nature*, 333: 134-139.

Numberg, H.W. (1984): The Volumetric Approach in Trace Metal Chemistry of Natural Waters and Atmospheric Precipitation, *Analyst. Chim. Acta*, 164: 1-21.

Obiri, Samuel (2007): Determination of Heavy Metals in Water from Boreholes in Dumasi in the Wassa West District of Western Region of Republic of Ghana, *Environ Monit Assess,* 130:455-463.

Olaniya, M.S., Sur, M.S., Bhide, A.D. and Swarnakar, S.N. (1998): Heavy Metal Pollution of Agricultural Soil and Vegetation due to Application of Municipal Solid Waste – A Case Study. *Indian J. Environ. Health*, 40, 160-168.

Olaniya, M.S.; Khandekar, M.P. and Bhide. A.D. (1998): Groundwater Pollution due to Refuse Leachate. *IJEP.* 18(10): 745-751.

Padmavathiamma, P.K. and Li, L.Y. (2007): Phytoremediation Technology: Hyper-accumulation Metals in Plants, *Water Air Soil Pollut*, DOI 10.1007/s11270-007-9401-5.

Palanivelu, K.; Priya, M.N.; Selvan, A.M. and Natesan, U. (2006): Water Quality Assessment in the Tsunami Affected Coastal Areas of Chennai, *Current Science*, 91 (5): 583-584.

Porter, J.J. (1970): The Changing Nature of Textile Processing and Waste Treatment Technology, Textile Chemist and Colourists, 2: 336.

Pujari, G.K. and Sinha, B.K. (1999): Studies on the Water and Soil Quality of Some Villages of Attabira Area Irrigated by Bargarg Main Canal Originated from Hirakund Reservoir of Orissa, *J. of Env. and Poll.*, 6(1): 71-76.

Ramraj, Athiya Afshan, Halappa Gowda, T.P. and Karanth, N.G.K. (2000): Sorption of Copper(II) and Lead(II) by Microbial Cultures during Growth. *Indian J. Environ. Health*, 42, 95-99.

Rao, N.S. and Rao, V.V.S.G. (1999): Pathlines of Pollutants Migration in Ground Water of the Visakhpatanam Urban Area, India, *Hydrological Process*, 13: 1381-1389.

Reddy, K.J. and Jianping Lin (2000): Nitrate Removal from Ground Water Using Catalytic Reduction. *Water Res.* 34 (3), pp: 995-1001.

Rhoades, J.D. (1987): Use of Saline Water for Irrigation, *Wat. Qual. Bull.*, 12: 14-20.

Richards, L.A. (1954): Diagnosis and Improvement of Saline and Alkali soils, US Deptt. Agri., edited Handbook, No. 60: 160.

Rizk, Z.S.; Alsharhan, A.S. and Wood, W.W. (2007): Sources of Dissolved Solids and Water in Wadi Al Bih aquifer, Ras Al Khaimah Emirate, United Arab Emirates, *Hydrogeology Journal,* DOI 10.1007/s10040-007-0188-7.

Royee, M.K.P. and Prakasham (2003): Water Characteristics of Dug and Tube Wells of Kollam Municipality, *IJEP*, 23(6): 607-612.

Saed, K.; Noor, M.M.M. and Yusuf, B. (2005): Sudarcane Bagasse as an Adsorbent for Dye Removal, *J. Ind. Poll. Control*, 21 (1): 1-10.

Saksena, R.K.; Sharma, M.L. and Jodha H.R. (1966): Quality of Ground Waters for Irrigation in Ahor Developmental Block, Jalore, *Ann. Arid Zone*, 5: 204-218.

Samy, D.I.A. and Gananarethinam, J.L. (1980): Effect of Distillery Effluents on the Growth of Three Aquatic Macrophytes, *J. Comp. Physiol. Ecol.*, 5(4): 290-295.

Sastry, K.V. and Pratima Rathee (1999): Ground Water Quality in Three Villages of Rohtak District. *J. Natcon*, 11(2): 175-182.

Seeber, P.R. (1962): Cation Hydrological Facies of Ground Water in the English Town Formation, New Jersey, In: Short Paper in Geology, Hydrology and Topography, USGC, Profes. Paper, 450B: 124-126.

Sharma, D.R. and Parihar, S.S. (1973): Effect of Depth and Salinity of Ground Water on Evaporation and Soil Salinization, *Indian J. Agric. Sci.*, 43: 582-586.

Sharma, K. and K.S. Patel (1996): Spectrophotometric Determination of Copper in Water. *Journal of Indian Chemical Society.* 73, pp: 443-444.

Sharma, K.P.; Sharma, K.; Bharadwaj, S.M. and Chaturvedi, R.K. (1999): Environmental Impact Assessment of Textile Printing Industries in Sanagar, Jaipur: A Case Study. *J. Int. Bot. Soc.*, 78: 71-74.

Sharma, K.P.; Sharma, K.; Bhardwaj, S.M. and Chaturvedi, R.K. (1999): Environment Impact Assessment of Textile Printing Industries in Sanganer, Jaipur: A Case Study. *J. Ind. Bot. Soc.* 78:71.

Sharma, P.D. (2002): Ecology and Environment, *Rastogi Publication*, pp: 585.

Sharma, S.; Jain, P.C. and Mathur, R. (1995): Quality Assessment of Ground Water in Municipal and Fringe Areas Near Gwalior, *IJEP*, 15(7): 534-538.

Sheth, K.N. and Desai, A.P. (2005): Study of Bio-kinetics of Textile Wastewater by Designing a Bench Scale Completely Mixed Activated Sludge Reactor Model, *J. Ind. Poll. Control*, 21 (1): 11-16.

Sheth, K.N. and Patel, M.R. (2001): Characterization, Treatment and Comparative Cost Analysis Studies of Textile Processing Wastewater of Vatva Industrial Complex, J. Engg. and Tech., S.P. University, 14.

Shivakumar, K.; Pandey, A.K. and Bhiksham, G. (1977): Toxic Trace Element Pollution in Ground Water Around Patancheru and Bollaram Industrial Area, A.P., India: A Graphical Approach, *Env. Monitor. Assess.*, 45 (1): 57-80.

Shrivastava V.S. and Patil B.H. (2003): Metallic and Some Physico-chemical Studies of Soil and Aquatic Sediments, *Eco. Env. Conserv.*, 9(1): 75-77.

Sial, R.A.; Chaudhary, M.F.; Abbas, S.T.; Latif, M.I. and Khan A.G. (2006): Quality of Effluents from Hattar Industrial Estate, *J. Zhejiang Univ. Sci. B,* 7(12): 974-980.

Siddiqui, Z.M. and Pathani, D. (2002): Studies on Heavy Metals in Surface and Ground Water of Jalandhar and Ludhiana Districts, *IJET*, 22(2): 201-206.

Singh, A.K. (2006): Chemistry of Arsenic in Ground Water of Genges-Brahmaputra River Basin, *Current Science*, 91 (5): 599-606.

Singh, B. and Bhumbla, D.R. (1968): Effect of Quality of Irrigation Water on Soil Properties, *J. Res.* (Punjab Agri. Univ.), 5: 166-171.

Singh, K.N.; Bains, S.S. and Dayanand (1969): Salinity Problem in High Water Table Areas: An Appraisal, *Indian J, Agron.*, 14: 31-34.

Singh, K.S. and Sharma, R.P. (1971): Studies on the Effects of Saline Irrigation Waters on Physico-chemical Properties of Some Soils of Rajasthan, *J. Indian Soc. Soil Sci.*, 18: 345-356.

Singh, T.B.; Jadon, S.P.S. and Mishra, G.J. (1994): Degradation of Water and Soil Quality of Parwanoo Area with Respect to Heavy Metals, *IJEP*, 14 (4): 282-287.

Souther, R.H. and Alsapaugh, T.A. (1957): Biological Treatment of Mixture of Textile Wastes and Domestic Sewage. *Textile,* 2 (1): 135-139.

Spiegel, H. (2002): Trace Element Accumulation in Selected Bioindicators Exposed to Emissions Along the Industrial Facilities of Danube Lowland, *Turk J. Chem.,* 26: 815-823.

Srinivas, C.; Piska, R.S. and Reddy, R. (2002): Ground Water Pollution due to the Industrial Effluents in Kothur Industrial Area, Mahaboonagar, A.P., *Asian J. Micobiol. Biotech. Env. Sci.*, 4(3): 39-42.

Stetzenbach; Klaws, J.; Irene M. Farnham; Vernon F. Hodge and Kevin H. Johannesson (1999): Using Multivariate Statistical Analysis of Ground Water Major Cation and Trace Element Concentrations to Evaluate Ground Water Flow in a Regional Aquifer, *Hydrol. Process.* 13: 2655-2673.

Thorat, P.R. and Pathade, G.R. (2001): Textile Waste: Characterization and Treatment, In: Environmental Pollution and Management of Wastewaters by Microbial Techniques (Eds.- Pathade, G.R. and Goel, P.K.), *ABD Publishers, Jaipur, India*, pp: 316-325.

Todd, D.K. (1980): Groundwater Hydrology, John Wiley, New York: 554.

Trevors, J.T. and Saier Jr., M.H. (2007): Regulation of Pollution, *Water Air Soil Pollut*, DOI 10.1007/s11270-007-9344-x.

Trivedi, R.K. and Goel, P.K. (1984): Chemical and Biological Methods for Water Pollution Studies, *Environmental Publication*, Karad, pp: 251.

Tyagi, P. and Budhi (2000): Degradation of Ground Water Quality due to Heavy Metals in Industrial Area of India: A Review, *Indian J. Env. Prot.*, 20 (3): 174-181.

Va´zquez, N.N.; Gil, M.A.; Esteves, J. L. and Narvarte, M. A. (2007): Monitoring Heavy Metal Pollution in San Antonio Bay, Rý´o Negro, Argentina, *Bull Environ Contam Toxicol*, DOI 10.1007/s00128-007-9084-z.

Vates, M.V. (1986): Septic Tank Density and Ground Water Contamination, *Ground Water*, 23(5): 586-590.

Verma, S.R. and Mathur, R.P. (1974): Studies on the Toxicity of Industrial Wastes to Macrobranchium Deyanum, *Indian J. Environ. Hlth.*, 16(1): 1-11.

Vijith, H. and Satheesh, R. (2007): Geographical Information System Based Assessment of Spatiotemporal Characteristics of Groundwater Quality of Upland Sub-watersheds of Meenachil River, Parts of Western Ghats, Kottayam District, Kerala, India, *Environ Geol*, DOI 10.1007/s00254-006-0612-7.

Vishwanath, G. and Ananthmurthy, K.S. (2002): Assessment of Ground Water Quality Around a Solid Waste Dump site, *Nat. Env. Poll. Tech.*, 1(4): 411- 413.

Walker, D.J.; Bernal, M.P. and Correal, E. (2007): The Influence of Heavy Metals and Mineral Nutrient Supply on *Bituminaria bituminosa*, *Water Air Soil Pollut*, DOI 10.1007/s11270-007-9422-0.

Walker, R. (1970): The Metabolism of Azo Compounds: A Review of the Literature, *Food Cosmetics Toxicology*, 8: 659-661.

Widyanto, L.S. (1975): The Effect of Industrial Pollutants on the Growth of Water Hyacinth (Eicchornia crassipes Mart Solm.), In: *Proceedings of the third Indonesian Weed Science Conference*, Bandung, pp: 328.

Williums, D.R. (1972): Metals, Ligands and Cancer, *Chemical Review*, 72 (3): 203-213.

Wint, A. (1981): The Disposal of Toxic Wastes, In: Industrial Effluent Treatment Vol. I (Eds.- Watler, J.K. and Wint, M.), pp: 1-19.

Yadav, A.K; P.K. Jain and Jyoti Sharma (2003): Assessment of Ground Water Quality of Behror Textile of Alwar Dist., Rajsthan. *Aquacult*, 4(2): 265-270.

Yadav, J.P. and Sumanlata (2003): Pollution of Fluoride in Ground Water in Bahadurgarh Block of Districts Jhajjar, Haryana, *IJEP*, 23(6): 680-686.

Yadav, R.K.; B. Goyal, R.K. Sharma; S.K. Dubey and P.S. Minhas (2002): Post Irrigation Impact of Domestic Sewage Effluent on Composition of Soils, Crops and Ground Water: A Case Study, *Environment International*, 28: 481-486.

Yu, F-Y; Li, C-W and Kang, S-F. (2005): Color, Dye and Doc Removal, and Acid Generation during Fenton Oxidation of Dyes. *Environmental Technology*, Vol. 26. pp: 537-544.

Yusuf, R.O. and Sonibare, J.A. (2004): Characterization of Textile Industries Effluents in Kaduna, Nigeria and Pollution Implications, *Globel Nest,* 6(3): 212-221.

Zheng, G.; Yue, L.; Li, Z and Chen, C. (2006): Assessment on Heavy Metals Pollution of Agricultural Soil in Guanzhong District, *J Geographical Sciences*, 16, (1) 2006 105-113 ISSN: 1009-637X.

Zilliox, Lothaire (1989): Industrial Impact on the Quality of Ground Water in a Large Basin: Case of the Rhine Aquifer. *Water International*, 14(2): 62-68.

Pages: 112-130

SOIL CONTAMINATION AND CONSERVATION

Edited by: Dr. Ezeaku Peter Ikemefuna; Dr. Pawan Kumar 'Bharti'

ISBN: 978-93-5056-737-1

Edition: 2015

Published by: Discovery Publishing House Pvt. Ltd., New Delhi (India)

Desertification in Nigeria *Causes, Effects and Combation*

Okolo C.C.* and **Ezeaku, P.I.**

ABSTRACT

Nigeria is a large country with a substantial part of its area extending into the Sudano-sahelian belt, which, together with the neighbouring northern Guinea savanna, constitutes the drylands of the country. With an estimated population of 113 million, human pressure on the land particularly in the marginal areas has continued to take its toll on the environment, resulting in desertification. Desertification is made very severe in the drylands of the country by increasing human attempts to exploit the resources of the ecological zone in the face of persistent drought. Before now, Nigeria has been tackling the problem of desertification the best way it could, but with little success. It is now obvious that the menace should be addressed in a holistic manner in order to ensure that the drylands of the country continue to support human and natural resources.

Key words: Desertification, dryland, sudano-sahelian belt, guinea savanna, drought.

Department of Soil Science, University of Nigeria Nsukka, Nigeria.

INTRODUCTION

Desertification is the degradation of land in arid and dry sub-humid areas due to various factors: including climatic variations and human activities (Nick and David, 1997). Desertification results chiefly from man- made activities; it is principally caused by over-grazing, over drafting of groundwater and diversion of water from rivers for human consumption and industrial use, all of these processes are fundamentally driven by overpopulation (Nasiru, 2007). Desertification occurs mainly in semi-arid areas (average annual rainfall less than 600mm) bordering on deserts. In Sahel, (the semi-arid area south of the Sahara Desert), for example, the desert moved southwards between 1950 and 1975.

Desertification constitutes one of the international environmental problems whose global importance has been recognized by the International community. This importance is clearly visible in the massive endorsement that issues that states have given to the United Nations convention to combat desertification in those countries experiencing serious drought and/or desertification, particularly in Africa adopted in 1994 (Nasiru, 2007). Desertification affects about one-sixth of the world's population, 70 per cent of all dry lands, amounting to 3.6 billion hectares, and one quarter of the total land area of the world. The most obvious impact of desertification, in addition to widespread poverty, is the degradation of 3.3 billion hectares of the total area of rangeland, constituting 73 percent of the rangeland with a low potential for human and animal carrying capacity; decline in soil fertility and soil structure on about 47 percent of the dryland areas constituting marginal rain fed cropland; and the degradation of irrigated cropland, amounting to 30 percent of the dryland areas with a high population density and agricultural potential(UNCCD, 1992).

LOCATION OF NIGERIA

Nigeria is located approximately between Latitudes 4o and 14o north of the Equator and between Longitudes 2° 2′ and 14° 30′ east of the Greenwich Meridian. To the north, it is bordered by the Republics of Niger and Chad, to the east by the Republic of Cameroon, to the south by the Atlantic Ocean and to the West by the Republic of Benin.

The surface area of the country is approximately 923,770 m2. About 35% of this land mass is believed to bearable while 15% is said to be used as pastures, 10% as forest reserve, 10% for settlements and the remaining 30% is considered uncultivable, for one reason or the other. However, another estimate puts the surface area as 91.07 million hectares, 57% of which is believed to be either under crops, or pastures while the remaining 43% is divided among forest, water bodies and other uses (Cleaver & Shreiber, 1994).

CLIMATE

By virtue of its location, Nigeria enjoys a warm tropical climatic condition with relatively high temperatures throughout the year and two seasons; the dry and wet seasons. The climate of the country is influenced by the interaction of two air masses: the relatively warm and moist tropical marine air mass (mT) which originates from the Atlantic Ocean and is associated with Southwest winds in Nigeria; and the relatively cool, dry and relatively stable tropical continental air mass (cTs) that originates from the Sahara Desert and is associated with the dry, cool and dusty North-East Trades (Harmattan). The boundary surface area between the two air masses is known as the Inter-tropical Discontinuity (ITD) or the Inter-tropical Convergence Zone (ITCZ). The ITD migrates north and south of the country bringing rainfall or dryness to different areas of the country at different times of the year. Roughly, its northward movement brings the wet season to all areas south of its location, while its southward migration brings the dry season to areas north of its location. In general, while there is hardly any dry season in the extreme southern tip of the country, the wet season hardly lasts for more than three months in the northeastern part of the country. Similarly, annual rainfall totals range from over 2,500mm in the south to less than 400mm in parts of the extreme north.

GEOLOGY, LANDFORM AND SOILS

The geology of Nigeria is dominated by igneous structures that form most of the highlands and hills. The rocks of the Basement Complex, mainly of igneous origin, are encountered in over 60% of the surface area.

Younger Granites are intruded into these rocks in Jos Plateau and environs. Volcanic rocks are also extruded on to the surface in places such as Jos Plateau and Adamawa Highlands. Areas of sedimentary formations are restricted to the coastal belt; the Niger-Benue Trough, including the southeastern scarp land and the Sokoto-Rima basin; and the Chad Basin.

The landforms can simply be classified into highlands, plateaus, hills, plains and river valley systems.

Suffice it to state that the landforms are more deeply dissected in the southern parts than in the northern parts. Indeed, except for the Eastern Highlands in Adamawa area and the Jos Plateau, basins characterized by broad gently sloping plains dominate the northern half of Nigeria. An extensive section of this area is identified as the High Plains of Hausa land (Udo, 1970).

The geology and the geomorphological processes that shaped the landforms have greatly influenced the soils. The major soil types in Nigeria, according to the FAO soil taxonomy legends are fluvisols, regosols, gleysols, acrisols, ferrasols, alisols, lixisols, cambisols, luvisols, nitosols, arenosols, and vertisols. These soil types vary in their potential for agricultural use as shown in Table1. Clearly none of these soils is rated as Class 1 with high productivity by the FAO. Indeed, over 48% of Nigerian soils fall into classes 4 and 5.

Table 7.1: Productivity Potential of Nigerian Soils

Soil Productivity Grade	FAO Productivity Classes	Km²	Area % of Total
High (1)	–	–	–
Good (2)	Fluvisols, Gleysols Regosols	50.4	5.52
Medium (3)	Lixisols, Cambisols, Luvisols, Nitosols	423.6	46.45
Low (4)	Acrisols, Ferralsols, Alisols, Vertisols	289.2	31.72
Low (5)	Arenosols, Nitosols	148.8	16.32

Source: Originally from FAO and reported in Agboola, S. A. 1979. An Agricultural Atlas of Nigeria, Oxford University Press, Oxford, Modified by IAR&T, Ibadan. 1996.

These are mainly vertisols, alisols, acrisols, ferrasols, and arenosol. These soils usually have low productivity due to inadequate moisture retention capacity and low organic matter. What is more, except for the ferrasols, they are the most dominant types found in the northern dry parts of the country.

DRAINAGE AND HYDROLOGY

There are three major drainage systems in the country. These are: the River Niger drainage system; the coastal drainage system and the Lake Chad inland drainage system. The River Niger drainage system consists of the River Niger and its tributaries, prominent among which are: the Benue, the Sokoto-Rima, the Kaduna, the Gongola and the Anambra. The Lake Chad inland drainage system draws the following inflowing rivers from Nigeria: the Komadougou-Yobe (with headstreams including Hadejia, Jama'are and Misau) and the Yedseram. However, the Chari and Lagone rivers from the Central African Republic constitute the most important inflow.

The coastal drainage system consists of rivers and short streams draining directly into the Atlantic Ocean. Two sub-sets of this system can be recognized. There is the eastern system consisting of rivers and streams east of the Niger delta such as the Cross, Imo, Qua Iboe and Kwa rivers. The western system consists of the Ogun, Oshun, Owena and Benin rivers. The total area of inland water bodies is estimated to be slightly over 12 million hectares as shown in Table 7.2.

The hydrology of the country is influenced by the geologic structure. Areas of igneous structure are dominated by surface runoff while the areas of sedimentary formation are characterized by ground water retention. Most of the Chad Basin and the Sokoto-Rima Basin in the drier north are associated more with groundwater than surface water.

Table 7.2: Summary of Water Surface Area of Lakes, Reservoirs and Major Rivers in Nigeria

Body of Water	Area (ha)	% of Total
Lake Chad (Nigerian Sector)	550,000	4.46
Kainji Lake	127,000	1.03
Major Rivers	10,812,210	87.62
Reservoirs	275,000	2.23
Flood Plains	575,000	4.66
Total	12,339.21	100

Source: Adapted from Ita *et al* (1985)

VEGETATION

There is hardly any vegetation that has not been affected by human activities in the country. Farming, logging, grazing, hunting, urbanization, road construction and other development activities by the rapidly expanding population have together reduced the nation's natural plant cover to isolated remnants. Based on the climatic conditions, the following vegetation types are recognized in the country: the mangrove and fresh water swamps, the rain forest, the Guinea Savanna, the Sudan Savanna and the Sahel in a south-north transect. Between the rain forest and the Guinea Savanna is a modified vegetation transition consisting of light deciduous forest and derived savanna.

The southern forest that is, both the swamps and the rain forest constitutes the country's main source of wood. The derived savanna zone, about 250km wide, was once the northern part of the forest zone, but transformed by such activities into a vegetation type consisting largely of deciduous trees and grasses. The vegetation still supplies some wood. Most of the remaining part of the country is the Sudan Savanna accounting for more than 25% of the surface area, and expanding at the expense of the Guinea Savanna. At the northeastern and northwestern corners of the country is the Sahel that ordinarily does not account for more than 5 - 10% of the surface area, but is now growing larger at the expense of the Sudan zone. Indeed, it is now more meaningful to take the two driest zones together as the sudano-sahelian zone.

This is the ecological zone described as the Nigerian dryland by many researchers, containing most of the rangeland of the country. This zone constitutes the main source of fodder and grazing land for livestock. However, there is also the expansion of cultivation and extreme climatic variations that combine to reduce the grazing areas, and degrade the zone, including changes in plant species.

AGRICULTURE

Agriculture in Nigeria involves four broad systems of land use: crop production, animal husbandry, fishery and forestry. Crop production involves three types of farming in the country: rotational fallow; semi-permanent or permanent cultivation; and mixed farming. There are variations of each type. For example, the permanent cultivation may be under rain-fed system, or irrigated system. Rotational fallow, land rotation type is common in sparsely populated areas. The system allows a cultivated field to rest for a few years (known as fallow years) before it is cultivated again. However, as the population of a place increases, the fallow period becomes shortened until a permanent cultivation is enthroned. It is an irony of fate that the dryland of Nigeria is where permanent cultivation, as a result of pressure of people on the land, is practiced more than in other areas.

Animal husbandry in Nigeria is mainly the pastoral type. This is a nomadic system under which the herdsmen, usually the Fulanis, move with the seasons, southwards as far as the deciduous forest during the dry season and northwards as far as the Sahel during the wet season. The system also has international dimensions as herders from the neighboring countries infiltrate into Nigeria during the dry season.

Mixed farming, that is, a mixture of crop and animal production, is also practiced on a permanent basis. This system combines semi-permanent crop farming with grass fallow for grazing. The plots are then rotated after one or two years. The combination varies. Where crop production predominates, the farmer keeps only a few animals. Where livestock dominates, crop production will be a minor activity, and the rangeland type of agriculture is practiced. The land use types indicating these agricultural activities are illustrated in Table 7.3.

Table 7.3: Land Use Patterns in Nigeria

Land Use	Area (Million ha)	% of Total
Cropland	30.96	34
Pasture	20.94	23
Forest	14.57	16
Rivers/lakes/Reservoirs	11.66	13
Others	12.93	14
Total	91.06	100

Sources: Cleaver and Shreiber, 1994. Reversing the Spiral; FAO: WRI/HED 1988 (p. 264-265); WRI 1992 (p. 262); Ita, 1993.

HOW WIDESPREAD IS DESERTIFICATION IN NIGERIA AND BEYOND?

Nigeria is a large country with a substantial part of its area extending into the Sudano-Sahelian belt, which, together with the neighbouring northern

Guinea savannah, constitutes the dry lands of the country. With an estimated population of 140 million, human pressure on the land particularly in the marginal areas has continued to take its toll on the environment, resulting in desertification. Desertification is made very severe in drylands of the country by increasing human attempts to exploit the resources of the ecological zone in the face of persistent drought.

Current research has proven that desertification is persistently affecting the eleven northern states and is also considered the most pressing environmental problem and accounts for about 73% out of the estimated total cost of about US$ 5.110 billion per annum the country is losing arising from environmental degradation (UNCCD, 1999). The extent and severity of desertification in Nigeria has not been fully established neither the rate of progression properly documented. Nevertheless, there is a general consensus that desertification is by far the most pressing environmental problem in the drylands parts of the country and even beyond. The visible sign of this phenomenon is the gradual shift in vegetation from grasses, bushes and occasional trees to grass and bushes; and in the final stages, expansive areas of desert-like sand. It has been estimated that between 50% and 75% of Adamawa, Bauchi, Borno, Jigawa, Kano, Katsina, Kebbi, Sokoto, Yobe and Zamfara states in Nigeria are being seriously affected by desertification. These states, with a population of about 50 million people account for about 43% of the country's total land area (Nasiru, 2007). In these areas, population pressure resulting in overgrazing and over exploitation of marginal lands has aggravated desertification and drought. Entire villages and major access roads have been buried under sand dunes in the extreme parts of the northern parts of Katsina, Sokoto, Jigawa, Borno and Yobe states. The pressure of the migrating human and livestock populations from these areas are absorbed by pressure point buffer states such as the Federal Capital territory, Plateau, Taraba, Niger, Kwara and Kaduna states. It is reported that these buffer states have about 10 - 15% of their land area threatened by desertification (UNCCD, 1999). This action leads to an intensified use of fragile and marginal ecosystems resulting into progressive degradation even in years of normal rainfall.

More so, about one third of the world's land surface is arid or semi-arid. It is predicted that global warming will increase the area of desert climates by 17% in the next century. The area at risk to desertification is thus large and likely to increase (Nasiru, 2007).

Worldwide, desertification is making approximately 12 million hectares useless for cultivation every year. This is equal to 10% of the total area of South Africa or 87% of the area of cultivated lands in our country (Nasiru, 2007). In the early 1980s it was estimated that, 61% of the 3257 million hectares of all productive drylands (lands where stock are grazed and crops grown, without irrigation) were moderately to severely desertified. The problem is clearly enormous. The soils in most part of the dryland, though well drained, are sandy, low in soil organic matter and are characterized by low water holding capacity as cited earlier. The only exception to this observation is the fadama soil that is fine-textured with a higher organic matter content and relatively higher water-holding capacity. Furthermore, this zone is the most grazed as well as where increasing drought incidents have caused changes in plant species, such as the invasion of the Kano area (Sudan) by thorn bushes native to the Sahel. It is also the zone where farmers have encroached on grazing reserves and climatically marginal areas, leading to increased incidence of pastoralists-farmers conflict and desertification.

Moreover, in terms of human activities, the dryland areas of Nigeria have been inhabited and cultivated for centuries. It is a zone where the period of fallow has been reduced to the barest minimum in many areas, or non-existent over a radius of 30km around some urban centers. Thus the pressure on the land is much more than it is in some other parts of the country.

The following table presents a listing of Nigeria's 36 States ranked in order of their total population based on preliminary 2006 census figures:

Sl. No.	States	Total Population
1.	Lagos State	9,113,605
2.	Kano State	9,401,288
3.	Kaduna State	6,113,503
4.	Katsina State	5,801,584
5.	Oyo State	5,580,894
6.	Rivers State	5,198,716
7.	Bauchi State	4,653,066
8.	Jigawa State	4,361,002
9.	Benue State	4,253,641
10.	Anambra State	4,177,828
11.	Borno State	4,171,104
12.	Delta State	4,112,445
13.	Imo State	3,927,563
14.	Niger State	3,954,772
15.	Akwa Ibom State	3,902,051
16.	Ogun State	3,751,140
17.	Sokoto State	3,702,676

(Contd...)

Sl. No.	States	Total Population
18.	Ondo State	3,460,877
19.	Osun State	3,416,959
20.	Kogi State	3,314,043
21.	Zamfara State	3,278,873
22.	Enugu State	3,267,837
23.	Kebbi State	3,256,541
24.	Edo State	3,233,366
25.	Plateau State	3,206,531
26.	Adamawa State	3,178,950
27.	Cross River State	2,882,988
28.	Abia State	2,845,370
29.	Ekiti State	2,398,357
30.	Kwara State	2,365,353
31.	Gombe State	2,365,040
32.	Yobe State	2,321,339
33.	Taraba State	2,294,800
34.	Ebonyi State	2,176,947
35.	Nasarawa State	1,869,377
36.	Bayelsa State	1,704,515
–	Abuja Federal Capital Territory	1,405,201

Population by State and Sex. (Source: www.population.gov.ng)

CAUSES OF DESERTIFICATION IN NIGERIA

Desertification in Nigeria arises from the demands of increased populations that settle on the land in order to grow crops and graze animals.

Natural Causes

The natural causes of desertification include the poor physical conditions of soils, vegetation, topography as well as the inherent extreme climatic variability as evidenced in periodic droughts. Climatic variation is perhaps the most important natural cause of desertification in the dry lands of Nigeria. The history of the Sudano-Sahelian zone of Nigeria is replete with severe and prolonged drought events, some lasting several years. The zone started the 20th century with a prolonged drought of 1903 culminating in that of 1911-1914. Other droughts included those of 1919, 1924, 1935 and 1951-1954. Rainfall was relatively abundant in the late 1950s and the early 1960s. Since then average rainfall has fallen below the 1930-1960 mean for almost three decades with lows in both 1972-1973 and 1984-1985. In terms of rainfall deficiency, river discharges and Lake Chad level, the period of 1983-1985 was the driest period in this century in the zone as the lake fell to its lowest level and shrank to its smallest area (Nasiru, 2007).

Human Activities

The anthropogenic factor is mainly the disruption of the ecological system caused by poor land use and ever increasing pressure put upon the available resources by the expanding population. More specifically, there are four primary causes, notably over-exploitation, overgrazing, deforestation and poor irrigation practices, and these are influenced by factors such as changes in population, climate and socio-economic conditions. It is obviously a complex inter-relationship, which includes: poor physical conditions in terms of soils, vegetation, topography and inherent extreme variability of climate as manifested in frequent drought; disruption in ecological balance caused by poor land use and ever increasing demand being made on the available resources by the expanding population and socio-economic systems of the affected areas; and improper land-use practices and poor land management.

In addition to the causes mentioned above according to Marugba (1999) and NAP (2000), the following are the main causes of desertification in Nigeria through anthropogenic factor.

1. Wood Extraction for Fuel and Construction

Without alternative sources of energy in the Sudano-Sahelian zone, the demand for fuel wood has been on steady increase by the increasing population and rapid urbanization despite the existing felling of trees (control) Edict in the various states. In addition, wood is also exploited for building, arts and crafts in this environment. The United Nations Sudano-Sahelian Office (UNSO) has identified forest depletion as the major agent of desertification in Nigeria. As a result of the demand for wood for construction, building, fuel, fishing industry and other uses, the removal of trees, herbaceous plants and grass cover from the fragile land of the Sahel will continue to accelerate the degradation of the soil to desert-like conditions.

2. Bush Burning

Bush burning is an agent in the process of desertification. Owing to the low relative humidity of the semi-arid zone coupled with very dry harmattan wind, there is always a high incidence of bush fires every dry season. The occurrence of fire within the zone can be attributed to bush burning by villagers during land clearing for agriculture, hunters who in search of game, set fire onto the vegetation, and cattle herdsmen who set fire to dry grass to stimulate growth of dormant grass buds.

Thus, desertification is a result of complex inter-relationships between social and natural system as illustrated and shown below.

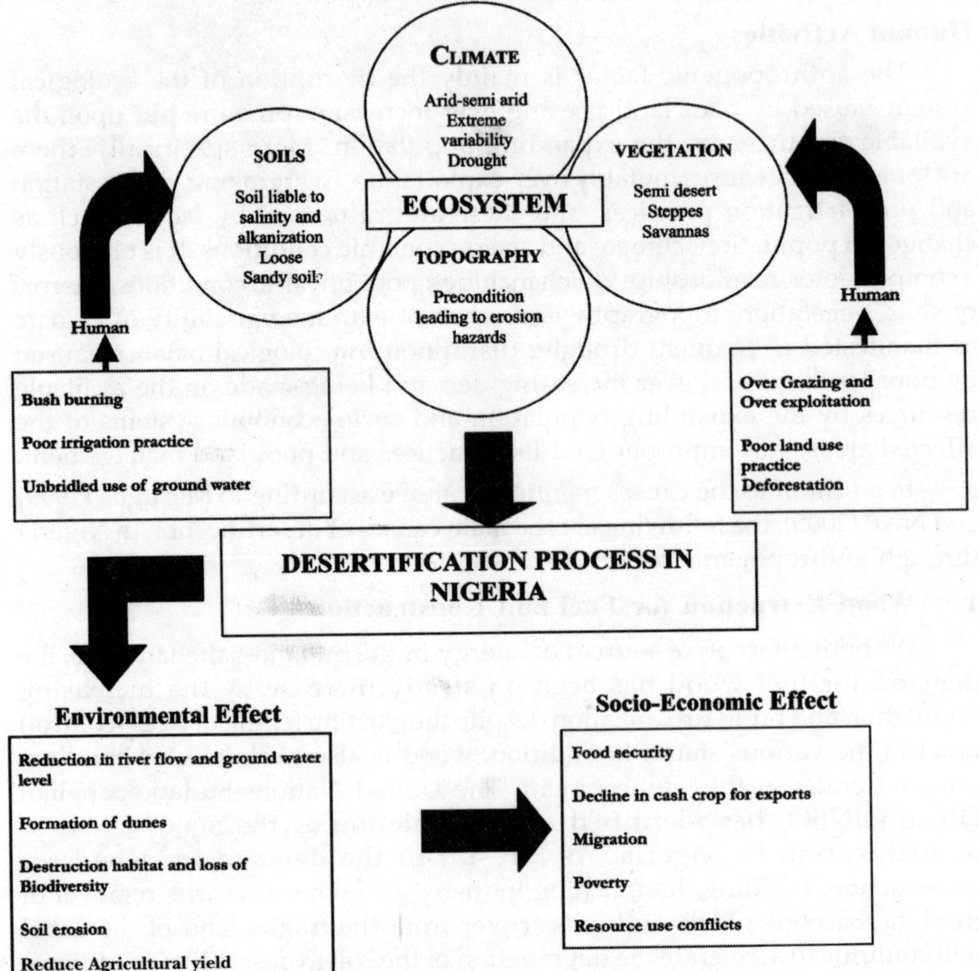

Fig. 7.1: Model of Desertification Processes in Nigeria (Adapted from Oladipo 1993)

3. Overgrazing

Overgrazing is one of the major causes of desertification worldwide. Plants of semi-arid areas are adapted to being eaten by sparsely scattered, large, grazing mammals which move in response to the patchy rainfall common to these regions. Early human pastoralists living in semi-arid areas copied this natural system. They moved their small groups of domestic animals in response to food and water availability. In modern times, the use of fences has prevented domestic and wild animals from moving in response to food availability, and overgrazing has often resulted.

Nevertheless, livestock population in Nigeria has been estimated to consist of 16 million cattle, about 13.5 million sheep, some 26 million goats, approximately 2.2 and 150 million pigs and poultry respectively (Gadzama, 1995). The dry lands of Nigeria is said to support much of the country's livestock economy, hosting about 90% of the cattle population. In Sudan and Sahel zones, which carry most of the livestock population, nomadic herdsmen graze their livestock throughout the area and are constantly in search of suitable pastures. Additional pressure is also put on pasture resources by livestock from neighbouring countries notably Cameroon, Chad and Niger respectively.

4. Cultivation of Marginal Land

Cultivation of marginal areas is one of the causes of desertification. In periods of higher than normal rainfall, people tend to extend farming activities into the marginal areas. When the years of plenty are followed by dry years, exposed land with very little vegetal cover is at the mercy of the winds. The fine clays and silts are carried away as dusts, and the sand drifts into dunes. Sand dunes can encroach on human habitats. Sand dunes move through a few different means, all of them assisted by wind. In major dust storm, dunes may move tens of meters through sheet flows, and the effect of this could be irreversible except through carefully planned rehabilitation programmes.

5. Faulty Irrigation Management

Irrigated cropping can turn land into desert if not properly designed and managed as a result of waterlogging, salinized or alkalinisation. This scenario is already a reality on a number of irrigated projects in Nigeria today, such as the Bakolori Irrigation, South Chad Irrigation and the Hadejia-Jamaare Irrigation projects.

6. Poverty

Perhaps the most subtle and often neglected cause of desertification is poverty. Although statistical data are hard to come-by, evidence seems to suggest that the vast majority of the inhabitants of the drylands of Nigeria live below the poverty level. To a large extent therefore, they depend heavily on the natural resources of the area. Thus, the well known interrelationship between poverty and environmental degradation obtains whereby poverty generates environmental degradation (desertification) which in turn accentuates poverty.

IMPACT OF DESERTIFICATION

Socio-economic Impact

Desertification has severe impact on food security, livelihood, socio-economic and cultural activities of the affected people. This has aggravated the food situation in the area resulting in low food security index. Drought causes a lot of economic disruption, for example, it was responsible for the drastic fall in the GDP of 18.4 percent in 1971-1972 and of 7.3 percent in 1972-1973 (at constant 1974-1975 prices). It was also seen as causing the rapid rise in price index for foodstuff and relative decline in non-oil exports.

Land and Water Resources

In addition to the socio-economic impacts, drought and desertification do have serious consequences on available water resources. Long term drought could adversely affect the level of upper ground water and stream flows, as well as the underground water. They also affect the level of large lakes, thereby affecting riparian access as in Lake Chad, which has receeded beyond the borders of Nigeria.

Resources Use Conflicts

Desertification and land degradation encourage economic and social strife as shown in wars of the horn in Africa in the last two decades. This is often accentuated by lack of proper natural resource planning and management as well as rapid population increase in the arid zones, and the diminishing environmental resource base. In the drylands of Nigeria, conflicts over land resources are focused areas of high productivity, especially those that provide seasonally critical resource such as the wetlands. The most of which have competitive uses amongst the various rural land users, notably farmers, herders, fishermen and hunters.

Destruction of Habitat and Loss of Bio-Diversity

The flora and fauna of the Sudano-Sahelian zone have been badly depleted as a result of climate variation and human mismanagement and/or over-exploitation of the environment. Some fauna species such as the sitodunga antelope, cheetah, lion, giraffe and elephant are endangered. Other endangered species are the crowned crane, the bustard, Palearctic migrants, ostriches and fulvov tree duck.

GOVERNMENTS EFFORTS AND WAYS OF COMBATING DESERTICATION PROBLEMS IN NIGERIA

The Nigerian Government, within the overall framework of protecting the Nigerian environment, has given prominence to the twin environmental problems of drought and desertification. The efforts are on National Policies, Institutional and Legislative framework, Sectoral Programmes and Partnership Building that have been in place to address the problem of drought and desertification. The current government policies are:

National Policies:

- *National Policy on Environment:* The policy clearly indicates synergies with other sub-sectors relating to population, culture, housing and human settlements, biological diversity, conservation of natural resources, land-use and soil conservation, agriculture, water resources, forestry, wildlife and protected areas, flood and erosion control and the cross-sectoral issues of public participation.

- *National Agricultural Policy:* Within the National Agricultural policy, there are sub-sectoral policies covering livestock, forest, food production, and land and water resources.
- *National Energy Policy:* The objectives of this policy is for the promotion of the use of renewable energy resources (wind, water) and improving efficiency of domestic energy utilization as well as minimizing and mitigating harmful practice of extracting energy from woods (plants).
- *National Forestry Policy and Action Plan:* It is a framework for halting deforestation and associated destructive impacts. Among its objectives are: protection of forests resources, achieving 25% forest coverage's in Nigeria and sustainable utilization of forest products.
- *National Environmental Action Plan and State Environmental Action Plans:* The policies, plans and programmes include: overall protection of the Nigerian environment, promotion of renewable energy technologies, conservation of threatened flora and fauna species, environmental education and awareness creation and reduction of resource use conflict among land users.
- *National Conservation Strategy:* The aim is to manage the ecosystems in such a way that they yield greatest sustainable benefit to present generations while maintaining the potential to meet the needs and aspirations of future generations in such a way that essential ecological processes and life support systems are maintained.
- *National Resources Conservation Action Plan:* This plan aims at collating and evaluating data and knowledge of natural resources with a view to developing programmes of action for management and sustainable use.
- *National Water Resources Master Plan (1995-2020):* The master plan aims at sustainable utilization of water resources, particularly in the semi-arid zone of the country.
- *National Biodiversity Strategy and Action Plan:* The goals and objectives are to conserve and enhance the sustainable use of the nation's biodiversity resources and to integrate biodiversity – planning considerations into national policy and decision making and the Green Agenda of the vision 2010.
- *National Agenda 21:* This is essentially designed to integrate environment and development, which seeks to attain sustainable development. Its main focus is on how to redress the major existing environmental problems.

- *National Economic Empowerment and Development Strategy (NEEDS):* NEEDS focuses on four key strategies: reorienting values, reducing poverty, creating wealth and generating employment.
- *National Action Plan to Combat Desertification:* This National Action Plan (NAP) is a report that spells out critical activities to be taken in a holistic manner to tackle the menace of desertification of the country.

Institutional and Legislative Framework

The establishment of FEPA by Decree 58 of 1998 was probably the most far-reaching initiative undertaken by the Federal Government of Nigeria for the purpose of addressing the multifarious environmental problems (drought and desertification inclusive) and protecting the Nigerian Environment. The Federal Environmental Protection Agency (FEPA) also facilitated the establishment of State Environmental Protection Agency (SEPAs) in the 36 states of the Federation and the Federal Capital Territory (FCT). Nigeria signed the Desertification convention on the 31st October, 1994 and ratified same on the 8th July, 1997 there by qualifying the country as a party to the convention with effect from 6th October, 1997. The creation of the Department of Drought and Desertification Amelioration in the Federal Ministry of Environment strengthens the existing institutional arrangement for more effective coordination of activities by Government towards the implementation of the CCD in the country.

Sectoral Programmes

In Nigeria, several sectoral and multi-sectoral programmes have been put in place over the years, to tackle the twin problem of drought and desertification. A brief review of some of these programmes is given below:

1. Management of Water Resources

Towards promoting sustainable utilisation of water resources in the drylands, Nigeria established River Basin Development Authorities (RBDAs) under the supervision of the Federal Ministry of water Resources. These are actively involved in development of water resources particularly for irrigation. These efforts include damming and diversion of rivers, and in some areas exploiting underground water. The RBDAs are also involved in improvement of community water supplies and provision of watering points in rangelands. The RBDAs that operate in the semi-arid region of Nigeria include the Sokoto-Rima, Hadejia-Jama'are, Upper Benue, Niger River and Chad Basin Development Authorities. The Federal Government of Nigeria, with World Bank assistance, has also implemented a programme tagged National Fadama Development Project for the purpose of optimally utilizing the water resources of the wetlands of Nigeria for small scale irrigation. The project was under the guidance and supervision of the Agricultural Development Programmes (ADPs) of the various states. The project provided gainful employment for the rural populace during the dry season thereby cutting down on the number of peasants engaged in off-season trade in firewood.

2. Forestry Programmes

An Arid Zone Afforestation Project (AZAP) was established by the Federal Government in 1976 to tackle the problems of desertification through the establishment of woodlots, shelterbelts and windbreaks. Over 10 million seedlings were raised annually between 1978 and 1984. About 150kilometers of shelterbelts, 3,680 hectares of woodlots, 24 boreholes, 70 tree nurseries, and Forestry Vocational Schools were established. The European Economic Community supported a pilot project in Katsina state covering a total area of 1.6 million hectares involving the establishment of shelterbelts, windbreaks, woodlots and trees on farmlands. In addition, the World Bank also financed a similar project in the five arid zone states. The emphasis is on farmer participation and extension. Areas of focus of the Forestry programme include the following; land use policy, fuel energy, mass tree planting campaign, preventing of bush fire, silvo-pastoral system and sand dune fixation.

3. Agricultural Development Programme

The Federal Government of Nigeria with World Bank assistance has expanded enormous resources to establish Agricultural Development Programmes (ADPs) in all the 36 states of the federation and the Federal capital territory. The ADPs operate the training and visit (T & V) system of unified extension system covering the areas of Crop Production and Protection, Livestock Production and Animal Health, Fisheries, Agro-forestry and gender related issues in Agriculture popularly referred to as Women in Agriculture. This unified extension system is employed for the dissemination of proven agricultural technologies (aimed at ensuring sustainable development) to the small-scale, resource poor farmers who are responsible for well over 90 percent of the national food production.

4. Energy Resources

Although Nigeria is blessed with abundant renewable resources, there is currently a heavy reliance on fuel wood and fossil fuels. Sourcing of fuel wood for domestic and commercial uses is a major cause of desertification in the arid zone states of Nigeria.

Currently, fuel wood is the dominant source of energy in the domestic sector. According to a report by the ECN, Nigeria consumes well over 50 million metric tonnes of fuel wood annually; a rate that exceeds the replenishment rate through various afforestation programmes. The Federal Government through the Energy Commission of Nigeria (ECN), has put in place the following programmes for the purpose of promoting optimal utilization of renewable resources with a view to reducing deforestation associated with fuel wood sourcing; training programmes on renewable energy technology, biogas and biomass utilization projects and solar photoroltaic electrification projects for remote rural areas. All energy-related environmental projects that are being implemented in Nigeria are guided by the National Policy Guidelines on Energy.

5. Integrated Programme Targeted at Poverty Alleviation

The Federal Government of Nigeria realises that poverty alleviation is a major weapon for combating desertification. Consequently, a number of poverty alleviation programmes have been put in place. Notable amongst these are the NorthEast Arid Zone Development Programme (NEAZDP), the FMENU/UNIMAID linkage model village project, the Katsina State Agricultural and Community Development Project (KSACDP), and the Sokoto Environmental Protection Programme (SEPP). The major components of this programme include water resources development and management (including irrigated agriculture), provision of micro-credit for the off season economic activities, cottage industries, livestock fattening, rural banking and popularisation of animal traction for land preparation for agricultural activities.

Building Partnerships

Government has recognised that the hydra-headed problem of desertification cannot be tackled by itself alone. To this end, it has facilitated the involvement of other actors including the private sector, Non-Governmental Organisations (NGOs), Community Based Organisations (CBOs) and Donors. At present, a number of NGOs are actively involved in the implementation of CCD in Nigeria. Some of them participated very actively in the negotiation process. The regional Annexes of the convention and the resolution on Urgent Action for Africa spell out the expected roles for NGOs as follows:

1. Action programmes, co-ordination mechanisms and partnerships.
2. Capacity building, education and public awareness.
3. Financial resources mechanisms.

ONGOING PROJECTS INITIATED BY THE FEDERAL GOVERNMENT AIMED AT COMBATING DESERTIFICATION

The following projects have been approved for implementation by the Federal Government of Nigeria as part of her effort in combating desertification.

- **The Greenbelt Project**: The Greenbelt project is an integrated and participatory scheme with the following components: nursery development, poverty reduction, promotion of livelihood, watershed management, rural water supply, micro-credit facility, eco-tourism, rural energy, biodiversity conservation, environmental education and awareness creation, capacity building and research.

- **Assessment and Preparation of Desertification Map of Nigeria**: A major output of the project will be the production of National Desertification map using satelite imaginary and GIS. This is of course in addition to yielding credible data on the extent, severity and rate of desertification in Nigeria.
- **Development of National Drought Forecasting and Early Warning System**: The capacity to predict the occurrence of drought will no doubt facilitate timely development of early warning systems for effective adoption of appropriate mitigating factors.
- **Nigeria-Niger Trans-boundary Ecosystem Management Project:** Integrated ecosystem management of Trans-boundary areas between Nigeria and Niger is a Global Environmental Facility (GEF) funded project aimed at creating conditions for sustainable integrated ecosystem management and thereby improve livelihoods in areas covered by the Maiduduri Agreement between the two countries.

CONCLUSION AND RECOMMENDATIONS

Despite the various national efforts/programmes discussed above, desertification continues to be a serious problem in the dry-land Nigeria. Desertification is a reversible process, but action must be taken immediately to reverse the process in areas where the threat is greatest before the processes reaches its conclusion and there is no longer the chance of recovery. In the dry-lands of Nigeria and in particular the north western and north eastern part has the highest priority because it is here that removal of natural vegetation and inappropriate cultivation methods are degrading and depleting valuable and limited biological, soil, and water resources at the fastest rate. In addition, the priority in combating desertification should be the implementation of preventive measures for lands that are not yet degraded, or which are only slightly degraded. However, the severely degraded areas should not be neglected.

In combating desertification, the participation of local communities, rural organisations, national governments, non-governmental organisations and international and regional organisations is essential.

Moreso, massive planting of drought resistant plants like moringa olifeira in those frontline northern states already under severe threat of desertification can affectively combat desertification and equally reclaim the vast portions of land.

REFERENCES

Cleaver K.M. and A.G. Shreiber, (1994): Reversing the Spiral, World Bank, Washington, D.C.

Gadzama, N.M (1995). Sustainable Development in the Arid Zone of Nigeria. Monographic series No. 1, Centre or Arid Zone Studies, University of Maiduguri, Nigeria. 32 pp.

Ita, E.O., Sado, E.K., Balogun, J.K., Padongari, A. and Ibitoye, B. (1985) Inventory Survey of Nigerian Inland Waters and Their Fishery Resources: A Preliminary Checklist of Inland Water Bodies in Nigeria with Special References to Ponds, Lakes, Reservoirs and Major Rivers. Kanji Resources Institute, Kanji Lake, New Bussa. Technical Report series No. 14.

NAP (2000). National Action Plan Report to Combat Desertification and Mitigate the Effect of Drought Towards the Implementation of the United Nations Convention to Combat Desertification and Mitigate the Effect of Drought in Nigeria.

Nasiru, I.M (2007). A Comprehensive Approach to Addressing Drought and Desertification in Nigeria. Universiti Teknologi Malaysia: Unpublished Master's Thesis. Nick Middleton and David Thomas (1997). World Atlas of Desertification; Second Edition, 1997.

Oladipo, E.O (1993). A Comprehensive Approach to Drought and Desertification in Northern Nigeria. Natural Hazards 8: 235-261.

Udo, R.K. (1970): Geographical Regions of Nigeria. Heinemann, Ibadan.

UNCCD (1992). Report of the United Nations Conference on Chapter 12. Retrieved October 22, 2006 from world wide www.unccd.int/convention/history/agenda21.php.

UNCCD (1999). National Report on the Implementation of United Nations Convention to Combat Desertification in those Countries Experiencing Serious Drought/or Desertification, Particularly in Africa for Submission at the Third Session of the Conference of the Parties, Recipe, Brazil.

http://www.bcb.uwc.ac.za/envfacts/facts/desertification.htm

http://en.wikipedia.org/wiki/List_of_Nigerian_states_by_population

***Pages:* 131-145**

SOIL CONTAMINATION AND CONSERVATION

***Edited by:* Dr. Ezeaku Peter Ikemefuna; Dr. Pawan Kumar 'Bharti'**

ISBN: 978-93-5056-737-1

***Edition:* 2015**

***Published by:* Discovery Publishing House Pvt. Ltd., New Delhi (India)**

Adoption of Organo-Minerals in Restoration of the Productivity of Degraded Lands in South Eastern Nigeria

Ezeaku, P.I. and **Edeh, I.G**

INTRODUCTION

Nigeria has a total of 92.4 million hectares of land out of which about 57% (52.668 million hectares) is under crop and pasture production. Although the aggregate production from these lands has sustained the population and the economy in the time past, the rapid increase in population and the need to diversify the economy in other non-agricultural sectors, has necessitated much pressure on the resources (Osuji, 2011). Thus, population growth has been a detrimental dynamic to the use and cultivation of land, leading to changes in cropping patterns; basically continuous cropping. This poses serious problem due to the fragile nature of soils in the humid tropics as well as high dependency on vegetative cover for moisture and stability (Osugiri, 1996).

The inhabitants of southeast Nigeria are predominantly farmers and crop production is centered on food crops such as cassava, yam, maize, rice, beans and cash crops such as oil palm, groundnut, cocoa and bananas. Over

Department of Soil Science, University of Nigeria, Nsukka.

80% of the area allotted to agricultural production is occupied by food crops (Akinyosoye, 1996). The rapid growth of population in the area over the past three decades results to more demands on arable land, which has adversely affected its resource base. Consequently, there is a breakdown of the old traditional land management practices, causing pressure on land and agricultural intensification with reduced fallow periods. In the absence of adequate soil management practices or the economic use of fertilizer and other additives (inputs), declining fallow periods result to accelerated leaching of nutrients, increased weed production, erosion and decreased moisture (Lal, 1983; IITA, 1992; Spore, 1994).

The threats and subsequent destruction of land by soil erosion and land degradation has been the subject for intensive debate in the literature (scherr and Satya 1997; Brabant, 1996). Over the years the destructive process has continued with increased intensity, quantum and rate, such that its devastating effects had subjected the communities to high risks of loss of lives, properties and the natural land that supports their livelihood including extreme difficulties in marketing their products. The land in south East Nigeria has been considered as low lying nature that exposes the surface areas to flooding, coastal and sheet erosion, thus, resulting to the removal of the affected soil (Urama, 2005). Soil fertility in this area is traditionally maintained through shifting cultivation and fallow. Increase in demand for land for agricultural activities and for other human activities has resulted in shortened periods available for land fallow. There has risen the need for intensive land cultivation to cater for the ever-increasing population.

Now that we are facing the greatest challenges of food insecurity resulting from the recent flooding that devastated some parts of the country coupled with the fast declining productivity of our soils, the need to increase soil productivity and also to restore the productivity of degraded lands has prompted the use of various soil amendments.Maintenance of high crop yields under intensive cultivation is possible only through the use of fertilizers. The use of chemical fertilizers to sustain cropping systems on a long term basis has not been very effective. It usually leads to a decline in soil organic matter content, soil acidification and soil physical degradation, which, consequently leads to increased soil erosion (Avery, 1995; Doran et al, 1996). The inorganic fertilizers are usually not available and are always rather expensive for the low – income, small - scale farmers. Organic manures can be used as an alternative for the inorganic fertilizers. They release nutrients rather slowly and steadily over a longer period and also improve the soil fertility status by activating the soil microbial biomass (Ayuso, 1996). Organic manure application sustains cropping system through better nutrient recycling, improved soil structure and increased soil water – holding capacity (Cook *et al*, 1982). They are however, required in rather large quantities to meet up with crops' nutrient supply. They are rarely available to small-scale farmers in the required large quantities (Nyathi et al, 1995). All these have prompted the growing trend of organo-minerals. In many parts of the World, emphasizes are greatly shifting from the simple use of either organic or inorganic fertilizers to combined use. Many research works has been done and is still on going on the use of organo-minerals to improve soil productivity. Organo-mineral fertilizer usage is expected to increase in the near future; therefore, a better understanding of its usage, handling, and soil behaviour is needed. The objective of this paper is to clearly outline the role of organo-minerals in the restoration of degraded lands in South Eastern Nigeria.

LAND DEGRADATION – A SURVEY OF THE LITERATURE

Land degradation remains the greatest problems in Nigeria. In addition, we still witness high levels of water and air pollution while efforts to reduce the rate of natural resources depletion and desertification are yet to yield significant results. Moreover the debt situation in Nigeria is still a major hindrance to sustainable development and poverty alleviation.

Perspective on Land Degradation

Land degradation has been severally defined by many but it revolves around soil surface removal, destruction of various components of soils, reduction in the natural component of the soil and the reduction in the productivity of the soil. Few of such definitions are outlined here;

- The United nations Convention to Combat Desertification (UNCCD, 1994) considers land degradation as a reduction or loss of the biological or economic productivity and complexity of rain fed cropland, irrigations cropland or range, pasture, forest and woodlands resulting from land uses or from a process or combination of processes including processes, arising from human activities and habitation patterns such as, soil erosion caused by wind/or water; deterioration of the physical, chemical, and biological or economic properties of soil and long term loss of natural vegetation.
- Global Environmental Fund (GEF, 2003) explained land degradation to be any form of deterioration of the natural potential of land that affects ecosystems integrity either in terms of reducing sustainable ecological productivity or in terms of reducing its sustainable and resilience.
- Land Degradation Assessment in Dry land (LADA, 2005) considered it as the reduction in the capacity of the land to perform ecosystems functions and services (including those of agro ecosystems and urban systems) that support society and development.

In addition to the usual types of land degradation that have been known for centuries (water, wind and mechanical erosion, physical, chemical and biological degradation), four other types have emerged in the last 50 years (Brabant, 2010) pollution (often chemical) due to agricultural, industrial, mining or commercial activities; loss of arable land due to urban construction; artificial radioactivity, sometimes accidental; land-use constraints associated with armed conflicts. Overall, 36 types of land degradation can be assessed. All are induced or aggravated by human activities, e.g. sheet erosion, silting, aridification, salinization, urbanization, etc.

Land Degradation in South Eastern Nigeria

Geopolitical speaking, the south eastern region of Nigeria is comprised of five states namely, Imo, Anambra, Abia, Enugu and Ebonyi States (Figure 8.1). It is the home of the Igbo speaking people of Nigeria. It is located within latitudes 4° 47″ 35″ N and 7° 7″ 44″ N, and longitudes 7° 54″ 26″ E and 8° 27″ 10″ E in the tropical rain forest zone of Nigeria, with mean maximum temperature of 27°C, and total annual rainfall exceeding 2500mm (Ezemonye and Emeribe, 2012). The region is largely agrarian and there is thus much dependence on land resources, due to its dense population averaged to about 1000 people/Km². This dependence on land has led to the over use of the land resources in the region, leading to the farming of agricultural lands annually.

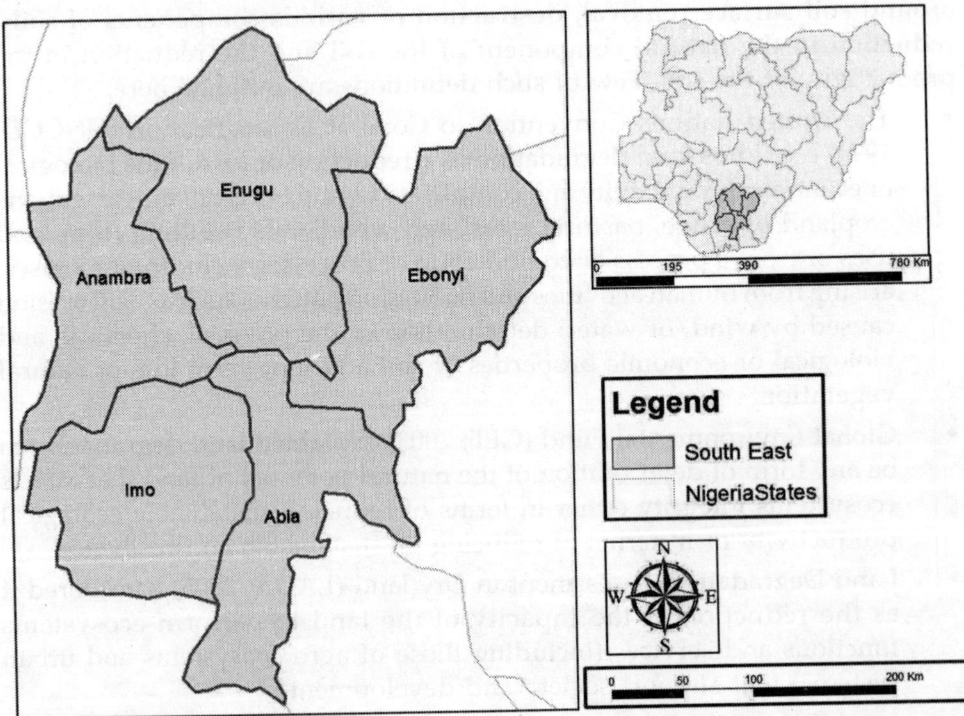

Fig. 8.1: Map of the South East Region of Nigeria Showing the Five Component States. Map of Nigeria is Inset

The nature of soil in the south east is the red earth with sand stones loose surface that is easily prone to damages by torrential rain and flood. Flooding occurs in Nigeria in three main forms: coastal flooding, river flooding and urban flooding. Urban flooding occur in towns located on flat or low lying terrain especially where little or no provision has been made for surface drainage, or where existing drainage has been blocked with municipal waste, refuse and eroded soil sediments. Extensive urban flooding is a phenomenon of every rainy session in Lagos, Maiduguri, Aba, Warri, Benin and Ibadan. The Anambra/Imo river basin has been described as undulating and underlain by the Imo Clay Shale of the Tertiary period, (Asadu et al., 1997).

The soil in the South East constitutes sandy stones loose surface that makes it vulnerable to attacks by floods and in some areas the steep slopes reinforces the rapid flow of rain water to wash away the soil including the vegetation and other nutrients. FAO (2006) records showed that soils in Africa (Acrisols, Ferralsols) are generally shallow, acidic and carbon poor when compared with the types in Europe (Luvisols, cambisols, chernozems). Decomposition of biomass is a rapid process in consistently warm temperatures, leaving little time for accumulation of humus. As a result, extensive layers of deep top soil are rare in Africa. The soil structure has been a major factor in the use of land in the south east and any threat to such structure renders the land unproductive and vulnerable to destruction.

The south east Nigeria has greatly been impacted by soil erosion. Gully erosion is particularly severe in Abia, Imo, Anambra, Enugu and Delta States. Anambra and Enugu States alone have over 50 active gully complexes, with some extending over 100 metres, 20 meters wide and 15 meters deep. This has largely been attributed to extensive use of land for agricultural purposes (over farming) due to high population density (Grove, 1951). All these factors facing land in South Eastern Nigeria has lead to increased land degradation.

Causes of Land Degradation

The causes of threats to land cannot be isolated from the natural and human activities. The natural factors in land degradation includes wind and water soil erosion, torrential rainfall, floods, landslides, desertification, drought, acid rain, acid and salt accumulation, retreating forests, climatic vagaries and sand dunes accumulation. Although it is pertinent to note that these natural factors are intensified by the anthropogenic factors. Land has been subjected to intensive pressure from human uses that induce degradation. The intensification of the use of fragile and marginal ecosystems has led to progressive degradation and continued desertification of marginal agricultural lands even in years of normal rainfall. Inappropriate agricultural practices, the destruction of watersheds, and the opening up of river banks and other critical areas have led to silting of river beds and loss of water courses. Uncontrolled use of agro-chemicals and the concomitant problems of chemical persistence in the soil in humid areas and soil-crust formation in arid climates have contributed to salinization and destruction of vast agricultural lands.

Petroleum prospecting with its attendant oil pollution problems (including spills, oil well blow-out, oil blast discharges, improper disposal of drilling mud) has created problems such as; the loss of aesthetic values of natural beaches, damage to marine wildlife, modification of the ecosystem through species elimination and the delay in biota (fauna and flora) succession and decrease in fishery resources.

Gas flaring and the resultant problems of ecosystem heat stress, acid rain and acid precipitation have prompted destruction of freshwater and forests resources in coastal areas of the country. Global estimates indicate that the flaring of petroleum associated gas in Nigeria alone accounts for 28% of the total gas flares in the world.

The problems of exposure to radiation, creation of artificial ponds associated with bad mining practices and non-reclamation of mining waste lands as provided for in the minerals Acts are common in the mine field of Jos Plateau, Enugu and other locations.

Excessive pressures on available urban resources, infrastructure and space, due to rural urban migration and the resultant problems of urban decay and squatter settlements are evident in Lagos, Port-Harcourt, Abuja and its satellite towns, Ibadan and Umuahia etc.

Uncontrolled logging and tree felling from which government generate paltry taxes accentuated by lack of re-stocking are the order of the day in many parts of the southern states of Nigeria. This carries with it losss of precious biological diversity. Many of our cities are turning into concrete jungle where plants are no longer used for home landscaping. Most recently areas earmarked as green belts and recreational areas are being systematically converted into building sites.

Other direct and indirect anthropogenic factors that leads to land degradation includes; overgrazing, poorly designed irrigation, pollution, fire and burning of vegetation, administration and institutional problems, poverty, population explosion and industrialization etc.

Impact of Land Degradation

The impact of land degradation can be felt and is been felt in all areas of life from the loss of soil nutrient down to international level. Its impact can be summarized into the following:

- Depreciation of the physical, chemical and biological properties of soil.
- Organic matter decline
- Carbon storage decline
- Soil moisture storage decline

- Loss of water for irrigation
- Compaction
- Salinization
- Landslides
- Soil contamination
- Soil sealing
- Loss of biodiversity
- Soil nutrient decline
- Soil deformation
- Land productivity decline
- Decline of vegetative cover
- Increased inputs at greater costs
- Loss of flexibility in land management
- Diversion of resources to reclamation
- Lower and less reliable food supply
- Lower incomes
- Abandonment by members of the communities, forcingautomatic or emergency migration on the people or their means of livelihood.
- Less food production
- Food insecurity
- Rural poverty and land degradation

Ways to Combat Land Degradation and Improve Agricultural Productivity

Ways to combat land degradation and improve agricultural productivity could be viewed from various point;

Information, Monitoring and Assessment of Land Degradation

This involves collection of data from conventional statistics, GIS database, Models, guidelines, digital soil maps, indicators, information systems etc. to understand the state and causative factors of land degradation. It also involves exchange of information and experiences.

Social Issues

(a) Stake Holders Participation: effective stake holders participation in land use plaaning and management is a key issue for the sustainable use of land by all resource users.

(b) Capacity Building: Nigeria need to seek for strong support by United Nations agencies to develop tools and capacities for integrated approaches to ecosystems and land use systems such as river basins, wet lands, mangroves and biosphere reserves.

Policy Issues

There is need to critically review property rights and land tenure systems laws so as to open up land marketing systems. Also formulation and implementation of policies that will open opportunities for training of young people in the various discipline of Soil Science, Crop Science, Animal Science, Agricultural Economics and other Agricultural related disciplines.

Land Restoration

Land restoration is the process by which land resources are restored to their former state or "baseline condition". This is the condition of the natural resource and its services which would have existed had environmental damage not occurred. Restoration involves land management practices which can remove, control, contain or reduce environmental risks, so that the site no longer poses any significant threat to human health or the environment. The need for land restoration by soil conservation techniques is critical to control environmental degradation, so that agricultural, and thus economic and social development can be sustained.

Remedial measures are defined as "any action, or combination of actions, including mitigating or interim measures to restore, rehabilitate or replace damaged natural resources and/or impaired services, or to provide an equivalent alternative to those resources or services" (European Commision 2004).

One approach to land restoration is to consider the transition from degraded to non- degraded land as two phases.

- The first phase is concerned with the abiotic barriers to successful restoration - this is the reclamation phase.
- The second (restoration) phase deals with the biotic barriers, and will involve measures designed to restore ecosystem function, services and structure.

Abiotic (Physical) Land Restoration Measures: Remediating land from a degraded to an "in- tact" state may first require engineering of the physical landscape. In the reclamation of degraded land, an understanding of the fundamental properties of soil and water, including hydrology, hydraulics and geotechnics is essential. These disciplines are also the basis for designing, laying out and re constructing the physical landscape of the site to minimize degradation processes, and protect the environment. Thus, land restoration often starts with the selection, design and engineering of appropriate physical structures such as channels, weirs, spillways, terraces, berms and culverts to control these environmental threats, and create a landscape suitable for the intended end land use. Once the abiotic/physical barriers to successful restoration are crossed, the second phase of the restoration process can be implemented, whereby the biotic/biological status of the site is restored.

Biotic (Biological) Land Restoration Measures: Abiotic or physical reclamation is only the first phase of land restoration. Restoring the ecological functions and services of a site, and preventing further degradation can be achieved with bio- and phyto-restoration techniques. Micro-organisms such as fungi, bacteria, vegetation and their enzymes can restore, rehabilitate and reclaim damaged soil resources. However, conditions must be favourable for this biota, and physical restoration alone may not be able to create a "healthy" substrate. Soil amendments (sources of carbon and nutrients) may be added (in the form of compost, organo-mineral fertilizers, treated sewage sludge etc.) to provide sustenance for (micro) biological communities.

USE OF ORGANO-MINERALS IN RESTORATION OF PRODUCTIVITY OF DEGRADED LANDS

Perspective on Organo-Mineral Fertilizers

Organo-mineral fertilizer is obtained bychemical reaction or by dry mixing of one or severalorganic fertilizers and/or one or several organic matrixes with one or several inorganic fertilizers. Organo-mineral fertilizers are obtained through blending or processing one or more organic materials with one or more mineral fertilizers to enhance their nutrient content and fertilizing value. This fertilizer group is made up of natural components, enriched and complemented with chemical elements for fast action. This type of fertilizer contains at least 25% in organic matter with 40% of its nitrogen content required to be of organic origin. The organic substances in this group serve as an added enrichment for the humus in the soil. Combined application of organic resources and inorganic inputs resources in agricultural production has gained increasing popularity in the recent years. Farmyard manure and crop residues are frequently the most widely used because of their availability to farmers. The most common inorganic fertilizers used in South Eastern Nigeria is NPK and urea while the most common organic fertilizers used is pig manure and poultry manure.

Need for Organo-Mineral Fertilizers

Due to the impacts of land degradation many farmers look for ways to improve the productivity of the soils so as to meet the increasing demand for food. This has lead to the need for additions of soil amendments to improve productivity. The Soil Science Society of America (SSSA) defined it as any material such as lime, gypsum,sawdust, compost, animal manures, crop residue or synthetic soilconditioners that is worked into thesoil or applied on the surface toenhance plant growth.

One of the forms of soil amendments been used is organic fertilizers. Organic fertilizers are made with natural raw materials which refer to our biodegradable wastes. They are mostly sourced from animal and plant residues. They are important primarily because of their organic matter content. All soils require the supply of organic matter as carrier of utilizable energy and nutrients for thesoil organisms, as well as for: improvement of soil structure and porosity; increase in water-holding capacity of soils; improvement of aeration; reducing soil temperature fluctuations; and storage of nutrients inexchangeable form. Even though organic fertilizers andother organic materials are likely to beused in the same area where they are produced, because of their bulky nature and high transportation cost, they may have to be imported from elsewhere if not available locally. Also it is not always available in the sufficient amount of quantity needed by the large scale farmers. They release nutrients very slowly which is also a disadvantage for the plants.

Another form of soil amendment is the inorganic fertilizer. They are made of synthetic artificial ingredients manufactured and ready to use on plant. The use of inorganic fertilizers make nutrients immediately available for the plants and the plants get the exact amount of nutrient needed. The disadvantages of this form of soil amendment are that it can get washed away easily (leeching); they are expensive; it can also lead to toxic build up and when it is not added in the exact amount then there is a possibility that the roots of the plants will get burnt.

The disadvantages surrounding the use of these two forms of soil amendments has lead to the arising need for the use of organo-mineral fertilizers- which is the combination of the two forms. The combined effect of using organic and inorganic fertilizers gives a complementary result. In this type of fertilizer the mineral nutrients are protected by the binding and absorption of the organic component, leading to a gradual release of nutrients in the soil and to a reduction of nutrient losses.A complementary use of organic manure and mineral fertilizers has been recommended for sustenance of long-term cropping in the tropics (Palm et al, 1997; Ipimoroti *et al*, 2002). High and sustained crop yields can be obtained with judicious and balanced NPK fertilization combined with organic matter amendment (Kang, 1990; Makinde et al, 1997). Organo-mineral fertilizer application will give the benefits of applying an organic fertilizer as well as applying a little dose of inorganic fertilizer.

Advantages of Organo-Mineral – Discussion of Findings in South Eastern Nigeria

Improves Gravimetric Moisture Content

Nweke and Nsoanya (2013) reported that the combination of poultry manure and NPK gave the highest gravimetric moisture content value than the sole application in Igbariam South Eastern Nigeria. The high gravimetric moisturecontent observed in plots amended with combined poultry manure and NPK fertilizer maybe due tochanges in the specific surface area of the soil material as a result of mixing the two. It might as well be influenced by thecolloidal and hydrophobic nature of the poultry manure.

Improves Soil Hydraulic Conductivity

Nweke and Nsoanya (2013) reported that the combination of poultry manure and NPK (PNPK) gave the highest soil hydraulic conductivity value than the sole application in Igbariam South Eastern Nigeria. The increase in hydraulic conductivity observed in mixed manure (PNPK) maybe as a result of higher pores in the plotsamended with PNPK manure. Higher saturatedhydraulic conductivity indicates better water transmission and hence reduction in waterlogging.

Reduction in Bulk Density of Soils

The results gotten by Nwite et al (2012) on short-term response of soil physical properties of an ultisol, and nutrient composition of fluted pumpkin to organic and inorganic fertilizer mixtures in Ishiagu Ebonyi State showed that integrated application of the organo-minerals and mineral fertilizer (rice husk dust + poultry droppings+ NPK) significantly reduced the soil bulk density than the sole application of these amendments. The lower bulk density obtained from the treated plots can be as a result of the improved soil structure, hence increase in the soil granulation and improving the soil porosity. More so, the decreased bulk density could equally be as result of increased microbial activity.

Improves Aggregate Stability

Nweke and Nsoanya (2013) reported that the combination of poultry manure and NPK (PNPK) gave the highest aggregate stability value than the sole application in Igbariam South Eastern Nigeria. The increased aggregate stability following manure application could be as a resultof cementing effects of organic matter in soilparticles. High level of organic matter, goodcolloidal nature of the soil and most importantly aluminum ions promote high soil aggregate stability (Trembley and Levy, 1993).

Improves Productivity of Soil by Increasing the Growth and Yield of Plants

Nweke and Nsoanya (2013) reported that the combination of poultry manure and NPK (PNPK) improved growth and grain yield of maize than the sole application in Igbariam South Eastern Nigeria. The increase in grainyield components can be due to the synergistic effect of combination of organic and inorganic fertilizer that enhanced nutrient release andavailability improved nitrogen and other macro and micro elements absorption by the maize plant.

Best yield and nitrogen uptake performance of maize was achieved with complementary application of 15 t/ha rice mill waste and 200 kg/ha inorganic NPK fertilizer in a research carried out by Nwaogu (2012) in Umudike Abia State.

A study carried out by Unagwu (2014) at the green house in University of Nigeria Nsukka indicated that complementary application of poultry manure and NPK to maize plant performed better than sole application. Also Unagwu, et al (2012) reported that for better yieldand productivity of maize crop, the use of 200Kg/ha NPK + 6t/ha Poultry Manure) in a soil limed to pH 5.5 is recommended.

Nweke et al (2013) also reported that based on the result of the study of pig manure and urea application, the organo mineral fertilizer (pig manure + urea) performed competitively better than all the other treatments applied and therefore can be used for effective maize production.

It was also recorded by Nwite et al that the integration of amendments (organic and inorganic fertilizers) statistically reduced crude fibre of fluted pumpkin relative to the sole application.

The significant influence of organomineral fertilizer on some growth and yield components of rice in Delta State as reported by Egbucha and Enujeke (2013) could be attributed to the synergistic effects of the treatment in rice physiological processes, restoring soil quality and increasing yield by the combination of the two nutrient sources (Brady and Weil, 1999).

From the study carried out by Asadu and Nwajiaku (2011) the use of only organic manure showed outstanding effects on yield of maize, but 0.25t/haN.P.K + 2.5t/ha pig dung combination was acomparable alternative.

Problems Associated with the Use of Organo-Minerals

All the scientific research carried out on effect of organo-minerals on soils in South Eastern Nigeria never indicated any disadvantages but generally there are some problems associated with organo-mineral usage in Nigeria and they are;

- The capacity of agricultural extension services in Nigeria to provide integrated soil fertility management technologies is low. Only a small share of agricultural extension agents in Nigeria was shown to provide advisory services on organic inputs. Most of their agricultural advisory services focused on improved seeds, fertilizers, and pesticides (Banful *et al*, 2010).
- Due to a lack of synchrony between nutrients released by soil organic matter and mineral fertilizer, nutrients especially nitrogen, are lost through leaching, volatilization, and denitrification.
- Proper evaluation and auditing of the land is not been done by farmers in the field before application of organic amendments.

Table 8.1: Adoption of Integrated Soil Fertility Management in Six Sub-Saharan African Countries

Soil Input	Rate of Farmers Adoption (%)					
	Kenya	Malawi	Mali	Niger	Nigeria	Uganda
Organic Input Alone	29.4	18.6	38.7	1.0	12.1	11.9
Synthetic Fertilizer Alone	10.5	70.8	16.3	0.1	45.3	6.1
Organic Input and Synthetic Fertilizer	19.6	14.7	17.7	0.0	7.5	2.0

Source: Nkonya, et al. (2011).

RECOMMENDATIONS

- There should be proper communication links between researches, extension agents and farmers, so that better handling, usage and application of organo-minerals can be implemented. This would go a long way to better improve productivity even in degraded lands.
- As pointed out by Myers et al., (1994) synchrony of organic and inorganic fertilizers can be promoted by manipulating plant demand (controlling planting date, duration of crop to be grown, use of crops with different growth patterns in multiple cropping systems).
- Evaluation and auditing - Carrying out a comprehensive and appropriate ecological audit of the site before application of any form of amendment is essential, because it will help assess the sustainability and give better information on the type of organo-mineral best suited for that particular land.
- Flooding is a threat to physical infrastructures and it also destroys farmlands including standing crops. Nigeria government should enforce environmental sanitation laws in towns and cities, ensure appropraiate management and maintenanace of dams, enforce compliance with town planning/urbanlaws/edicts and ensure appropriate maintenance of existing drainage channels.
- Solid wastes, chemicals, hazardous and radioactive waste constitute pollution that also results to land degradation. Nigeria government should encourage the phasing out of processes that produce high risks because of hazardous waste generation, carry out environmental audits of existing industries to improve hazardous waste management and promote the development and adoption of appropriate technologies for the conversion of organic municipal solid waste to compost and encourage markets for its use as soil conditioners.
- Easy access to scientific and technological information.
- Huge financial investments are needed to implement the various programmes and activities therefore adequate budgetary provision for policy formulation and implementation of the National Policy on Environment should be ensured.

CONCLUSION

The use of organic fertilizers and inorganic fertilizers together to increase productivity and sustainability of land is increasing and the benefit greatly supersedes the sole usage of either organic or inorganic fertilizers. If proper dissemination of information to farmers is carried out the problems of low productivity, poverty, food insecurity and land degradation would be greatly reduced.

REFERENCES

Akanbi, W.B., Akande, M.O., Baiyewu, R.A. and Akinfasoye,J.O., (2000). *The Effect of Maize Stover Compost and Nitrogen Fertilizer on Growth, Yield and Nitrogen Uptake of Amaranth.* Moor Journal of Agric. Research., 1(1): 6-15.

Akinyosoye, V.O. (1996). *An Introduction to Senior Tropical Agriculture for West Africa.* Macmillan Lagos, Nigeria Press.

Asadu, C.L.A., Okorji, E.C. and Onah, F.O., (1997). *Edaphic Socio-economic and Cultural Changes due to Irrigated Rice Cultivation in Eastern Nigeria.* Global Journal of Pure and Applied Sciences 3(1), 3-8.

Asadu, C.L.A. and Nwajiaku, I.M., (2011). *The Effects of Four Ratios of Organic to Inorganic Manures on Soil Physicochemical Properties and Maize Yield.* Agro-Science Technology Engineering and Mechanization Journal. Vol. 10 No. 2.

Avery, D.T., (1995). *Saving the Planet with Pesticides and Plastics: The Environmental Triumph of Highyielding Farming.* Hudson Institute. Indianapolis, IN., pp: 44.

Ayuso, M.A., Pascal, J.A., Garcia C. and Hernadez, T., (1996). *Evaluation of Urban Wastes for Agricultural Use.* Soil Science and Plant Nutrition. 142(1): 105-111.

Banful,B., Nkonya,E. and Oboh, V., (2010). *Constraints to Fertilizer Use in Nigeria: Insights from Agricultural Extension Service.* IFPRI Discussion Paper 1010 (Washington, DC: International Food Policy Research Institute,)

Brabant, P., Darracq, S., Egue, K. and Simoneaux, V., (1996).*Collection Notice Explosion,* No. 112. Editions ORSTOM, Department Milieux 34 Paris.

Brabant, P., (2010). *A Land Degradation Assessment and Mapping Method.* A Standard Guideline Proposal. Les dossiers thématiques du CSFD. Nº8. November 2010. CSFD/ Agropolis International, Montpellier, France. 52 pp.

Brady, N.C. and Weil, R.R., (1999). *The Nature and Properties of Soil.* 12th" Edition Delhi, Pearson Educational Publishers.

Cook, G.W., (1982). *Fertilizing for Maximum Yield.* Granad Technical Books. 3rd Ed. Granada Publishing Limited, London.,pp: 465.

Egbuchua, C.N. and Enujeke, E.C., (2013). *Effects of Different Levels of Organomineral Fertilizer on the Yield and Yield Components of Rice (Oryza Sativa L.) In A Coastal Flood Plain Soil, Nigeria.* Journal of Agriculture and Veterinary Science. pp. 01-05.

Nkonya,E., Place, F., Pender, J., Mwanjololo, M., Okhimamhe,A., Kato, E., Crespo, S., Ndjeunga, J. and Traore,S., (2011). *Climate Risk Management through Sustainable Land Management in Sub- Saharan Africa.* International Food Policy Research Institute. Paper 01126, pp. 32.

European Commission, (2004). Directive 2004/35/Ce of the European Parliament and of the Council of 21 April 2004 on Environmental Liability with Regard to the Prevention and Remedying of Environmental Damage. Directive 2004/35/EC (OJ L 143, 30.4.2004,). Official Journal of the European Union. 30.4.

Ezemonye, M.N. and Emeribe, C.N., (2012). *Rainfall Erosivity in Southeastern Nigeria. Ethiopian Journal of Environmental Studies and Management (EJESM), 5 (2), 112-122.*

FAO, (2006). *Assessment of Use Pressure, State, and Response in Sub-Saharan Africa,* Internal FAO (Zero Draft) May (PDF-B-Activity 1-1 WIP v8.doc).

Ipimoroti, R.R., Daniel, M.A. and Obatolu, C.R., (2002). *Effect of Organo – Mineral Fertilizer on Tea Growth at Kusuku, Mambilla Plateau, Nigeria.* Moor Journal of Agric. Research., 3(2): 180-183. 8.

Kang, B.T. and Balasubranian,V., (1990). *Long-Term Fertilizer Trial on Alfisols in West Africa.* In: Transactions of XIV International Soil Science Society Congress. Kyoto, Japan., pp: 350.

Lal, R., (1983). *Erosion Caused Productivity Decline in Soils of the Humid Tropics.* Soil Taxonomy News No. 5 pp. 4-11.

Makinde, E.A., Akande M.O. and Agboola,A.A., (2001). *Effects of Fertilizer Type on Performance of Melon in a Maize-melon Intercrop.* ASSET Series A, (2): 151-158. 12. Palm, C.A., R.K.J. Myers and S.M. Nandwa, 1997.

Nwaogu, E.N., (2012). *Effects of Organo-mineral Fertilization on Nitrogen, Yield and Yield Sustainability Responses of Maize in Rainforest Ecology of South Eastern Nigeria.* International Journal of Applied Research and Technology ISSN 2277-0585.

Nweke, I.A. and Nsoanya, L.N., (2013). *Effect of Poultry Manure and Inorganic Fertilizer on the Performance of Maize and Selected Physical Properties of Igbariam South Eastern Nigeria.* International Journal of Agriculture and Rural Development.

Nweke, I.A., Nsoanya, L.N. and Okolie, E.C., (2013). *Effect of Organo-Mineral Fertilizer on Growth and Yield of Maize of Igbariam South Eastern Nigeria.* International Journal of Agriculture and Rural Development.

Nwite J.C., Ogbodo., E.N., Obalum, S.E., Igbo, V.C. and Igwe,C.A., (2013). *Short-term response of Soil Physical properties of an Ultisol, and Nutrient composition of Fluted Pumpkin to Organic and Inorganic Fertilizer mixtures.* Journal of Biology, Agriculture and Healthcare ISSN 2224-3208 Vol 2, No. 10, 2012 195 IOSR.

Nyathi, P. and Campbell, B.M., (1995). *The Effect of Tree Leaf Litter, Manure, Inorganic Fertilizer and their Combinations on Above-ground Production and Grain Yield of Maize.* African Crop Science Journal, 3(4): 451-456.

Osugiri, I.I., (1996). *Effect of Population Pressure on Agricultural Productivity in Imo State, Nigeria.* Unpublished M.Sc. Thesis, Dept of Agric. Economics University of Nigeria Nsukka.

Osuji, E.E., (2011*). Land Use Patterns and Effects on Agricultural Productivity in Ikeduru Local Government Area, Imo State.* Unpublished M.Sc. Thesis, Department of Agricultural Economics, FUTO, Owerri, Nigeria.

Scherr, S.J., andSatya Y., (1997) *Land Degradation in the Developing World: Issues and PolicyOptions for 2020* International Food Policy Research Institute 2020 Brief 44.

Unagwu, B.O., AsaduC.L.A. and Ezeaku, P.I., (2012). *Maize Response to Organic and Inorganic (Poultry manure) and Inorganic Fertilizers (NPK 15-15-15) at Different Soil pH Levels.* International Journal of Environmental Sciences Vol.1 No. 2. pp. 126-134.

Urama, J.C., (2005). *Land Use Intensification and Environmental Degradation: Empirical Evidence from Irrigated and Rain-fed Farms in South Eastern Nigeria.* Journal of Environmental Management 75, 199-217.

***Pages:* 146-153**

SOIL CONTAMINATION AND CONSERVATION

Edited by: **Dr. Ezeaku Peter Ikemefuna; Dr. Pawan Kumar 'Bharti'**

ISBN: 978-93-5056-737-1

Edition: **2015**

Published by: **Discovery Publishing House Pvt. Ltd., New Delhi (India)**

Environmental Implication of Solid Mineral Mining on Selected Soil Properties in Enyigba, Southeastern Nigeria

*Okolo, C.C., Akamigbo, F.O.R. and Ezeaku, P.I.

ABSTRACT

This research was conducted to evaluate the environmental impact of solid minerals mining at the Enyigba Lead-Zinc mining district in Abakaliki Local Government Area of Ebonyi State, Southeastern Nigeria and to ascertain the present state of soil physical properties and heavy metal status of the surface (0-15 cm) and subsurface (15-30cm) soil. In the study, two factors were considered: factor A - Soil depths (surface soil: 0-15 cm and subsurface soil: 15-30 cm) and factor B - Distances from mine pits (100 m, 200 m, 300 m, 400 m and 500 m away from mine pit). These were compared alongside a control (located 1.5 km away from Enyigba mining vicinity). Core and auger soil samples were collected and analysed in the laboratory following standard methods. Results showed that the bulk density value of the mine area was higher than the control. The values of total porosity in all distances and depths were significant, recording a reverse trend compared to bulk density values. The

Department of Soil Science, University of Nigeria Nsukka, Nigeria.

textural class of the distances and depths were predominantly sandy clay loam as well as the control, though higher values of clay were obtained at lower depths (15-30 cm) at both mine area and control. Heavy metal concentrations of the mine area were higher compared to the control. There was decreasing heavy metal concentration with increasing distance from the mine pit. The heavy metal concentrations (As 0.166 mg/kg, Cu 2.042 mg/kg, Pb 0.498 mg/kg and Zn 4.769 mg/kg) at mine area were within the acceptable limits in soil with the exception of cadmium (Cd 11.097 mg/kg). Though the concentrations of these metals in soils with the exception of cadmium were found to be low compared to WHO regulatory limits, contamination of soil with heavy metals even in traces is considered a serious environmental concern as these elements can persist in soil for a long time with chances of increasing their concentrations with time.

Key words: soil, solid mineral mining, contamination, WHO, Nigeria.

INTRODUCTION

Mining is one of the potential sources of heavy metals in the environment and can be described as series of activities geared towards the extraction of minerals. It is well established that one of the primary anthropogenic sources of heavy metal is mine (Goyer, 1996). Thus mines have significant negative environmental impacts such as pollution of water bodies and farmlands as well as changes of the landscape with subsequent typical changes in flora and fauna (Aremu *et al.*, 2010). These negative environmental impacts can vary from one mine site to another and depend on a variety of factors, such as the sensitivity of the local terrain, composition of the mineral being mined, analytical methods employed and adherence to stipulated environmental regulations. Mining causes large amount of destruction of the environment in the form of alteration of landscape, deterioration of vast land areas, extinction of wild life, destruction of natural habitat, changes in river regime, dust inhalation and air emissions (Ezeaku and Alaci, 2008). During mining, a fine grind of the ore is often necessary to release metals and minerals, so the mining industry produces enormous quantities of the fine rock particles, in sizes ranging from sand-sized down to as low as a few microns (USEPA, 1994). Heavy metal contamination of agricultural soils and crops in the vicinity of mining areas has been regarded as a great environmental concern (Wcislo *et al.* 2002; Liu *et al.* 2005a; Kachenko and Sinh, 2006).

The main objective of the study was to assess the negative externalities of lead-zinc mining on the soil and water properties of Enyigba Ebonyi State, Southeastern Nigeria, where open cast mining predominate. The result will give an insight to the level of heavy metal contamination in the study area with regards to the environmental implication of solid mineral mining and especially to aid relevant stakeholders in environmental and agricultural land use planning to ensure soil productivity optimization.

MATERIALS AND METHODS

Study Area

The study was conducted at Enyigba in Abakaliki Local Government Area of Ebonyi State. Enyigba is 14 km southeast of Abakaliki in Southeast Nigeria (Fig. 9.1). The area of study lies between latitudes 6° 07′ N and 6° 12′ N and longitudes 8° 05′ E and 8° 10′ E as obtained with a handheld GPS in the derived savanna vegetation zone. The area experiences bimodal pattern of rainfall (April – July and September – November) with short dry spell in August normally called ''August break''. The total mean rainfall is between 1700 to 2000 mm. At the onset of rainfall it is torrential and violent, sometimes lasting for 1-2 hours. The minimum and maximum temperatures are 27° C and 31° C respectively while relative humidity is in the range of 60-80% (ODNRI, 1989).

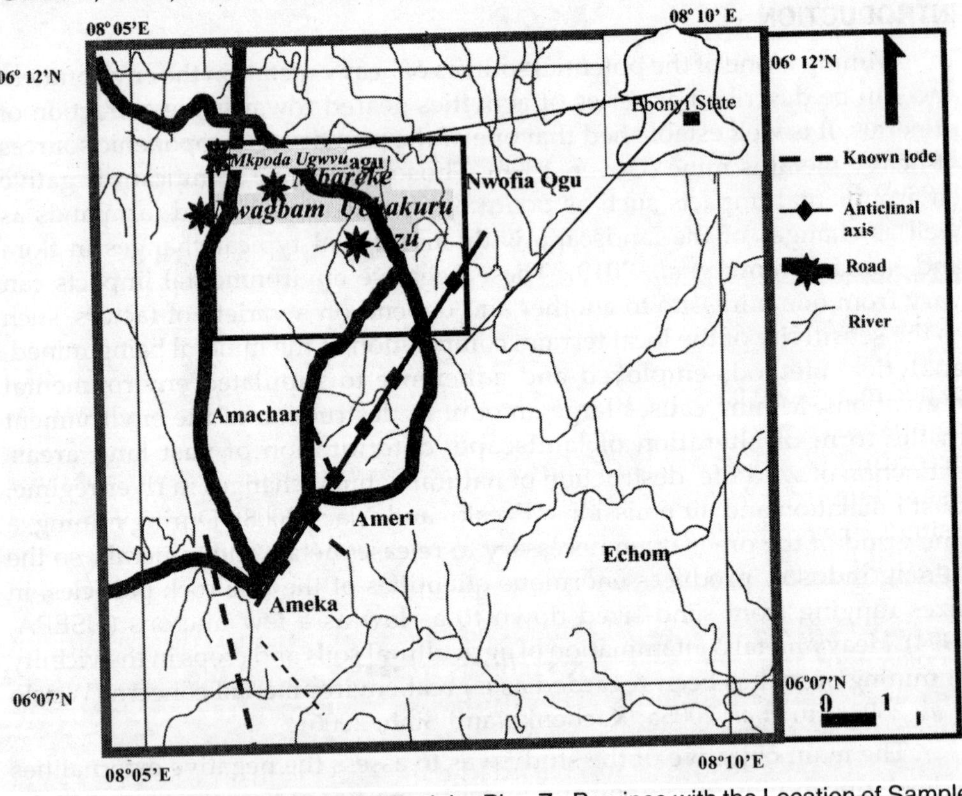

Fig. 9.1: The Physiographic Map of Enyigba Pb – Zn Province with the Location of Sample Points (Modified from Orajaka, 1965)

FIELD SAMPLING

Four mine sites were selected for the study. Each sampling site was given geographical coordinates using a hand-held global positioning system (GPS). Auger soil samples (0-15 and 15-30 cm) were collected starting from

100 m away from the mine site and at 100 m intervals up till 500 m (i.e, 100 m, 200 m, 300 m, 400 m, 500 m distance). Core soil samples were also collected at similar distances. At each mine site, sampling was done eastwards and westwards. Similarly, a control site was selected at a distance of 1.5 km away from the Enyibga mining vicinity and soil samples collected at depths 0-15 cm and 15-30 cm. The core samples were used for soil bulk density and total porosity determination while the auger soil samples were air-dried and passed through 2 mm sieve and used for heavy metal extraction and routine analysis.

SAMPLE TREATMENT AND LABORATORY DETERMINATIONS

Particle size analysis of the soil was determined using the Bouyoucos hydrometer method as described by Gee and Bauder (1986). Bulk density was determined on the core samples by core method as described by Anderson and Ingram (1993). Lead (Pb) was determined by Sulphide Method as described by Vogel (1965). Copper (Cu) was determined by Ferrocyanide Method as described by Alexeyev (1969). Zinc (Zn) was determined by EDTA Titration Method as described by Jackson (1969). Arsenic (As) was determined by Bicarbonate Method Using Starch Indicator as described by Alexeyev (1969). Cadmium (Cd) was determined using Xylenol Orange Indicator as described by Vogel (1965).

EXPERIMENTAL DESIGN AND DATA ANALYSIS

This study was considered as a factorial experiment in which distance from the mine pit and soil depth were two factors under consideration. The experiment was laid out in 2 X 5 factorial in RCBD replicated four times compared alongside a control. Analysis of variance (ANOVA) was done according to Obi (2002) and significantly different means were separated using F-LSD at 5% level of probability. The statistical analysis was done using Genstat Discovery Edition 3 (Genstat, 2003).

RESULTS AND DISCUSSION

The soils percentage of coarse and fine sand generally decreased with increasing depth, while the clay contents increased down the profile. There was no definite trend in the particle size distribution across the distances but coarse sand dominated the total sand fraction in all distances. The control surface soil and subsurface soil recorded the highest values of 31% and 45 % for silt and clay respectively compared to the soils of mine area. The texture of the soil is related to its parent material (Akamigbo and Asadu, 1983), and this accounts for the similarity in textural classes obtained irrespective of locations, distances and soil depths. This is expected as soil texture is mainly inherited from the soil forming parent materials. The highest bulk density value of 1.79 Mgm^{-3} was recorded at 300 m subsurface soil of mine area and was higher than the control both at the surface soil (1.51 Mgm^{-3}) and subsurface soil (1.66 Mgm^{-3}). The high bulk density value observed in mine area may be due to removal of vegetative cover arising from series of mining activities.

Results of heavy metal concentration indicate that for each sampling distance, the concentrations were highest at the surface soil and decreased with depth. The 100 meter distance evidently recorded significantly ($p < 0.05$) higher mean values for As (0.228 mg/kg), Cd (23.89 mg/kg), Cu (2.85 mg/kg), Pb (0.725 mg/kg) and Zn (5.838 mg/kg) compared to other distances. In general, the heavy metal levels in Enyigba mine area decreased in the order Cd>Zn>Cu>Pb>As in the surface soil and Cd>Zn>Cu>Pb>As in the subsurface soil. The soil type of the control showed the same trend of Cd>Zn>Cu>Pb>As. These results are at variance both in trend and values with the results of previous investigation which showed the order Zn>Pb>Mn>Cu>Ni>Cu>Cd in Enyigba mine soil and Mn>Zn>Pb>Ni>Cu>Cd in Abakaliki (Chukwuma, 1994).

ENVIRONMENTAL IMPLICATIONS

Destruction of vegetative cover and changes in landscape constitute major consequences of surface mining as evidenced in the study area (Plate 9.1). Vegetative cover destruction gives rise to increased run-off leading to soil erosion, alteration of soil microbial activities, loss of farm land for cultivation and relative decrease in crop yield. Numerous abandoned mine pits observed in the study area is an environmental threat leading to land degradation and subsequent changes in landscape. It is pertinent to restore all those observed abandoned mine pits (Plate 9.2) and to return them to their original uses in such a way that agricultural production can be resumed as early as possible considering the increasing population growth and the need for quality food supply, i.e. the site should be rehabilitated.

CONCLUSION

Results of the study showed high bulk density in mine area compared to the control. The result further revealed that highest heavy metal concentrations were obtained at the 100 m surface soil than the subsurface soil, suggesting a lower reception of heavy metals by the latter. The observed heavy metal concentrations in the study area were found to be below critical limits in soil with the exception of cadmium, thus they might not present direct environmental threat, although potentially, they could remobilize (with rainfall) and affect aquatic systems.

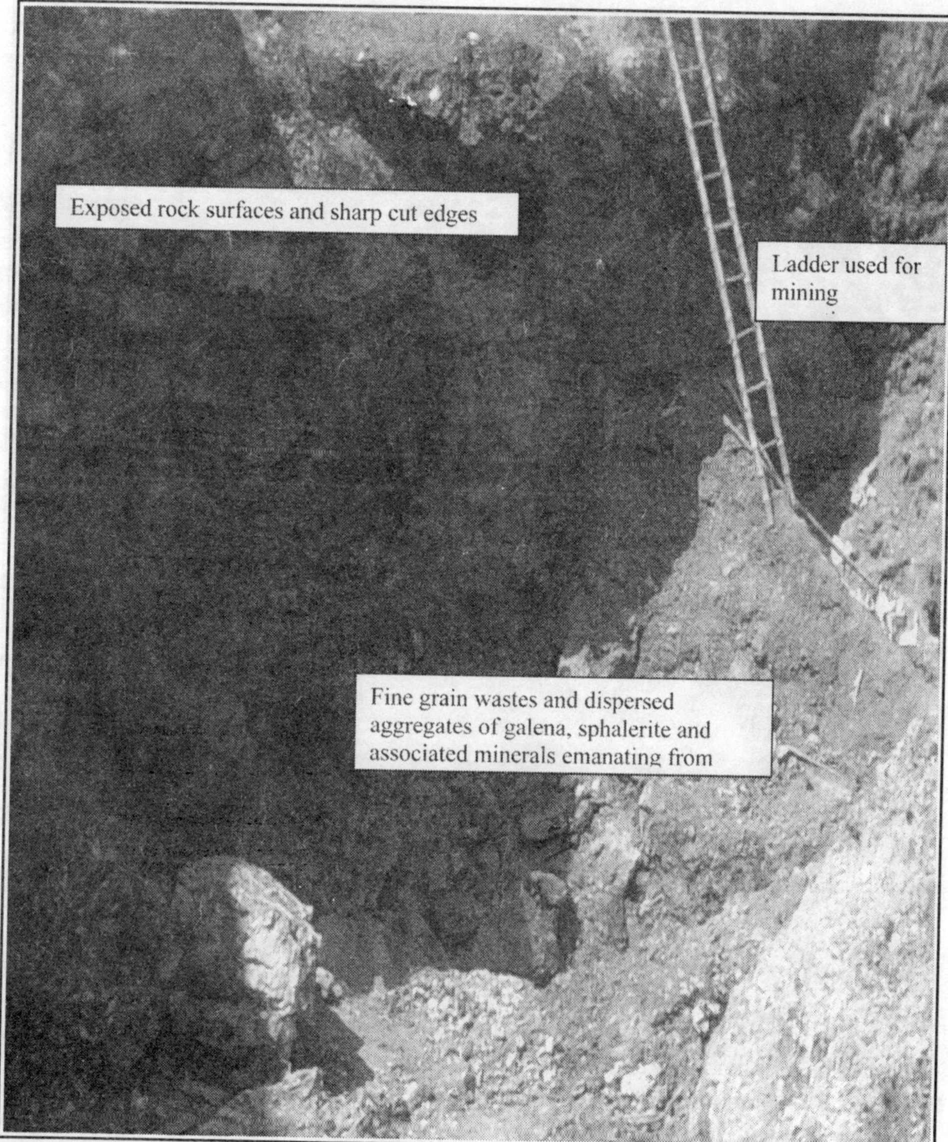

Plate 9.1: Dry mine pit with exposed rock surface and sharp cut edges, evidence of manual extraction processes giving rise to dispersed aggregates of galena, sphalerite and other associated minerals

Plate 9.2: A 30 ft mine pit filled with water after mine was abandoned with heaps of fine-grained wastes surrounding it

REFERENCES

Akamigbo, F.O.R and Asadu, C.L.A (1983). Influence of Parent Materials on the Soils of Southeastern Nigeria. East African Agric. For. J. 48: 81-91.

Alexeyev, V (1969). Colorimetry in Quantitative Analysis, 2nd Edition. MIR Publishers, Moscow.

Anderson, J.M. And J.S.I Ingram (1993). Tropical Soils Biology and Fertility. A Handbook of Methods, 2nd Ed; CAB International, Wallingford U.K. pp. 221.

Chukwuma, C (1994). Evaluating Baseline Data for Trace Elements, pH, Organic Matter Content and Bulk Density in Agricultural Soils in Nigeria. Water Air and Soil Pollution, Kluwer Academic Publishers', Amserdam. pp 13-34.

Ezeaku, P.I and Alaci, D (2008). Analytical Situations of Land Degradation and Sustainable Management Strategies in Africa. Pakistan J. Agric. Soc. Sci., 4: 42-52 (http://www.fspublishers.org).

Gee, G.W., and Bauder, J.W. (1986). Particle Size Analysis. P. 383-411. In: Klute, A. (Ed.). Methods of Soil Analysis Part I. Physical and Mineralogical Methods. Agronomy Monograph No. 9 (2nd Ed.) Am. Soc. of Agron., Madison, W.I.

Genstat (2003). GENSTAT 5.0 Release 4.23 DE, Discovery Edition_ 2. Lanves Agric. Trust, Rothamsted Experimental Station Press, UK.

Goyer, R.A. (1996). Results of Lead Research: Prenatal Exposure and Neurological Consequences: Environmental Health Perspect. 7704: 1050.

Jackson, M.L (1969). Soil Chemical Analysis. Advance Course, Dept. of Soil Science, University of Wisconsin, Madison, Wisconsin.

Kachenko, A.G and Singh, B (2006). Heavy Metals Contamination in Vegetables Grown in Urban and Metal Smelter Contaminated Sites in Australia. *Water, Air and Soil Pollution*, 169: 101-123. Doi: 1007/S11270-006-2027-1.

Liu,Y, S., Gao,Y., Wang, K.W., Mai, X.H., Chen, G.D and Xu, T.W (2005a). Etiology Study on Alimentary Tract Malignant Tumor in Villages of High Occurrence. China Tropical Medicine 5, 1139-1141 (in Chinese).

Obi, I.U (2002). Statistical Methods of Detecting Differences Between Treatment Means and Research Methodology Issues in Laboratory and Field Experiments. Second Edition. AP Express Publisher Limited. Nsukka –Nigeria.

Orajaka, S (1965). The Geology of Enyigba Lead-zinc Lodes, Abakaliki Division, Eastern Nigeria, journ. Min. Geol. Vol. 2, pp. 65-70.

Overseas Development of Natural Resources Institute(ODNRI)(1989). Nigeria Profile of Agricultural Potential, ODA, United Kingdom.

USEPA (1994). Design and Evaluation of Tailings Dams. Technical Report – EPA530-R-94-038. USEPA, Office of Solid Waste, Special Waste Branch, Washington, DC.

Vogel, A.I (1965). Complexometric (Largely EDTA) Titrations (In Textbook of Quantitative Inorganic Analysis) pp. 319-320, 324, 444, 454-455, 801-802.

Wcislo, E., Ioven, D., Kucharski, R and Szdzuj, J (2002). Human Health Risk Assessment Case Study of an Abandoned Metal Smelter in Poland. Chemosphere, 47, 507-515. Doi: 1016/S0045-6535 (01) 00301-0.

Pages: **154-178**

SOIL CONTAMINATION AND CONSERVATION

Edited by: **Dr. Ezeaku Peter Ikemefuna; Dr. Pawan Kumar 'Bharti'**

ISBN: 978-93-5056-737-1

Edition: **2015**

Published by: **Discovery Publishing House Pvt. Ltd., New Delhi (India)**

Transect Approach for Assessing Soil Variability in Eroded Landscapes of Shillong Plateau, Meghalaya

B.P.Bhaskar*, R.K.Saxena, Dipak Sarkar Utpal Baruah[1] and P.S.Butte

ABSTRACT

The mountainous environment of Shillong plateau in Meghalaya state, India has great variety of ecotopes and landscape diversity leading to various soil types with specific risks and potentials. The soil sequences of Ultisols and associated subgroups of Inceptisols and Entisols on eroded landscapes of Shillong Plateau were examined in four transects for assessing variability of soil properties. The highland soils have unique combination of soil properties (such as thickness of A horizons, organic matter, base satuation and aluminium saturation) directly related to functional horizons (argillic, sombric, kandic and cambic).

The soils on hill slopes were well drained with extremely to strongly acid and dark brown to reddish brown matrix . A numerical model was used to cluster

National Bureau of Soil Survey and Land Use Planning, Division of Soil Resource Studies, Amravati road, Nagpur - 440 010, Maharashtra, India.

1 National Bureau of Soil Survey and land use Planning, Regional centre, Jamuguri road, Rowriah, Jorhat, Assam.785 005, India.

highland soils into three groups . The coefficient of variation for A horizons was more than 50 per cent for organic carbon and per cent base saturation in Group A soils whereas for A horizon thickness, per cent silt and clay, effective cation exchange capacity, per cent base saturation, free iron and manganese contents in Group B soils. The B horizons in showed high variability for redness rating and organic carbon for Group A soils and off dithionite Fe and Mn for Group B soils. The variability analysis was helpful in identifying soil properties linked to soil taxonomy and to assess functional characteristics related to changes in morphology, texture and chemistry in highlands.

Key words: Shillong plateau, soil variability, soil taxonomy, dendrogram.

INTRODUCTION

Soil surveys have traditionally overlooked soil variability within map units due to scale limitations and inadequate quantitative data. The three issues related to soil variability assessment are (i) location of sample points, (ii) size of sample, and (iii) total number of samples to be collected (Upchurch and Edmonds, 1991). Variability of soil input data can strongly influence the reliability of the results of logical, empirical and physical models of soil and landscape processes (Burrough, 1993; Foussereau, *et al.*, 1993; Wilding, *et al.*, 1994). With growing interests in landscape perspective to address diverse environmental and natural resource issues, an adequate understanding of soil variability as a function of space and time becomes essential. However, in spite of voluminous literature published in the past three decades or so, knowledge about soil variability is still dispersed and requires further synthesis (Burrough, 1993; Heuvelink and Webster, 2001).

The optimum scales for characterizing soil landscape processes affecting the development of catena (a sequence of related soils that differ primarily because of topography and drainage) are unknown and represent a major research need (Moore, *et al.*, 1993). However, the mode and magnitude of such changes depend on where the soil is located in the landscape (spatial location) and which soil type or specific soil property is of concern. Transect method on hill slopes was employed to workout soil variability of Machakos district Kenya by Ellenkamp (2004). Transect sampling, an optimized cluster sampling' allows the investigation of environmental gradients that commonly occur along a landscape continuum and for regional relations with parent material, climate and land use. Transect data showed that the slope length to be the dominant factor affecting erosion (Kreznor, *et al.*, 1989).

Increasing solum thickness in downslope was explained by the effect of erosion on the upper and deposition at the lower slopes. Silt, organic carbon and Fe_o and Fe_d contents significantly decreased downslope in North East Brazil (Agbenin and Tiessen, 1995) because of slash and burn agriculture on the lower slopes and the changes in redox conditions caused by periodic waterlogging. Numerical procedures were applied to avoid classification schemes based on logical keys and to assess similarity by sorting procedure (Campbell, *et al.*, 1970). The soil pH has lease variability on slopes but increases with depth (Ogunkunle and Ataga, 1985) where as organic matter and % clay range from moderate to high variability in the Alfisols of southwestern Nigeria (Ogunkunle, 1993) and available phosphorus and potassium be highly variable (Wollenhaupt *et al.*, 1997).

The striking similar results were reported using both laboratory and field morphology of soil catena of Miami soil family (Hole and Hironaka, 1960). The soil variability analysis in Shillong plateau of Meghalaya with great landscape diversity, variety of ecotopes, different climatic conditions and various soil types with specific risks and potentials.was undertaken with an objective to demonstrate dependence of soil variability as a function of landscape and the soil property in question. and to quantify the variability of soil type and selected soil properties at landscape level.

MATERIALS AND METHODS

Characteristics of Study Site

The study site is from Myllieum to Pynursala is a part Shillong plateau . Meghalaya (25°15 to 25°30 N and 94°45 to 92°00 E, Fig. 10.1) with an elevational range of 2000 m in the northern part of Shillong to 1200 m towards the southern part of East Khasi Hills district. The terrain is mostly hilly with deep gorges to river valleys and ravines in Mawsynram and Shella-Bholaganj bordering Bangladesh. The altitudinal differences coupled with varied physiography contributes to climatic variations in the Shillong plateau of Meghalaya state. The climate is humid tropical with well-defined wet and dry cycles. The distribution of rainfall is erratic and ranges from 11418mm near Cherrapunji to 2014 mm near Shillong (Nair, *et al.*, 1983). The soil moisture regime is udic in hills and hill slopes with thermic soil temperature regime. The mean annual rainfall is about 2490 mm with highest rainfall of 12,500 mm in the Cherrapunji - Mawsynram region with very high humidity (62% to 91%) in the rainy season. About 75% of the total annual rainfall is received between June and September. August, with a mean minimum temperature of 18. 8°C and mean maximum temperature of 26. 8°C is the warmest month of the year, while January, with a mean minimum temperature of 4.8°C and mean maximum temperature of 15 8C is the coldest month. The period between March and May, with relatively high temperature and scanty rains, represents mild-summer.

The vegetation of Shillong - Cherrapunji plateaux may be classified under subtropical broad-leaved wet hill forest (Champion and Seth, 1968). The Shillong plateau with Archean gneissic basement and late Cretaceous-Tertiary sediments along southern margin is bounded by the Brahmaputra graben in the north and Dauki fault in the south. The Shillong plateau occupies a unique position in the Precambrian history of the Indian plate both geodynamically and seismically (Mazumdar 1986 and Acharyya, 2005).

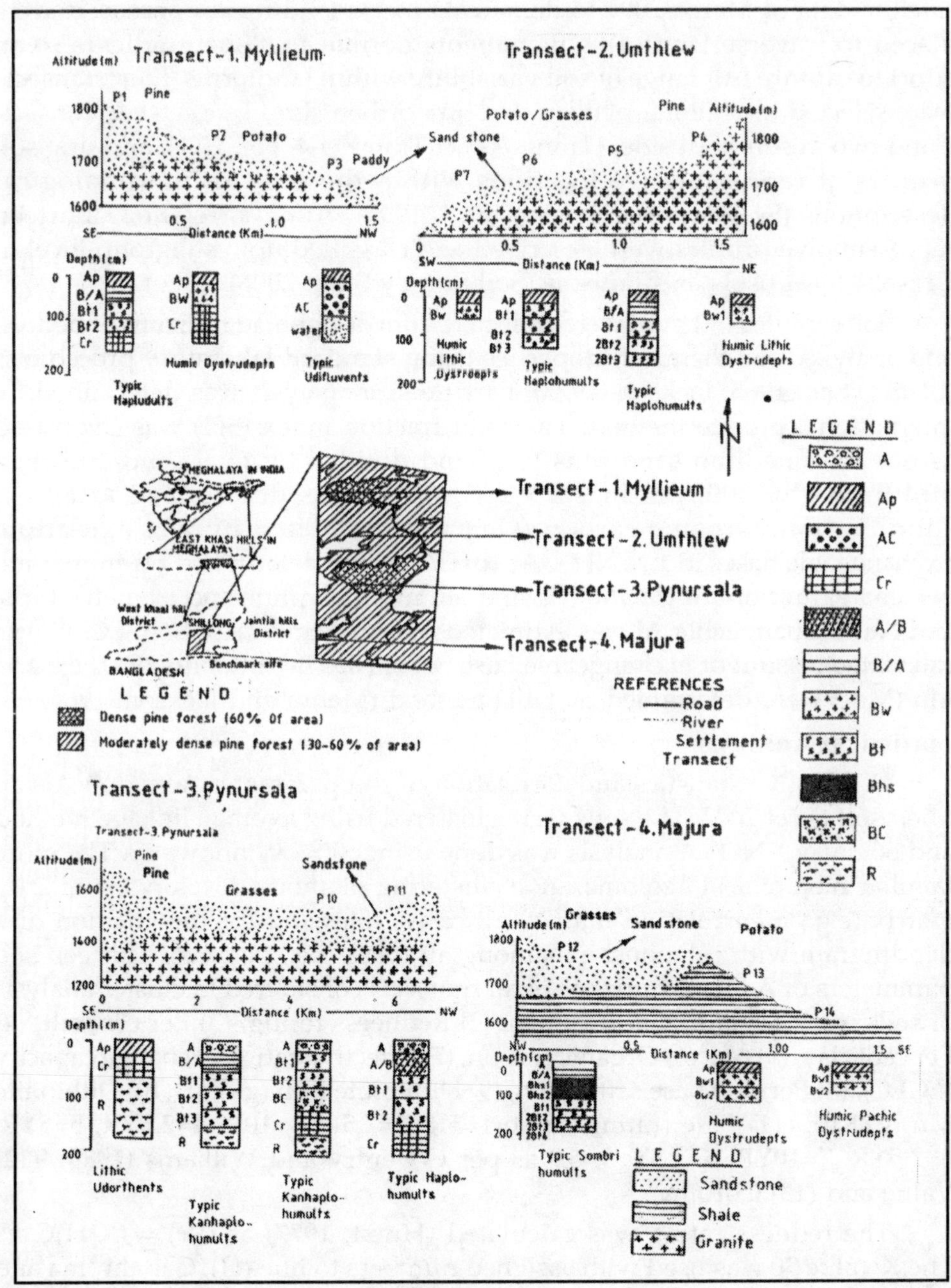

Fig. 10.1: Location of Soil Transects in Highlands of Shillong Plateau, Meghalaya

Transects and Soil Descriptions

A reconnaissance survey was performed at a scale of 1:50,000 using Survey of India toposheet No. 78 O/15 and the Indian Remote Sensing-ID satellite data of March 2001 to demarcate major land forms. Transects were placed to traverse landforms increments normal to slope gradients in an effort to capture full range of soil variability within landforms. Four transects were selected in Shillong plateau (two in northen side, Tansect-1 & Tansect-2 and two in southern side, (Transect-3 & Transect-4, Fig. 10.1). and dug soil profiles at representative locations within the unit for morphological descriptions (Soil Survey Division Staff, 1995). After correlation, fourteen representative profiles were described and classified upto subgroup level in Ultisols, Inceptisols and Entisols (Soil Survey Staff, 2006).

Soil samples (<2 mm) were collected from designated horizons of pedons and analyzed for chemical properties using standard laboratory procedures (Black, *et al.*, 1965; Jackson, 1973). Particle size analysis was determined by international pipette method; The sand fraction index (SFI) was calculated as per cent medium sand plus fine sand divided by total sand and then multiplied by 100. pH in 1:2.5 soil/water was determined after 1 h equilibration. Organic carbon (OC) was estimated by wet oxidation. Exchangeable bases in 1 N NH_4OAc (pH 7.0) were determined by employing versenate titration for Ca and Mg and atomic absorption spectrometry for K and Na. Exchangeable Al was estimated by extraction in1N KCl. ECEC was calculated as sum of exchangeable bases plus Al. The dithionite Fe (Fe_d) and Mn (Mn_d) were determined by CBD method (Mehra and Jackson, 1960).

Statistical Analysis

Descriptive statistics and correlation of soil parameters was done using Microsoft excel 2007. The soils were clustered using average linkage method and one way ANOVA analysis was done using SPSS Windows 10. The more familiar hierarchical agglomerative clustering methods develop a similarity matrix (e.g., a correlation matrix) all cases, allowing for the creation of a dendrogram with relationships among all cases (i.e., pedons). Thirteen soil parameters of A and B horizons of all transects considered in cluster analysis of soils were: (1) Horizon thickness, (2) Redneess rating, (3) Per cent silt, (4) Per cent clay, (5) pH, (6) Organic carbon, (7) Effective cation exchange capacity (ECEC), (8) Per cent base saturation, (9) Dithionite iron (g/kg), (10) Dithionite Mn (g/Kg), (11) Hue (rating value 1=5R, 2=7.5R, 3=10R, 4=2.5YR, 5=5YR, 6=7.5YR, 7=10YR, 8=2.5Y, 9=5Y as per Coventry and Williams (1983), (12) Value and (13) Chroma.

The redness rating was calculated (Hurst, 1977) as (Rr) = $(K-H)CV^{-1}$. The K value 30 was used with assigned numbers to hue (H), C is chroma and V is value.

RESULTS AND DISCUSSION

Soil Characteristics and Classification

The main morphological and physico - chemical properties of the pedons in four transects of Shillong plateau are strongly linked not only to the climate but also to their position in the landscape. The sand stone capping over Archean Genessic basement in highlands of Shillong plateau was broadly divided into three landscape units such as:- summits, middle slopes and foot slopes. The summits standout as highest, more or less solitary flattened areas exhibiting etching process of deep weathered mantle caused by high infiltration and strong chemical weathering (Driessen and Dual, 1991). The middle slopes are gullied with rock faces because of severe erosion and rapid run off where as at dissected foot slopes, the soils are shallow with the presence of red clay subsoils. The characteristics of soil transects are discussed below:

The Myllieum Transect-1

The summit soils are deep, loamy, dark brown Ap and reddish brown B horizons (Table 10.1., P1). The illuvial argillic horizons are present in summit soil (P1, Table 10.2) with 1.5 to 1.7 fold increase of clay in B horizons relative to the surface. Many soils have stronger chroma, redder hue and larger structural units to designate as argillic (Soil Survey Staff, 2006). These subsoil horizons are extremely to strongly acid at pine sites (Table 10.3) but differentiated based on organic carbon and base saturation to classify as Typic Hapludults (P1). It was proposed to use *alumic* adjective at subgroup level as these soils have 60 per cent aluminum saturation (Bhaskar, *et al.*, 2009). The soils on shoulder slopes (P2) have dark brown, sandy loam texturedand an organic carbon > 1% in A horizons with base saturation <50 per cent in -Bw horizons to classify under Humic Dystrudepts . The soils on footslopes with dark grey,loamy sand textures and AC horizons are classified as Typic Udifluvents (P3).

The Umthlew transect-2

The summit soils (P4) have dark brown umbric epipedons and thin yellowish red cambic horizons (mean thickness of 27 cm) with 21.5 per cent clay, 30 g/kg organic carbon, 35.5 g/kg of dithionite iron (Fe_d) and 15 per cent base saturation. These soils have less than 15 per cent clay content in surface layers (Table 10.2) due to continuous eluviation process as favoured by high rainfall in the areas. These soils are extremely acid (pH<4.5, Table 10.3) with poor base status and effective cation exchange capacity. This soil is classified as Humic Lithic Dystrudepts with lithic contact with in 50cm. The soils on middle slopes (P5 & P6) are strongly associated with dark brown organic enriched umbric epipedons (0.9% organic carbon) and dark reddish brown to reddish brown argillic subsurface horizons. In acid environments, considerable loss of clay and iron in subsurface horizons indicates destruction of argillic horizons (P5 and P6, Bhaskar, *et al.*, 2004a). This soil is classified as Typic Haplohumults. The soils on foot slopes (P7) are shallow, dark yellowish brown, loamy textured and have dark brown cambic subsurface. This soil is extremely acid (pH < 4.5) with poor base status, lithic contact with in 50cm and low effective cation exchange capacity. This soil is classified as Humic Lithic Dystrudepts.

The Pynursala Transect-3

The soils on summits (Lithic Udorthents, P8) have shallow, dark brown, sandy loam texture with lithic contact with in 50cm. The soils on middle slopes in Shillong plateau are severely truncated with lithological discontinuity and no clay films posing a problem in recognizing argillic/kandic horizons. The soils on middle slopes (P9 & P10) have less than 15 per cent clay in surface horizon with more than 3 per cent in B horizons. These soils with kandic horizon (<12 cmol/kg apparent ECEC and CEC of <16 cmol/kg) are classified as Typic Kanhaplohumults. The soils on foot slopes (P11) are deep and have dark grey, silty clay loam to dark brown, silty loam.textures with depth. This soils has an organic carbon content more than 1 per cent throughout the profile with very strong acid and less than 15 per cent of base saturation. This soil is classified as Typic Haplohumults.

The Majura Transect 4

The soils on summits (P12) have reddish brown to dark yellowish brown and dark brown matrix with abrupt textures of silt loam to sandy loam, loam and clay loam. The textural variations is futher confirmed with abrupt sand to silt ratio of 0.43 in Ap to 1.97 in Bhs1 horizon to 2.1 in IIBt2 and then 0.46 in IIBt4 horizons for distinguishing lithological discontinuities (Stolt, *et al.*, 1993, Rutledge, *et al.*, 1975 and Bhaskar, *et al.*, 2004b). Similarly, the sand fraction index in corresponding horizons is varied from 80.7 in Bhs1 to 27.8 per cent in IIBt4 horizons (Table 2). This soil is classified as Typic sombrihumults having sombric horizon with strong leaching, low base status (<15 per cent) and strong acid (Table 10.1). The soils on middle slopes (P13) have dark brown to strong brown and silty clay loam to silt loam textures. This soil is strongly acid with poor base status and an organic carbon more than 1 per cent to classify under Humic Dystrudepts. The soils on foot slopes (P14) have 50 cm organic enriched A horizons and sandy clay loam textures. The occurrence of colluvial soils on summits and foot slopes of highlands of Shillong were reported by Bhaskar *et al.* (2009) and in Machakos district Kenya by Ellenkamp (2004). These cambic horizons have highly weathered colluviums as evident from Fed/Fet ratio >0.7 (Rebertus and Boul, 1985). These soils are classified as Humic Pachic Dystrudepts.

Table 10.1: Morphology of Soil

Site/Soil Taxonomy	Depth (cm)	Horizon	Matrix Colour	Texture	Structure	Consistence	Roots	Boundary	RR
Transect 1:- Myllieum Profile1.Typic Hapludults- (1755 m above msl) (25°29'40" N l-91°48'26"E) - pine	0-13	A p	10YR4/3	l	vf 1 Sbk	-ss,sp	vf,f-c	cs	7.5
	13-30	B/A	10YR4/4	cl	f1sbk	-s,p	vf,f,m-c	cs	10
	30-48	B t2	5YR4/4	cl	m1sbk	-s,p	m-c	cs	15
	48-70	B t3	5YR4/6	cl	m1sbk	-s,p	m-c	cw	22.5
	70-100	Cr	2.5YR4/6	scl	–	–	–	–	26.3
Profile-2. Humic Dystrudepts- (1735 m above msl) (25°29'39" N - 91°48'31" E).-.pine forest	0-23	Ap	10YR4/3	sl	vf 1sbk	-s,p	vf,f-m	cs	7.5
	23-52	BW	5YR5/6	sl	vf 1sbk	-s,p	f,m-c	cw	18
	52-105	Cr	10YR7/4	sl	–	–	–	–	5.7
Profile-3.Typic Udifluvents(1662m above msl) (25°29'42"N -91°48'48" E) -rice	0-25	Ap	10YR3/1	ls	m1sbk	ss,sp	vf,f-m	cs	3.3
	25-50	AC	10YR7/6	s	gr	so,po	vf,f-m	cw	8.6
Transect 2:-Umthlew Profile 4. Humic Lithic Dystrudepts-(1669.1m) (25°25'59"N - 91°5148" E) - potato	0-17	Ap	10YR4/4	l	f2sbk	s,p	f,m-c	cs	10
	17-45	Bw	7.5YR4/4	cl	f2sbk	s,p	f,m-f	cw	12.5
Profile 5.- Typic Haplohumults - (1686.1m) (25°25'58"N-91°51'50" E) - potato/pine	0-17	Ap	7.5YR3/4	sl	f1sbk	ss,sp	vf,f-m	cs	16.6
	17-36	Bt1	5YR4/4	l	m1sbk	ss,sp	vf,f-m	gs	15.0
	36-75	Bt2	5YR4/4	l	m1sbk	s,p	m-f	gs	15.0
	75-95	Bt3	5YR3/4	cl	m1sbk	s,p	m-f	gs	20.0
Profile 6.-Typic Haplohumults - (1724.9m) (25°25'55"N -91°51'46 "E) - grasscover	0-13	Ap	10YR3/3	l	f1sbk	ss,sp	vf,f-m	cs	10
	13-44	B/A	7.5YR4/4	cl	m1sbk	s,p	f-m	gw	12.5
	44-57	Bt1	5YR4/4	cl	m2sbk	s,p	f-c	gs	15
	57-90	2Bt2	5YR3/4	c	m2sbk	s,p	f-c	gw	20
	90-105	2Bt3	5YR3/4	c	m1sbk	s,p	c-f	gi	20
Profile 7. Humic-Lithic Dystrudepts–(1795.2m) (25°25'47" N - 91°51'47" E)- pine	0-10	Ap	7.5YR3/2	l	f1sbk	ss,sp	f,m-c	as	8.3
	10-46	Bw	5YR4/6	cl	f1sbk	s,p	f,m-c	aw	22.5

(Table Contd...)

Site/Soil Taxonomy	Depth (cm)	Horizon	Matrix Colour	Texture	Structure	Consistence	Roots	Boundary	RR
Transect 3:- Pynursala Profile 8. Lithic Udorthents-(1407.59m) (25°19'31" N-91°53'54"E)-grasscover	0-15	Ap	10YR3/4	sl	gr	ss,sp	vf,f-m	cs	13.3
	15-40	Cr	7.5YR4/6	l	vf1sbk	s,p	-	cw	18.8
Profile 9-Typic Kanhaplohumults–(1390.3m) (25°19'30"N-91°53'51"E)-grass cover	0-18	Ap	7.5YR4/6	ls	gr	ss,sp	vf,f-m	cs	18.8
	18-41	BA	7.5YR6/6	ls	f1sbk	ss,sp	vf,f-f	cw	12.5
	41-72	Bt1	7.5YR5/6	scl	f1sbk	ss,sp	-	cw	15
	72-98	Bt2	7.5YR6/6	cl	m1sbk	ss,sp	-	gs	12.5
	98-110	Bt3	7.5YR5/6	cl	m1sbk	s,p	-	-	15
Profile 10 Typic Kanhaplohumults (1386.7m) (25°19'09"N-91°53'20"E)- grass cover	0-19	A	10YR3/3	sl	gr	so,po	vf,f-c	as	10
	19-43	Bt1	5YR5/8	scl	m1sbk	s,p	f,m-f	cs	24
	43-56	Bt2	5YR5/8	sc	m2sbk	s,p	f,m-f	gs	24
	56-76	Bt3	7.5YR5/8	scl	m2sbk	s,p	c-f	gw	20
	76-109	BC	2.5YR4/6	scl	m2sbk	ss,sp	-	gw	26.3
	109-196	Cr	2.5YR7/6	scl	f1sbk	ss,sp	-	gi	15
Profile 11- Typic Haplohumults (1631.52m) (25°19'30"N-91°52'23"E)-grass cover	0-20	Ap	10YR3/2	l	gr	ss,sp	vf,f-c	cs	6.6
	20-69	A/B	7.5YR4/4	cl	m1sbk	s,p	vf,f-f	cs	12.5
	69-110	Bt1	7.5YR4/4	cl	m1sbk	s,p	vf,f-f	cs	12.5
	110-140	Bt2	7.5YR4/4	cl	m1sbk	s,p	-	cs	12.5
Transect 4. Majura Profile 12. Typic Sombrihumults (1804.2m) (25°26'33"N-91°49'30"E) - grass cover	0-13	Ap	5YR4/4	sl	f1sbk	ss,sp	vf,f-c	cs	15.0
	13-48	B/A	10YR3/4	l	m1sbk	ss,sp	vf,f-c	gw	13.3
	48-77	Bhs1	7.5YR3/2	cl	m1sbk	s,p	f-c	gw	8.3
	77-102	Bhs2	7.5YR3/2	sc	m2sbk	vs,vp	f-c	cs	8.3
	102-127	Bt1	7.5YR4/4	sc	m2sbk	vs,vp	-	cw	12.5
	127-152	IIBt2	10YR3/3	c	m2sbk	vs,vp	-	gs	10.0
	152-174	IIBt3	10YR3/3	c	m2sbk	vs,vp	-	gw	10.0
	174-199	IIBt4	7.5YR3/2	c	m2sbk	vs,vp	-	-	8.3
Profile13. Humic Dystrudepts (1807.3m) (25°26'31"N-91°49'30"E) - potato	0-20	Ap	10YR4/3	slL	gr	ss,sp	vf,f-m	as	7.5
	20-58	Bw1	7.5YR5/8	cl	m2sbk	ss,sp	f-f	gw	36
	58-89	Bw2	7.5YR5/8	cl	m2sbk	ss ,sp	f-f	gw	36
Profile14. Humic Pachi Dystrudepts (1522.7m) (25°26'14"N-91°49'28"E)-potato	0-18	Ap	10YR2/2	l	f1sbk	ss,sp	c,m-m	cs	10
	18-46	Bw1	10YR4/3	cl	m2sbk	s,p	-	gs	7.5
	46-70	Bw2	10YR4/3	cl	m2sbk	s,p	-	gs	7.5

Table 10.2: Particle Size Distribution in Soils

Profile Number/Classification	Depth (cm)	Horizon	Sand						Silt	Clay	Sand/ Silt	Sfi
			Very Coarse	Coarse	Medium	Fine	Very fine	Total				
P1. Typic Hapludults	0-13	Ap	17.3	7.1	5.0	2.7	1.7	33.8	40.2	26.0	0.84	22.8
	13-30	B/A	12.4	6.3	4.4	2.8	0.9	26.8	46.7	26.5	0.57	26.9
	30-48	Bt1	11.5	5.0	3.1	2.4	0.3	22.3	37.7	40.0	0.59	24.7
	48-70	Bt2	7.5	5.3	4.3	3.2	0.5	20.8	34.7	44.5	0.59	36.1
	70-100	Cr	15.1	10.6	10.1	8.2	4.0	48.0	23	29	2.09	38.1
P 2. Humic Dystrudepts	0-23	Ap	25.8	13.6	12.8	9.5	5.3	67.0	12.9	23.5	5.19	33.3
	23-52	BW	23.3	10.8	15.2	10.0	4.3	63.6	11.0	16.0	5.78	39.6
	52-105	Cr	18.4	18.5	20.0	11.9	4.2	73.0	9.0	15.5	8.11	43.7
P 3. *Typic Udifluvents*	0-25	Ap	31.3	15.2	15.7	10.1	3.2	75.5	9.0	15.5	8.3	34.2
	25-50	AC	31.8	15.7	19.3	14.1	3.6	84.5	5.5	10.0	15.3	39.5
P4. Humic. Lithic Dystrudepts	0-17	Ap	–	0.3	2.2	17.1	24.6	44.2	43.3	12.5	1.02	43.7
	17-45	Bw	0.2	0.2	2.4	19.2	22.5	44.5	42.5	13.0	1.05	48.5
P5. Typic Haplohumults	0-17	Ap	2.0	2.1	3.2	7.8	9.0	24.1	55.9	20.0	0.43	45.6
	17-36	Bt1	0.3	0.4	1.6	10.3	31.7	44.3	45.2	10.5	0.98	26.9
	36-75	Bt2	0.1	0.2	1.7	17.5	25.4	44.9	41.1	14.0	1.09	42.8
	75-95	Bt3	0.4	0.3	2.6	11.8	21.0	36.1	44.4	19.5	0.81	39.9
P 6. Typic Haplohumults	0-13	Ap	1.6	1.9	4.8	8.6	8.2	25.1	53.4	21.5	0.47	53.4
	13-44	B/A	0.5	0.4	3.0	14.2	27.0	45.1	44.4	10.5	1.02	38.1
	44-57	Bt1	0.2	0.4	2.4	21.4	15.7	40.1	42.9	17.0	0.92	59.4

(Table Contd...)

Profile Number/Classification	Depth (cm)	P^H	O C gkg⁻¹	ECEC (cmol (p+) kg⁻¹)	Base Saturation (%)	Exchangeable Bases (cmol (p+) kg⁻¹)						CBD Extractable (mgkg⁻¹)
	57-90	2Bt2	0.6	0.4	2.7	15.3	15.5	34.5	42.5	23.0	0.81	52.2
	90-105	2Bt3	0.3	0.7	3.9	21.7	13.7	40.3	39.2	20.5	1.03	63.5
P7. Humic .Lithic Dystrudepts	0-10	Ap	7.5	7.2	5.8	3.2	0.8	24.5	47.5	28.0	0.52	36.7
	10-46	Bw	1.4	2.1	3.7	1.9	1.8	10.9	59.6	29.5	0.18	51.4
P8. LithicUdorthents	0-15	Ap	6.6	5.0	19.3	21.1	6.3	58.3	23.7	18.0	2.46	69.3
P9-Typic Kanhaphumults	0-18	Ap	0.2	0.3	8.2	48.9	24.1	81.7	10.3	8.0	7.93	69.9
	18-41	BA	-	0.2	6.3	47.3	25.2	79.0	12.5	8.5	6.32	67.8
	41-72	Bt1	0.2	0.5	7.6	48.8	21.9	79.0	11.5	9.5	6.86	71.4
	72-98	Bt2	0.5	1.4	11.5	41.6	15.2	70.2	16.3	13.5	4.31	75.6
	98-110	Bt3	0.2	0.3	6.2	26.0	14.3	47.0	30.5	22.5	1.54	68.5
P10. Typic Kanhaphumults	0-19	A	5.2	8.2	22.7	32.9	9.2	78.2	9.3	12.5	8.41	71.1
	19-43	Bt1	3.3	4.0	14.1	15.4	9.4	46.2	15.8	38.0	2.92	63.9
	43-56	Bt2	1.1	2.6	22.4	27.1	6.4	59.6	11.4	29.0	5.22	83.1
	56-76	Bt3	1.5	2.1	18.1	28.0	11.9	61.6	13.9	24.5	4.33	74.8
	76-109	BC	0.3	1.9	27.9	33.5	5.7	69.3	7.2	23.5	9.62	89.2
	109-196	Cr	0.5	0.5	1.7	27.6	35.0	65.3	15.7	19.0	4.15	44.8
P11- Typic Haplohumults	0-20	Ap	1.3	1.7	7.4	6.1	1.6	18.1	61.4	20.5	0.29	74.5
	20-69	A/B	1.2	1.6	6.3	13.0	9.2	31.3	51.7	17.0	0.61	61.7
	69-110	Bt1	1.0	1.3	5.0	7.5	5.0	19.8	57.2	23.0	0.35	63.1
	110-140	Bt2	1.2	1.8	6.5	8.6	3.7	21.8	54.7	23.5	0.40	69.3
P12. Typic Sombrihumults	0-13	Ap	4.7	3.4	4.3	6.8	6.3	25.5	60.0	14.5	0.43	43.5
	13-48	B/A	3.4	2.5	3.3	5.9	9.4	24.5	60.5	15.0	0.41	37.6
	48-77	Bhs1	1.0	0.9	13.7	34.7	9.7	60.0	30.5	9.5	1.97	80.7
	77-102	Bhs2	2.6	11.6	21.4	10.3	2.2	48.1	35.9	16.0	1.34	65.9
	102-127	Bt1	1.8	2.6	12.5	15.3	4.1	36.3	41.2	22.5	0.88	76.6
	127-152	IIBt2	0.3	0.5	7.5	35.4	14.2	57.9	27.6	14.5	2.10	74.1
	152-174	IIBt3	0.5	1.1	2.4	17.7	19.3	41.0	48.0	11.0	0.85	49.0
	174-199	IIBt4	9.8	5.5	3.5	2.9	1.3	23.0	49.5	27.5	0.46	27.8

(Table Contd…)

Profile Number/Classification	Depth (cm)	P^H	O C gkg^{-1}	ECEC (cmol (p+) kg^{-1})	Base Saturation (%)	Exchangeable Bases (cmol (p+) kg^{-1})						CBD Extractable ($mgkg^{-1}$)
P13. Humic Dystrudepts	0-20	Ap	3.4	3.1	3.2	4.2	4.4	18.3	50.7	31.0	0.36	40.4
	20-58	Bw1	1.2	2.1	4.2	8.0	9.0	24.5	53.5	22.0	0.46	49.8
	58-89	Bw2	2.5	1.7	3.1	3.1	2.6	13.0	70.0	17.0	0.19	47.7
P14. Humic Pachic Dystrudepts	0-18	Ap	0.3	0.7	2.2	14.1	20.7	38.0	49.0	13.0	0.78	42.9
	18-46	Bw1	0.9	1.8	6.1	14.2	7.7	30.7	47.8	21.5	0.64	66.1
	46-70	Bw2	3.4	9.4	21.9	10.9	2.0	47.6	20.4	32.0	2.33	68.9

Table 10.3: Chemical Properties of Soils

						Ca^{2+}	Mg^{2+}	Na^{+}	K^{+}	Al^{3+}	H^{+}	Fe	Mn
P1. Typic Hapludults	0-13	5.1	3.07	4.66	21	0.88	0.56	0.28	0.15	2.51	0.28	25950	76
	13-30	5.3	2.62	4.80	25	0.66	1.26	0.34	0.11	2.03	0.40	25250	110
	30-48	5.0	0.12	4.95	18	0.88	0.32	0.21	0.12	3.11	0.31	30325	158
	48-70	5.2	0.67	4.45	27	1.1	0.58	0.24	0.10	2.15	0.28	30825	146
	70-100	5.7	0.20	3.18	86	1.1	0.58	1.18	0.05	-	0.27	19550	88
P 2. Humic Dystrudepts	0-23	5.2	2.46	3.37	42	0.66	1.02	0.23	0.11	1.08	0.27	7050	81
	23-52	5.1	1.26	3.41	34	0.66	0.78	0.19	0.07	1.19	0.52	6450	36
	52-105	5.3	0.18	1.73	31	0.44	0.52	0.17	0.06	0.36	0.18	3250	76
P 3. *Typic Udifluvents*	0-25	5.7	2.93	2.40	37	1.10	0.34	0.26	0.07	0.36	0.27	5225	43
	25-50	5.5	1.06	2.99	92	0.88	1.04	0.22	0.07	0.36	0.42	5300	28
P4. Humic .Lithic Dystrudepts	0-17	4.0	19.6	4.56	11	0.88	0.32	0.27	0.21	2.39	0.49	35900	669
	17-45	3.8	21.8	5.04	11	0.88	0.32	0.23	0.19	2.99	0.43	34225	507
P5. Typic Haplohumults	0-17	3.6	46.2	5.99	18	1.98	0.66	0.33	0.23	2.39	0.40	34450	611
	17-36	3.9	21.6	6.04	27	1.1	2.02	0.21	0.19	1.91	0.61	36525	779
	36-75	3.8	14.4	5.1	12	0.66	0.54	0.23	0.16	3.11	0.40	36675	525
	75-95	4.1	14.8	4.41	17	1.1	0.82	0.27	0.15	1.67	0.40	32900	548
P 6. Typic Haplohumults	0-13	4.0	35.2	4.23	12	0.66	0.78	0.22	0.14	1.91	0.52	21150	600
	13-44	4.0	18.0	3.84	12	0.66	0.54	0.23	0.16	1.91	0.34	26800	825
	44-57	4.0	16.3	4.18	11	0.66	0.54	0.23	0.14	2.39	0.22	19175	650
	57-90	4.3	13.0	3.82	13	0.88	0.56	0.20	0.11	1.67	0.40	17375	700
	90-105	4.2	11.4	3.45	33	0.88	0.56	0.18	0.12	1.56	0.15	21550	675
P7. Humic .Lithic Dystrudepts	0-10	4.4	15.0	1.85	15	0.88	0.32	0.14	0.06	0.24	0.21	22550	575
	10-46	4.3	37.8	3.48	9	0.66	0.48	0.17	0.10	1.56	0.51	28825	100
P8. LithicUdorthents	0-15	3.9	5.1	4.70	17	0.88	0.56	0.23	0.15	2.39	0.49	20400	25
P9. Typic Kanhaphumults	0-18	3.9	8.3	2.25	34	0.66	0.24	0.16	0.11	0.96	0.12	3575	50
	18-41	3.9	3.1	2.05	35	0.66	0.24	0.10	0.06	0.84	0.15	6675	450
	41-72	4.1	1.8	2.09	32	0.44	0.52	0.10	0.04	0.84	0.15	6900	19
	72-98	4.0	1.0	2.70	27	0.66	0.24	0.21	0.06	1.20	0.33	6375	19
	98-110	4.1	3.3	3.63	25	0.88	0.32	0.25	0.11	2.03	0.04	8950	50

(Table Contd...)

						Ca^{2+}	Mg^{2+}	Na^{+}	K^{+}	Al^{3+}	H^{+}	Fe	Mn
P 10. Typic Kanhaphumults	0-19	5.2	22.0	3.30	32	0.44	1.0	0.17	0.07	1.20	0.42	19875	25
	19-43	5.2	5.5	4.38	20	0.22	0.74	0.20	0.07	2.51	0.64	54750	50
	43-56	5.4	2.4	2.7	39	0.44	1.0	0.13	0.05	0.72	0.36	46175	99
	56-76	5.3	1.2	3.4	35	0.66	0.78	0.12	0.04	1.56	0.24	33425	137
	76-109	5.4	0.4	2.85	24	0.66	0.30	0.13	0.05	1.44	0.27	38350	400
	109-196	5.4	0.2	2.81	30	0.88	0.32	0.24	0.13	0.48	0.76	24200	20
P 11. Typic Haplohumults	0-20	4.6	38.2	6.44	12	0.88	0.8	0.30	0.23	3.59	0.64	6000	75
	20-69	4.7	17.1	4.51	13	0.44	0.76	0.28	0.15	2.51	0.37	21425	125
	69-110	4.9	12.7	4.19	13	0.88	0.56	0.26	0.15	2.15	0.19	30550	425
	110-140	5.1	11.7	4.09	17	0.88	1.04	0.31	0.15	1.44	0.27	9050	305
P 12. Typic Sombrihumults	0-13	5.1	37.2	3.34	12	0.44	1.0	0.28	0.18	1.32	0.12	21525	351
	13-48	5.0	21.0	3.40	9	0.66	0.48	0.24	0.13	1.44	0.45	14950	159
	48-77	5.1	27.5	3.43	9	0.88	0.32	0.32	0.20	0.84	0.87	12950	109
	77-102	5.2	27.3	2.80	7	0.66	0.24	0.28	0.18	1.08	0.36	12125	121
	102-127	4.9	16.8	3.97	11	0.88	0.32	0.29	0.23	2.15	0.10	8925	397
	127-152	5.2	14.1	3.55	12	0.66	0.48	0.26	0.26	1.32	0.57	8100	548
	152-174	5.2	18.2	3.96	8	0.66	0.48	0.24	0.24	1.91	0.43	8500	538
	174-199	5.2	17.6	4.06	7	0.66	0.48	0.20	0.20	2.15	0.37	8850	511
P 13. Humic Dystrudepts	0-20	5.0	48.2	4.15	9	0.66	0.48	0.20	0.20	2.27	0.34	24275	74
	20-58	5.5	4.1	1.96	13	0.44	0.52	0.14	0.14	0.60	0.12	19600	127
	58-89	5.5	2.7	2.64	14	0.66	0.48	0.15	0.15	1.32	0.03	24600	161
P 14. Humic Pachic Dystrudepts	0-18	4.2	56.0	5.18	6	0.88	0.32	032	0.24	2.99	0.43	24275	85
	18-46	4.8	17.8	5.27	8	0.66	0.48	0.48	0.23	2.87	0.55	19600	94
	46-70	5.1	9.9	5.59	12	0.88	0.80	0.80	0.23	2.51	0.37	24600	146

Descriptive Statistics

The variability of soil properties such as horizon thickness, redness ratinf and profile darkness index related to topography is discussed (Table 10.4).

Horizon Thickness

The mean thickness of A horizon in four soil transects is 26.89 cm with standard deviation (sd) of 13.7 . Transect wise analysis shows that the mean thickness of A horizon is 35.7 cm in T1, 23.8 cm in T2 and T3 and 28.7cm in T4 with 75.9 percent of coefficient of variation(cv) for T2 and 40 to 49 per cent for other transects The mean thickness of B horizon is 59.3cm with 25.6 cm of standard deviation and coefficient of variation of 43 per cent (cv). It is further observed that the variation in mean thickness of B horizon is 45 per cent in T-2 as against the 13 per cent in T-4. The exponential relation between thickness of A horizon and elevation is expressed in regression equation as:

$Y = e^{0.001x}$ (R^2 = - 0.40*) where Y = thickness of A horizon (cm), X= elevation (metres). This relation is significant at 5 level. Similar kind of relationship between thickness of A horizon and elevation were reported in forest soils of Southern Taiwan by Chen Chi Tsat, *et al.* (2001).

Redness Rating (RR)

The mean redness rating is 10.7 for all transect data for A horizon with a cv of 35.3 per cent . The A horizon in T1, has redness rating 8.5 which is less than the mean of all transects with cv of 59.5 per cent. The decrease of redness rating of A horizons is due to topographic influence where in occurrence of dark grey Typic Ustifluvents were reported (Bhaskar, *et al.*, 2004b). In general, the mean redness rating is 16.8 to 22.2 in B horizons with cv of 77.9 per cent in T4. The redness rating of B horizons has a significant positive relation with Fe_d contents and its relation expressed for approximation as:

- Redness rating (Y) = $0.03(Fe_d)^3 - 0.66(Fe_d)^2 + 6.03(Fe_d)$, R^2 =0.37*, significant at 5% level).

This kind of polynominal equation were successfully employed in explaining relation of landform parameters with soil properties of transect data in Iowa (Walker, *et al.*, 1968 a and b). The relation of redness rating with hematite content was reported in various soils by Torrent *et al.* (1983).

Profile Darkness index

The profile darkness index (PDI, Thomson and Bell, 1996) was calculated as = " A horizon thickness/(Value X Chroma)+1. The PDI values are generally varied from 1.5 to 3.6 in upland soils but a value of 6.5 recorded in P3. The PDI values increase with the thickness of A horizons.The low PDI values in highland soils is due to thin A horizons showing a positive relation with elevation .Its relation is expressed in polynominal equation at 3rd order level as:

PDI (Y)= $-3E\text{-}08x^3 + 7E\text{-}0.5x^2 - 0.057x$ R^2=0.214) where x is elevation in metre.

Table 10.4: Transect wise Descriptive Statistics for Particle Size Distribution in Highland Soils

Statistical Parameters	Sand (%)						Silt (%)	Clay (%)	Sand/ Silt	Sf	Horizon Thickness (cm)		Redness Rating	
	Very Coarse	Coarse	Medium	Fine	Very fine	Total					A	B	A	B
Transect-1														
Mean	19.7	10.9	11.2	7.6	2.8	52.4	23.0	24.6	4.7	33.9	35.7	32.5	8.5	22.2
SD	8.5	4.9	6.7	4.5	1.8	24.8	15.3	11.0	4.8	6.8	14.4	10.6	5.1	
cv(%)	43.1	44.6	59.9	58.4	64.7	47.3	66.7	44.9	102.2	20.6	40.3	32.6	59.5	
Transect-2														
Mean	1.3	1.3	3.1	13.0	16.6	35.2	46.3	18.4	0.8	46.3	23.7	50.8	11.5	17.5
SD	2.0	1.9	1.2	6.47	9.7	10.9	6.1	6.2	0.30	9.9	17.9	22.9	3.6	4.1
cv(%)	164.8	150	39.4	49.5	58.3	30.8	13.3	33.7	37.25	21.4	75.9	45.3	31.1	23.6
Transect-3														
Mean	1.6	2.0	11.9	27.0	12.7	55.4	25.1	19.4	4.1	69.8	23.8	89.7	11.4	16.8
SD	1.9	2.1	7.7	14.6	9.3	22.2	19.4	7.9	3.0	9.7	11.7	20.5	3.9	6.2
cv(%)	118.5	105.0	65.1	53.7	73.1	40.2	77.1	41.1	74.9	13.9	49.3	22.9	34.8	36.5
Transect-4														
Mean	2.6	3.5	7.3	11.4	7.9	32.9	47.2	19.8	0.9	53.1	28.7	58.3	10.8	17.1
SD	2.5	3.3	6.9	8.7	6.4	13.2	13.5	6.9	0.7	15.4	13.7	7.6	3.1	13.3
cv(%)	95.1	95.4	94.1	75.7	81.7	40.0	28.6	34.9	77.6	29.1	47.8	13.0	28.8	77.9
All trasects														
Mean	5.2	3.8	8.4	16.2	10.6	28.7	48.6	22.7	0.8	52.6	26.9	59.3	10.7	17.7
SD	8.1	4.5	7.0	12.5	9.0	12.8	16.0	7.5	0.8	12.0	13.7	25.6	3.8	8.3
cv(%)	153.9	118.3	82.5	77.0	85.1	46.0	51.1	40.7	123.3	32.2	51.0	43.1	35.3	46.9

The profile darkness index was influenced by organic C content and dithionite Fe (Fe_d) with high variability between horizons. The profile darkness index has significant negative relation with organic carbon (R^2 = -0.78**, Significant at 1% level) and dithionite Fe (R^2 = 0.37* Significant at 5%level) and expressed its relation in polynominal eqations as:

PDI (y)= -7E-05 (organic carbon)^3 -0.015 (organic carbon)^2 + 0.395 (organic carbon), R^2=-0.78**),

PDI(y) =-0.000(Fe_d)^2 +0.347(Fe_d) (R^2=-0.37*).

Particle Size Distribution

The particle size data shows that medium and fine sand contribute 35 to 45 per cent of total sand in northern side and more than 50 per cent in southern side (Table 10.4). The soils in T1 have 52 per cent of sand, 23.1 per cent of silt and 24 per cent of clay. Among sand fractions, the variation accounts 65 per cent for very fine sand (mean of 2.85%) and 60 per cent for medium sand (mean of 11.2%). The sand fraction index has low variation (20.6 per cent of cv) with mean of 33.89 per cent but recorded high variation for sand to silt (cv of 102 per cent). The low per cent of variation for silt is in T2 (13.3% of cv) and T4 (28.58 per cent of cv) but for sand, the variation is 30.87% in T2 and 40% in T4 and for clay, the variation is 33.76% in T2 and 34.9% in T4. In transect 3, the coefficient of variation is 77 per cent for silt and 40 per cent for sand and clay. The variability related to side slopes and contribution of lower solum in highlands is explained with sand/silt, profile darkness index, organic carbon and dithionite Fe. The high variability of sand/silt ratio and sand fraction index (Table 10.4) are very much helpful to distinguish lithological discontinuities in P6, P9 & P10. In general, sand to silt ratio shows high variation (123% of cv) with a mean of 0.79. In general, sand fractions have shown very high variability (>77 per cent of cv) in all transects.

Chemical Properties

The statistical summary of chemical properties shows that pH of soils have low coefficient of variation (12.9%) with mean of 4.75 indicating very strongly acid with low effective cation exchange capacity (ECEC of 3.79 cmol($^+$)kg^{-1} and 29.48% of cv), low base saturation (mean of 21.8% and cv of 76%) and low exchangeable bases(<1 c mol($^+$)kg). Among bases, Na and Mg have cv more than 50%. The coefficient of variation is more than 70% for dithionite Fe in transect 1 & 3 and 74 to 110.9% for Mn contents in transect 3 & 4 (Table 10.5). These values are similar to those found in neighbouring regions within Shillong plateau (Nair and Chamuha, 1988). This kind of results expected in subgroups of Ultisols and associated soils in which considerable weathering, leaching and clay illuviation have occurred. Similar kind of variability of soil properties were reported in Blue Ridge highlands of Virginia by Stolt, *et al*. (1993). The variability of properties are more in B horizons due to substantial change in pedogenesis, colluvial processes and weathering in ordering properties than A horizons. Similar findings were reported by Mausbach, *et al.* (1980) and Wilding and Drees (1983).

Based on coefficent of variation (Wilding, 1985), the variability of soil properties in four transects are grouped as least variable (<15%), moderately variable (15 to 35%) and highly variable (>35%). Among physical properties, silt is the least variable in transect 2, sand fraction index in transect -3 and thickness of B horizon in transect-4. The sand, silt and clay fractions are highly variable in transect 2 and 4 where as moderaltely variable of sand and clay in transect -2 and sily and clay in transect -4. The high variability of A horizon thickness and redness rating is recorded in all transects under study. Among chemical properties, soil pH is the least variable in all transects (Table 10.5) whereas ECEC, ExCa, ExK, ExH as moderately variable (T1), ECEC, ExNa, ExK, total Fe and Mn (T2), ECEC and ExCa in transect-3 and ECEC, base saturation, EXCa and K in Transect -4. Organic matter, base saturation, exchangeable magnesium, sodium and aluminium, total Fe and manganese are highly variable in transects under study. Similar results have been reported for tropical soils (Wollenhaupt, *et al.*, 1997 and Oku, *et al.*, 2010)

Clustering of Soils

The soils are clustered into three groups based on similarity of thirteen soil characteristics (Fig. 10.2). The Group-I includes the five soils of which two are on summits (P1, Typic Hapludults & P10, Typic Kanhapludults), two on foot slopes (P11, Typic Haplohumults & P14, Humic Pachic Dystrudepts) and one on middle slopes (P13, Humic Dystrudepts). The Group-II includes three soils such as P9 on middle slopes (Typic Kanhapludults), P12 on summits (Typic Sombrihumults) and P7 on foot slopes (Humic Lithic Dystrudepts). The soils in three landscape positions viz. summits (P4, Humic Lithic Dytrudepts), foot and middle slopes (P5 & P6, Typic Haplohumults) in transect -2 are clustered in Group-III. Even though, the soil groups donot closely associated with landscape and resemble the soil classification. Similar observations in grouping of red, grey and yellow soils in Central North Queensland were reported by Coventry and Williams (1983). The distribution of numerically classified soil groups along four transects shows coincidence of boundaries between the field and numerical groups in southern side of transects 3 & 4 with Group-II and Group-I soil sequence but do not coincide in transects of northern side (T1 & T2). A similar results were reported by Campbell *et al.* (1970) from a numerical classification of some alluvial soils in the northern part of Swan Coastal plain of Western Australia.

Table 10.5: Transect wise Descriptive Statistics for Chemical Properties

Statistical Parameters	pH	O C gkg^{-1} kg^{-1}	ECEC cmol (+)	Base Saturation (%)	Exchangeable bases (cmol (+) kg^{-1}						Total mgkg^{-1}	
					Ca	Mg	Na	K	Al	H	Fe	Mn
Transect-1												
Mean	5.31	1.46	3.59	41.3	0.84	0.70	0.33	0.09	0.67	0.32	15917.5	84.2
SD	0.25	1.19	1.09	26.18	0.23	0.32	0.30	0.03	0.43	0.09	11482.1	43.8
cv(%)	4.65	82.29	30.31	63.39	27.17	44.99	90.9	34.9	63.61	30.69	72.13	53.01
Transect-2												
Mean	4.03	21.93	4.31	15.46	0.91	0.65	0.22	0.15	1.98	0.39	28315.3	597.2
Sd	0.23	10.86	1.12	7.03	0.36	0.44	0.05	0.05	0.73	0.13	7214.2	176.4
cv(%)	5.68	49.52	25.96	45.47	39.12	67.73	21.69	31.28	36.91	34.09	25.5	29.5
Transect-3												
Mean	4.69	8.38	3.51	25.31	0.66	0.59	0.19	0.10	1.62	0.34	21042.19	142.13
SD	0.62	10.23	1.17	8.99	0.21	0.29	0.07	0.054	0.84	0.21	15845.1	157.62
cv(%)	13.1	122.1	33.38	35.53	32.19	49.49	35.67	54.12	52.24	60.73	75.30	110.9
Transect-4												
Mean	5.07	22.74	3.81	9.78	0.69	0.49	0.3	0.20	1.77	0.37	16633.9	244.36
SD	0.32	15.46	1.03	2.52	0.15	0.19	0.17	0.04	0.75	0.22	6684.9	182.39
cv(%)	6.25	67.94	27.06	25.72	21.1	40.17	55.3	20.16	42.15	61.26	40.19	74.63
All transects												
Mean	4.75	14.19	3.79	21.81	0.76	0.59	0.26	0.14	1.72	0.36	20694.81	269.83
SD	0.61	13.91	1.12	16.76	0.26	0.32	0.17	0.06	0.82	0.17	11908.31	248.21
cv(%)	12.9	97.9	29.48	76.83	34.21	53.3	64.63	45.37	47.78	49.7	57.54	91.98

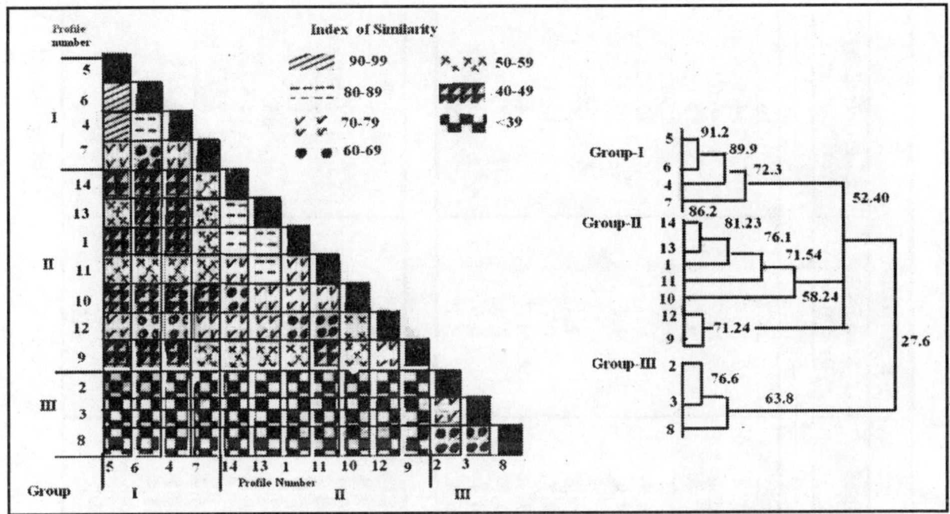

Fig. 10.2: Similarity Matrix and Dendrogram of Soils on Highlands of Shillong Plateau

Variability of Soil Groups

The coefficients of variation are means by which variability of soil properties are expressed and compared regardless of units or orders of magnitude (Harrandine, 1949 and Stolt, *et al.*, 1993). The statistical analysis to examine horizon wise variability (Table 10.6) clearly shows that the mean thickness of A horizon is 33cm for Group -II soils (cv of 61 per cent) with mean redness rating of 13, organic carbon of 19.2 g/kg (cv of 85 per cent) and base saturation of 20.3 per cent (cv of 58.7 per cent). The mean thickness of B horizon is 72 cm in Group-I (cv of 39 per cent) with redness rating of 20. The mean organic carbon in B horizons is relatively high in Group-II (21.6g/kg, cv of 85.1%) and Group–III soils (17.4g/kg, cv of 23.7%) and have redness rating almost similar to that of A horizons (15.8 for Group -III & 14.3 for Group-II soils). The Group-I soils have mean redness rating of 20 in B horizons which is three times more to A horizons (8.8 redness rating, Table 10.6). The mean clay content in B horizons is 27.5% for Group-I soils (20.6% in A horizon) and 19.4% in Group-II soils (16.9% in A horizons) but slightly decrease in clay content of 15.9% in Group-III soils as compared to A horizon (16.9%). The dithionite Fe (Fe_d) and Mn (Mn_d) contents are high in B horizons of Group-I soils (27.7g/kg for Fe & 177.8 mg/kg for Mn) as compared to A horizons but its values are low in B horizons of other Groups. The coefficient of variation (>50%) is reported in A horizon for organic carbon (63%) and base saturation (66.1%) for Group-I soils, A horizon thickness, per cent silt and clay, organic carbon, effective cation exchange capacity, chroma and dithionite iron for Group-II soils and horizon thickness alone for Group -III soils. The properties of B horizons show more than 50% of cv for redness rating and organic carbon in Group-I soils but in Group-II soils, organic carbon, per cent base saturation, dithionite iron and manganese are highly variable with cv more than 50%.

Table 10.6: Horizon wise Variability of Soil Properties in Highland Soils

Soil Properties	A Horizon			B Horizon		
	Mean	Standard Deviation	Coefficient of Variation (%)	Mean	Standard Deviation	Coefficient of Variation (%)
Group-I						
Horizon thickness (cm)	21.4	4.9	22.8	72.2	28.3	39.1
Redness rating	8.85	1.5	17.6	20.4	11.0	54.1
Per cent silt	42.9	19.8	46.3	39.6	19.3	48.6
Per cent clay	20.6	8.1	39.1	27.5	9.1	33.1
pH	4.8	0.44	8.9	5.2	0.26	4.98
Organic carbon (g/kg)	33.4	21.3	63.7	6.9	6.7	97.6
Effective cation exchange capacity (cmol/kg)	4.8	1.2	30.4	4.0	1.2	30.4
Per cent base saturation	16.5	10.9	66.1	17.6	7.4	41.9
Fe_d (g/kg)	20.0	8.1	40.6	27.71	9.2	33.4
Mn_d (mg/kg)	70.8	27.5	38.1	177.8	61.7	34.7
Hue	7	–	–	5.9	0.8	13.3
Value	3.2	0.8	26.1	4.4	0.6	13.7
Chroma	2.6	0.54	21.1	5.5	2.1	38.2
Group - II						
Horizon thickness (cm)	33	20.2	61.3	53	16.52	31.1
Redness rating	13	4.1	31.4	14.9	7.3	49.3
Per cent silt	39.6	25.2	63.7	40.9	20.2	49.4
Per cent clay	16.9	10.1	59.5	19.4	8.8	45.3
pH	4.5	0.6	13.5	4.5	0.5	11.8
Organic carbon(g/kg)	19.2	16.31	84.95	21.6	18.4	85.1
Effective cation exchange capacity (cmol/kg)	5.8	6.55	113.4	3.1	0.5	14.8
Per cent base saturation	20.3	11.9	58.7	15.4	11.7	75.9
Fe_d (g/kg)	16.5	9.7	58.8	16.5	11.2	67.7
Mn_d (mg/kg	400.3	155.9	38.9	85.4	55.3	64.6
Hue	5.7	0.6	10.2	5.8	0.7	12.6
Value	3.7	0.6	15.7	4.2	1.3	30.2
Chroma	4	2	50.0	5.1	1.5	29.2

(Table Contd...)

Soil Properties	A Horizon			B Horizon		
	Mean	Standard Deviation	Coefficient of Variation (%)	Mean	Standard Deviation	Coefficient of Variation (%)
Group - III						
Horizon thickness (cm)	26	15.6	59.9	55.7	25.4	45.7
Redness rating	12.6	3.5	27.8	15.8	2.9	18.9
Per cent silt	49.4	6.3	12.8	42.5	1.0	2.4
Per cent clay	16.5	4.2	25.6	15.9	3.8	23.5
pH	3.9	0.2	5.9	3.9	0.2	4.8
Organic carbon (g/kg)	30.8	13.8	44.8	17.4	4.1	23.7
Effective cation exchange capacity (cmol/kg)	4.9	1.0	20.8	4.7	0.7	15.9
Per cent base saturation	13.7	3.8	27.7	16.2	4.5	27.9
Fe_d (g/kg)	31.5	6.5	20.7	29.7	8.9	30.0
Mn_d (mg/kg)	664.3	51.2	7.7	599.8	85.4	14.2
Hue	6.6	0.6	8.7	5.4	0.5	9.6
Value	3.3	0.6	17.3	3.8	0.3	7.5

Similarily, the numerical techniques were used for predictive value for soil properties in deep sandy soils viz., chroma for Cu, Mn, pH and exchangeable K and value for cation exchange properties and Exchangeable Mg and Ca (Russel and Moore, 1967).

CONCLUSION

Four toposequences in highlands of Shillong Plateau are considered to determine the range of variation in soil properties and expressed in terms of coefficient of variation. These soils are strongly acid with umbric epipedons, thick red, argillic or sombric B horizons in summits and backslopes. The dark red B horizons in highland soils are the relict features of paleosols commonly associated with humid climate and needs special attention in soil correlation work. The thickness of A horizon had an exponential relation with elevation but have poor relation with profile darkness index. The profile darkness index for A horizons has negative relation with organic carbon and dithionite Fe. The redness rating in B horizons has a strong correlation with Fe_d contents. The soil transect data showed high variability of thickness of A horizon, thickness of red argillic B horizons, organic carbon, sand to silt ratio, per cent base saturation, dithionite iron and manganese contents. The Group A soils have coefficient of variation more than 50per cent for organic carbon, A horizon thickness and base saturation wherer as A horizon thickness, per cent silt and clay, organic carbon, effective cation exchange capacity, chroma and dithionite iron for Group B soils. The B horizons have more than 50 per cent of cv for redness rating and organic carbon in Group A soils and organic carbon, per cent base saturation, dithionite iron and manganese for Group B soils.

REFERENCES

Acharrya, S.K. (2005): Geology and Tectonics of NE India. *Journal of Geophysics,* XXVI (1), 35-4.

Agbenin, J.O. and Tiessen, H. (1995): Soil Properties and Their Variations on Two Contiguous Hill Slopes in North East Brazil. *Catena,* 24: 147-161.

Bhaskar, B.P., J.P. Mishra, U. Baruah, S. Vadivelu, T.K. Sen, P.S. Butte, and D.P. Dutta. (2004b): Soils on Hill Slopes of Narang-Kongripara Watershed in Meghalaya. *Journal of the Indian Society of Soil Science,* 52(2):125-133.

Bhaskar, B.P., Saxena,R.K., Vadivelu, S., Baruah, U., Butte,P.S. and Dutta,. D.P. (2004a): Pedogenesis in High Altitude Soils of Meghalaya Plateau. *Agropedology,* 14: 9-23.

Bhaskar, B.P., Saxena, R.K., Vadivelu, S., Baruah, U., Dipak Sarkar, Raja, P. and Butte, P.S. (2009): Intricacy in Classification of Pine Growing Soils in Shillong Plateau, Meghalaya, India. *Soil Survey Horizons,* 50(1): 11-16.

Black, C.A., D.D. Evans, L.E. Ensminger, J.L. White, and F.E. Clark. (1965): *Methods of Soil Analysis.* Part 1. ASA, Madison, WI.

Burrough, P.A.(1993): Soil Variability: A Late 20th Century View. Soils and Fertilizers 56: 529-562.

Campbell, N.A., Mulcahy, M.J. and Mcarthur, W.M. (1970): Numerical Classification of Soil Profiles on the Basis of Field Morphological Properties. *Australian Journal of Soil Research,* 8: 43-58.

Champion H.G. and Seth S.K. (1968): *Revised Survey of Forest Types of India.*, Government of India Press, Delhi, India.

Chen-Chi Tasi, Zueng-sang Chen, Chin-Tzer Duh and Fu-Wen Hrong. (2001): Prediction of Soil Depth Using a Soil-landscape Regession Model: A Case Study on Forest Soils in Southern Taiwan.*Proc. Natl.Sci.counc.ROC(B)*., 25: 34-39.

Coventry, R.J. and Williams, W.T. (1983): Numerical Examination of a Field Classification of Some Red, Yellow and Grey Earth Profiles. *Australian Journal of Soil Research,* 21: 343-357.

Driessen, P.M. and Dudal, R. (1991): *The Major Soils of the World. Lecture Notes on Their Geography, Formation, Properties and Use.* Agricultural University, Wageningen, Department of Soil Science and Geology in Association with Katholieke Universiteit. Leuven, Institute for Land and Water Management.

Ellenkamp, G.R. (2004): Soil Variability and Landascape in the Machakos District, Kenya. SFI80318, Thesis. Wageningen, The Netherlands.

Foussereau, X., Hornsby, A.G., and Brown, R.B. (1993): Accounting for Variability within Map Units when Linking a Pesticide Fate Model to Soil Survey.*Geoderma,* 60: 257-276.

Harradine, F.F.(1949): The Variability of Soil Properties in Relation to Stage of Profile Deveopment. *Soil Science Society of America Proceedings,* 14: 302-311.

Heuvelink, G.B.M., Webster, R. (2001): Modelling Soil Variation: Past, Present, and Future. *Geoderma,* 100: 269-301.

Hole, F.D. and Horonaka, M.(1960): An Experiment in Ordination of Some Soil Profiles. *Proceedings of Soil Science Society of America,* 24: 309-312.

Hurst, V.J.(1977): Visual Estimation of Iron in Saprolite. *Geological Society of American Bul letin,* 88: 174-176.

Jackson, M.L. (1973): *Soil chemical Analysis.* Prentice Hall of India, New Delhi.

Kreznor, R.W., Kenneth, R., Olson. Banwart, W.L. and Johnson, D.L.(1989): Soil Landscape and Erosion Relationships in a Northwest Illinois Watershed. *Soil Science Society of America Journal,* 53: 1763-1771.

Majumdar, S.K.(1986): The Precambrian Framework of Part of the Khasi Hills, Meghalaya. *Recent Geological Survey of India,* 117: 1-59.

Mausbach, M.J., Brasher, B.R., Yeck, R.D. and Nettleton, W.D.(1980): Variability of Measured Properties in Morphologically Matched Pedons. *Soil Science Society of America Journal,* 44: 358-363.

Mehra, O.P. and Jackson.M.L.(1960): Iron Oxide Removal from Soils and Clays by Dithionite-citrate System Buffered with Sodium Bicarbonate.*7th Natl. Conf. Clays Clay Miner.* 7: 317-327.

Moore, I.D., Turner, A.K., Wilson, J.P., Jenson, S.K., and Band, L.E. (1993): GIS and Land Surface-subsurface Modeling. pp. 196-230 in Goodchild, M.F., Parks, B.O. and Steyaert, L.T., eds, *Environmental Modeling with GIS.* New York: Oxford University Press.

Nair, K.M., Baruah, U. and Chamuah.G.S. (1983): Soil Survey Report of East Khasi Hills District, Meghalaya. Report. 522. NBSS&LUP, Nagpur.

Nair, K.M., and Chamuah.G.S. (1988): Characteristics and Classification of Some Pine Forest Soils of Meghalaya. *Journal of the Indian Society of Soil Science,* 36: 142-145.

Ogunkunle, A.O. and Ataga, D.O. (1985): Further Investigation into Soil Heterogeneity and Sampling Procedure Under Oil Palm. Nigeria Institute Oil Palm Research., VII: 40-50.

Ogunkunle, A.O. (1993): Variation of Some Soil Properties Along Two Toposequences on Qtile Schist and Banded Genesis in Southern Nigeria. Geoderma, 30(4): 397-402.

Oku, E., Essoka, A and Thom, E. (2010): Variability in Soil Properties Along an Udalf Toposequence in the Humid Forest Zone of Nigeria. Kasetsart J. (Nat. Sci.), 44: 564-573

Rebertus, R.A. and Boul, S.W. (1985): Iron Distributionin Developmental Sequence of Soils from Mica Gneiss and Schist. *Soil Science Society of America Journal,* 49: 713-720.

Russel, J.S. and Moore, A.W. (1967): Use of Numerical Method in Determining Affinities Between Some Deep Sandy Soils. *Geoderma,* 1: 47-68.

Rutledge, E.M., Holowaychuk, N., Hall, G.F. and Wilding, L.P. (1975): Loess in Ohio in Relation to Several Possible Source Areas: 1. Physical and Chemical Properties. *Soil Science Society of America Proceedings,* 39: 1125-1132.

Soil Survey Division Staff (1995): *Soil Survey Manual.* Agri Handb. 18. U.S. Dept. Agric. Indian Print, Scientific Publishers, Jodhpur.

Soil Survey Staff. (2006): *Keys to Soil Taxonomy*: 19th . USDA-NRCS, Washington, DC.

Stolt, M.H., Baker, J.C. and Simpson, T.W.(1993): Soil-landscape Relationships in Virgin ia: 1. Soil Variability and Parent Material Uniformity. *Soil Science Society of America Journal,* 57: 414-421.

Torrent, J., Schwertmann, U., Fechter, H. and Alferez, F.(1983): Quantitative Relationships Between Soil Colour and Hematite Content. *Soil Science,* 136: 354-358.

Thompson, J.A. and Bell, J.C. (1996): Color Index for Identifying Hydric Conditions for Seasonally Saturated Mollisols in Minnesota. *Soil Science Society of America journal,* 60: 1979-1988.

Walker, P.H., Hall, G.F. and Protz, R. (1968a): Soil Trends and Variability Across Selected Landscapes in Iowa. *Soil Science Society of America Proceeding,* 32: 97-101.

Walker, P.H., Hall, G.F. and Protz, R. (1968b): Relation Between Landform Parameters and Soil Properties. *Soil Science Society of America Proceedings,* 32: 101-104.

Wilding, L.P. (1985): Spatial Variability: Its Documentation, Accommodation and Implications to Soil Surveys. p. 166-189. In .Nielsen, D.R. and Bouma, J.(ed). *Soil Spatial Variability.* Proc.Workshop of the ISSS and SSSA, Las Vegas, NV30, Nov-1, Dec.1984. Pudoc. Wageningen, Netherlands.

Wilding, L.P. and Drees, L.R.(1983): Spatial Variability and Pedology. p. 83-116. in L.P. Wilding *et al.* (ed). *Pedogenesis and Soil Taxonomy.* 1. *Concepts and Interactions,* Elsevier, Amsterdam.

Wilding L.P., J. Bouma, and D.W. Boss. (1994): Impact of Spatial Variability on Interpretive Modeling. In: Bryant R.B. and R.W. Arnold - Quantitative Modeling of Soil Forming Processes. SSSA Special Publ., No., 39: 61-75.

Wollenhaupt, N.C, D.J. Mulla and C.A. Gotway Crawford. (1997): Soil Sampling and Interpolation Techniques for Mapping Spatial Variability of Soil Properties, pp. 19-53. In F.J.Pierce and E.J. Sadler (eds.). The State of Specific Management for Agriculture. American Society of Agronomy, Madison. Wisconsin. 19-53

Upchurch, D.R., and Edmonds, W.J. (1991): Statistical Procedures for Specific Objectives, in Spatial Variabilities of Soils and Landforms, edited by M.J. Mausbach and L.P. Wilding, pp. 49-71, SSSA Special Publication, No. 28, *Soil Science Society of America,* Madison, WI, 1991.

Pages: 179-184

SOIL CONTAMINATION AND CONSERVATION

Edited by: Dr. Ezeaku Peter Ikemefuna; Dr. Pawan Kumar 'Bharti'

ISBN: 978-93-5056-737-1

Edition: 2015

Published by: Discovery Publishing House Pvt. Ltd., New Delhi (India)

Effect of Nickel Concentrations on *Amaranthus spinosus* Uptake of Nutrients and Heavy Metals in Soil

Osu Charles I.[*1] and **Isaac, Issac U.**[2]

ABSTRACT

This study was conducted to evaluate the effect of different concentrations of nickel on uptake of essential and non-essential nutrients by green amaranth (*Amaranthus spinosus*). A plot of farmland in university of port Harcourt Research farm was randomly sampled from the surface (0-10 cm) and analyzed in the laboratory before treatment and thirty days after treatment and sowing. The nickel treatment of the samples showed inhibitive effects on absorption of nutrients by green amaranth.

Increasing the concentration of nickel from 10 ppm to 25ppm showed a significant decrease in uptake of available nutrients, which ranged from 30.71-20.12%, P; 39.60-15.38%, N; 19.71-10.04%, Fe; 54.84-25.25%, Zn; 35.18-10.38%, K; 17.20-2.46%, Pb; and 39.68-18.42% Cd as compared to control (57.85-20.02%). Nickel concentration of 10ppm reduced nutrient uptake slightly.

1* Department of Pure and Industrial Chemistry, University of Port Harcourt, PMB, 5323, Port Harcourt, Rivers State. Nigeria.

However, nickel concentration of 25 ppm produced the lowest amount of all nutrients absorbed. The study suggests that cultivation of green amaranth in nickel polluted soil should be avoided or appropriate control measures be adopted to maintain the nickel content of the soil below damage threshold level.

Key words: Sorption, nutrients, metals, nickel, *Amaranthus spinosus*.

INTRODUCTION

Complex interactions involving weathering of rock minerals, decaying organic matter, animals and microbes take place to form inorganic minerals in soil. These mineral nutrients are absorbed as ions in soil water by roots of plants. However, lots of factors influence nutrients uptake by plants. Soil itself or other elements may tie up nutrients; high or low pH can also make minerals unavailable to plants (Singh *et al.*, 2007). More so, it is almost near impossible to envisage a soil without trace amount of heavy metals and most of the heavy metals are essential elements for living organisms, but their excess amounts are generally harmful to plants, animals and human health (Azevedo and Lea, 2005; Jarup, 2003). Nickel is a first-row transition metal with chemical and physical characteristics ideally suitable to biological activity. Divalent nickel is the only oxidation state of nickel that is likely to be of any importance to higher plants. Nevertheless, Ni^{2+} forms an array of complexes with a variety of coordination numbers and geometries.

Naturally, nickel occurs widely in the environment; being release through both natural and anthropogenic sources (DEPA, 2005a; Cempel and Nikel, 2006). The phytoavailability of nickel has been correlated with free nickel ion activity in soil solution, hence, plant uptake is also dependent on soil pH, organic matter content and iron –manganese oxide (Massoura *et al.*, 2006; Rooney *et al.*, 2007; Ge *et al.*, 2000).

Plants have two transport systems: low affinity and high affinity. With the low affinity transport system, plants can absorb Ni^{2+} ions at the low concentration of 4.4 ppb. With the high affinity transport system, plants can take up 1.8 ppm of Ni^{2+} ions. Nickel is readily re-translocated within the plant, probably as a complex with organic acids, such as citrate, at $pH < 5$, or an amino acid, such as histidine, at $pH > 6.5$ (Brown, 2006).

Further studies showed that most nickel applied as a soluble salt is bound within the skin and does not reach systematic circulation (Hostynek et al., 2001; Turkhall et al., 2008). Currently, contamination of soil in cultivation field with toxic heavy metals such as nickel is a threat to agriculture, hence the present study is to investigate the effect of different nickel concentrations on *Amaranthus spinosus* uptake of nutrients and heavy metals in Soil from University of Port Harcourt research farmland.

MATERIALS AND METHODS

Sample Collection, Preparation and Analysis

A plot of farmland in University of Port Harcourt Research farm was randomly sampled from the surface (0-10 cm) and seeds of green Amaranth (*Amaranthus spinosus*) samples were collected from National Root Crop Research Institute, Umudike. Different nickel concentration (0 ppm (control), 10 ppm, 15 ppm, 20 ppm and 25 ppm) was made from nickel acetate (NiOAc) salts using de-ionized water. The collected soil samples were analyzed for nutrients and heavy metals before treatment. The soil (500g) was slowly mixed thoroughly with the different concentrations (200ml) of solution using a glass rod and left to equilibrate for one day. Five (5) seeds of green Amaranth Were sown in 35cm diameter porous pots filled with 200g of treated soil which has some percentage of clay, 1oam and silt with pH range of 6.81-7.22 at room temperature and the porous pots were watered with distilled water as described by Houshmandfar and Tehrani (2008) for a period of 30 days. After which the plant were removed and the contents of soil were determined according to Jackson (1973).

Table 11.1: Concentration Levels of the Nutrients Before Treatment

P (ppm)	N (ppm)	Fe (ppm)	Zn (ppm)	K (ppm)	Pb (ppm)	Cd (ppm)
39.880	0.143	3.668.10	153.500	258.800	2.440	0.750
33.470	0.101	4213.00	161.10	311.810	1.400	0.630
31.610	0.093	5,135.30	169.800	226.630	4.750	0.590
34.130	0.101	5381.30	149.000	202.590	1.470	0.430
32.200	0.169	3729.00	171.500	333.400	3.030	0.380

Table 11.2: Comparison of Nutrients/Heavy Metal Absorption with Different Concentrations of Nickel Treatment

Ni Treatment (ppm)	N (%)	P (%)	K (%)	Fe (%)	Zn (%)	Pb (%)	Cd (%)
0.0	52.44	49.37	38.29	20.78	57.85	20.02	56.00
10.0	39.60	30.70	35.18	19.71	54.84	17.20	39.68
15.0	24.73	25.49	22.46	11.24	36.93	16.10	23.73
20.0	20.79	21.12	13.98	10.89	36.70	14.42	18.60
25.0	15.38	21.40	10.38	10.04	25.25	2.46	18.42

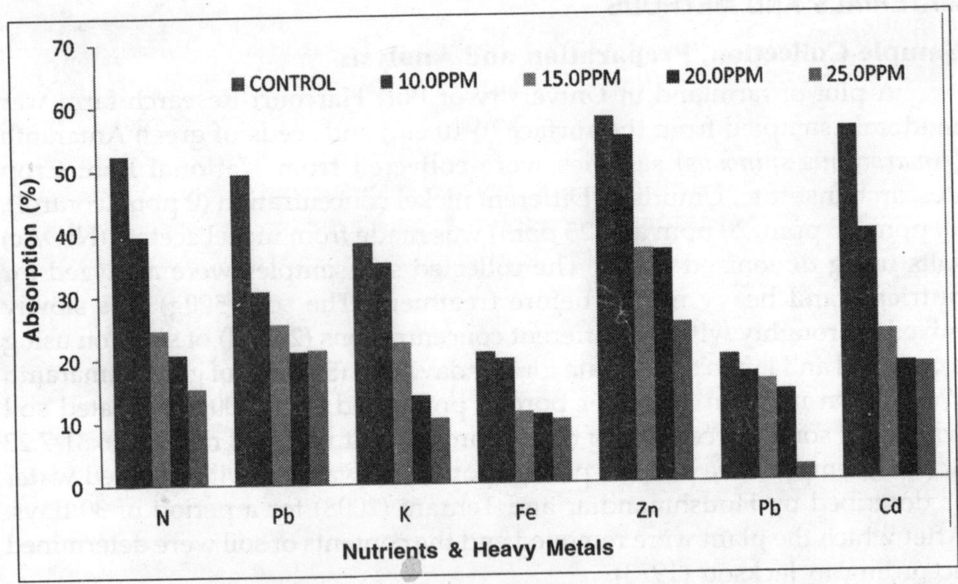

Fig. 11.1: Comparison of Nutrients/Heavy Metal Absorption with Different Concentrations of Nickel Treatment

RESULTS AND DISCUSSION

Evaluation of Nutrients Absorption by Green Amaranth (*Amaranthus spinosus*)

Absorption percentage of green amaranth was adversely affected due to application of nickel at different concentrations. Nickel treatment of the soil sample inhibited absorption of nutrients and heavy metals (lead and cadmium) significantly. The plant absorbed the nutrients best in the non-nickel treated (control) sample with values, 52.44%, N; 49.37%, P; 38.29%, K; 20.78%, Fe; 57.85%, Zn; 20.02%, Pb; and 56.00%, Cd. Absorption percentage was markedly suppressed At different nickel concentrations, the adsorption percentage was markedly suppressed with range of 15.38 -39.60%, N; 21.40 -30.70%, P; 10.38-35.18%, K; 10.04-19.71%, Fe; 25.25-54.84%, Zn; 2.46-17.20%, Pb; and 18.42-39.68%, Cd of 25ppm (figure 11.1 and table 11.2). As the concentration of nickel is increasing the percentage of all the metals and non-metals adsorbed by the soil decreases as a result of nickel stress (Houshmandfar and Moraghebi, 2011).

The comparison of the effects of different nickel treatment on the various elements (nutrients and heavy metals) is as shown in table 2. Amongst the elements, zinc showed highest percentage (54.84%) absorption at 10ppm nickel treatment. Cadmium followed with 39.68% at 10ppm nickel treatment phosphorous, also followed with 30.7% (10ppm) nickel treatment. However, no marked difference was seen in Iron (19.71%) and lead (17.20%) uptake.

Metal toxicity and inhibitive efficiency are important factors to be considered when examining plant uptake of nutrients. The effect of toxic substances such as nickel on plants uptake of nutrients is dependent on the amount or concentration of such toxic substance taken up by plant in the environment.

Plant ability to survive starts during germination or seedling growth. Its vulnerability or otherwise is dependent on its response to metal stress [Vange et al., 2004; Houshmandfar and Moraghebi, 2011]. We have investigated how nickel treatment affect uptake of nutrients by green amaranth plant. Nickel treatment decreased the absorption of plant nutrients and heavy metals by green amaranth plant. This reduction is indicative of the fact that if nickel is present in excess amount is capable of and responsible for producing toxic effects resulting in reduced plant development. This decrease in nutrient absorption efficiency of plants is in conformity with hosts of researchers (Houshmandfar and Moraghebi, 2011; Shafiq and Iqbal , 2005). Houshmandfar and Moraghebi, (2011) Observed that decrease in plants uptake of nutrient, may be attributed to accumulation on the plants body (seed) thus weakening the uptake control mechanism. This inhibition of nutrients uptake is also attributed to bonding of negative (soil) and positive (metal) charge because metal binds with hydroxyl (OH^-), and carboxyl group (COOH) and phenolic groups of soil. The physiological effect of metals on plants cellular interactions is also considered as probable contributor to nutrient inhibition (Houshmandfar and Moraghebi, 2011).

CONCLUSION

Increase in the concentration of nickel resulted in decrease in the absorption percentage of nutrients of green amaranth. Nickel, heavy metal has the capacity to form complexes as noted in literature. Hence, specific adsorption of nutrients through ligand exchange on hydroxylated surface sites of oxides or edges of clay (silicates) large. More so, humic acids (decomposed product of manure) bond with heavy metals (Nickel) at low pH. On the other hand, at high pH, humic acids may form aqueous complexes with metals such as nickel which has greater mobility than non-complex forms. Therefore, cultivation of green amaranth in nickel polluted soils should be avoided. Appropriate control measures should be adopted to maintain the nickel content of the soil below its threshold limit before green amaranth is planted. The environmental quality standard would be further enhanced given the identified toxic concentration of nickel (25ppm). This finding has also showcased the potential of green amaranth (Amaranthus spinosus.) as an effective tool for coordinating crop management programmes in nickel contaminated areas. Above all, research studies with nickel stress can be productive in proffering solutions to numerous agricultural challenges, including metal pollution.

REFERENCES

Azevedo RA, Lea PJ (2005). Toxic Metals in Plants. Braz. J. Plant Physiol., 17: 1.

Brown, P. H. 2006. "Nickel." In *Handbook of Plant Nutrition*, Edited by A.V. Barker and D.J. Pilbeam, 395-410. Boca Raton, FL: CRC Press Taylor & Francis Group.

Cempel M, Nikel G (2006). Nickel: A Review of its Sources and Environmental Toxicology. Polish J. of Environ. Stud., 15(3): 375-382.

DEPA (2005a). Draft Risk Assessment. Nickel (CAS No: 7440-02-0), EINECS No: 231- 111- 4. Copenhagen: Danish Environmental Protection Agency.

Ge Y, Murray P, Hendershot WH (2000). Trace Metal Speciation and Bioavailability in Urban Soils. Environ. Poll., 107: 137-144.

Hostynek J.J, Dreher F, Nakada T, Schwindt D, Angbogu A, Mailbach HI (2001). Human Stratum Corneum Adsorption of Nickel Salts. Investigation of Depth Profiles by Tape Stripping *in vivo*. Acta Dermato- Venereological, Supplement, 212: 11-18.

Houshmandfar A, Tehrani MM (2008). The Study of Zinc and Lead Extraction Potential by Safflower Plant, Plant Ecosyst., 14: 77-86.

Houshmandfar A. and F. Moraghebi, (2011). Effect of Mixed Cadmium, Copper, Nickel and Zinc on Seed Germination and Seedling Growth of Safflower, Afri. J. Agric Res. 6(5): 1182-1187.

Jackson, M.L., 1973. Soil Chemical Analysis. Prentic Hall of India Private Limited, New Delhi.

Jarup L (2003). Hazard of Heavy Metal Contamination. Br. Med. Bull., 68: 167-182.

Massoura ST, Echevarria G, Becquer T, Ghanbaja J, Leclerc- cessac E, Morel J- L (2006). Control of Nickel Availability by Nickel Bearing Mineral in Natural and Anthropogenic Soils. Geoderma, 136: 28- 37.

Rooney CP, Zhao F-J, McGrath SP (2007). Phytotoxicity of Nickel in a Range of Europian Soils: Influence of Soil Properties, Ni Solubility and Speciation. Environ. Pollution, 145: 596-605.

Shafiq M, Iqbal MZ (2005). The Toxicity Effects of Heavy Metals on Germination and Seedling Growth of *Cassia siamea* Lamk. J. New Seeds, 7: 95-105.

Singh D, Nath K, Sharma Yk (2007). Response of Wheat Seed, Germination and Seedling Growth Under Copper Stress. J. Environmental Biol., 28(8): 409-414.

Turkhall R.M, Skowronski GA, Abdel- Rahman MS (2008). Effects of Soil and Aging on the Dermal Bioavailability of Hydrocarbons and Metals in Soil. Int. J. Soil Sediment Water, 1(1): 1-13.

Vange V, Hevchand I, Vandvik V (2004). Does Seed Mass and Family Affect Germination and Juvenile Performance in *Knautia Arvensis*? A Study Using Failure Time Methods. Acta Oecol., 25(3): 169-178.

Pages: 185-193

SOIL CONTAMINATION AND CONSERVATION

Edited by: Dr. Ezeaku Peter Ikemefuna; Dr. Pawan Kumar 'Bharti'

ISBN: 978-93-5056-737-1

Edition: 2015

Published by: Discovery Publishing House Pvt. Ltd., New Delhi (India)

Assessment of Soil Quality in Textile Industrial Area at Panipat City (Haryana), India

Pawan Kumar 'Bharti'[*1, 2, 3] and **Pawan Kumar Tyagi**[1]

ABSTRACT

In this modern industrial era, the waste problem in land lies in the leaching process, such as quantum of liquid wastes leachates slowly through the layers of soil beneath and contaminate the water resources deep down the land, however, the problem of soil pollution differs from air and water pollution in the respect of pollutants remains direct contact with the soil for relatively long period. The wide industrialization and increasing consumption pattern has changed the very complexion, texture, characteristics and nature of soil especially in industrial area. Thus soil is getting heavily polluted day by day by addition of toxic materials.

1 Department of Zoology and Environmental Sciences, Gurukula Kangri University, Haridwar (Uttarakhand) - 249 404, India.

2 Society for Environment, Health, Awareness of Nutrition & Toxicology (SEHAT-India), 1775, Sohanganj, Near Clock Tower, Delhi - 7, India.

3 Antarctica Laboratory, R & D Division, Shriram Institute for Industrial Research, Delhi - 7, India.

The present work deals with the preliminary assessment of soil quality near textile industrial area to understand the impact of textile pollution on soil environment. Hence the investigation has been undertaken to assess the extent of heavy metal in soil. Samples of soil were analyzed for heavy metals, viz. Mn, Ni, Fe, Cu, Cd, Pb and Zn, using atomic absorption spectrophotometry. Some physico-chemical characteristics of soil were found altered in comparison to control site.

Key words: Soil contamination, Soil quality, Industrial Pollution, heavy metals.

INTRODUCTION

In the recent years, there has been a growing concern with environmental protection. This can be achieved either by decreasing the afflux of pollutants to the environment or by their removal from contaminated media. The former is a feasible choice only for pollutants of anthropogenic origin, whereas, the latter is unavoidable for those of natural origin (Gomez-Serrano *et al.*, 1998). The presence of heavy metals in the environment has been of great concern to scientists and engineers because of their increased discharge, toxic nature, and other adverse effects on surroundings.

Pollution of environment with heavy metals is a serious problem. Besides causing specific toxicity symptoms, these metals may also contribute to global warming by destroying the atmosphere ozone layer like atmosphere methane, nitrous oxide and sulphur dioxide because of potentially harmful effects on human and animal health, few toxic metals (lead, cadmium, mercury, arsenic, and chromium). It is major concern to ecologist or researcher, because air or water pollution from point and non-point sources may contribute significantly to the load of metals on natural ecosystem (Mani *et al.*, 2005). The pollution load in wastewater posed by textile industry is very high and affects soil quality and other environmental components in many ways. Discharges of textile waste on land and used for agricultural purpose have also affected the crop and soil productivity due to high dissolved salts. The suspended solids, which are present in the waste, may carry out clogging of soil pores. The sodium, which is present in the waste, may lead to hardening of texture of soil, thereby preventing penetration of roots in soil (Bharti, 2007).

MATERIALS AND METHODS

Small scale textile industries and many dye houses are situated in scattered manner on Jatal road in industrial area in Panipat city. A study was conducted in adjoining agricultural fields of industrial area in Panipat region. The soil samples were collected randomly from industrial area, where the textile industrial effluent drain is flowing and ultimately ends up into a large pond. A control site for parallel analysis was selected in other agricultural area of non-industrial region 10 Km far from dye houses. All the collected soil samples were analyzed by the standard methods (Trivedi and Goel, 1984).

RESULTS AND DISCUSSION

Many industrial drains and huge amount of liquid waste water from textile dye houses consists of many types of organic and inorganic pollutants especially heavy metals are found in Panipat city. These heavy metals and other pollutants have leached in soil system and ultimately accumulated and deteriorate the ground water resources of industrial area. Sometimes people used industrial waste water of textile industries directly for irrigation of their dry crops. Polluted water and industrial effluents may contaminate the basic structure and chemical composition of natural soil of the region due to increasing industrialization (Malik and Bharti, 2007).

Soil's physico-chemical parameters may demonstrate the pollution status in the industrial region, so, physical and chemical characteristics are important for the assessment of contamination and pollution load. There is not any significant variation in the temperature of agricultural soil (17.4-27.8 °C) and control soil (17.5-27.8 °C). The chemical processes and activities of microorganism which convert plant nutrients into available forms are also materially influenced by temperature. Removal of excess water from soil may facilitate changes in soil temperature. Humus content, good tillage, dark color of soil are the some other factors which influence the soil temperature (Miller and Turk, 2002).

Water held in the soil pores with varying degrees of tenacity depending on the amount of water present and the size of pores in soils. Depending on the soil, as much as one forth to two thirds of the moisture may remain in the soil after the plants have wilted or died due to the lack of soil water. Water holding capacity was found similar in agricultural soil (36.1-43.7%) and control soil (36.8-44.2%) with much difference between soil and sediment. Yuandong *et al.*, (2006) described the similar trend of water holding capacity on the basis of soil texture and chemical composition in the agricultural soil system. The amount of pore space is determined by the arrangement of the solid particles. If the particles lie close together, as in stands or compact sub-soils, the total porosity is low. If they are arranged in porous aggregates, as is often the case in medium textured soils high in organic matter, the pore space per unit volume will be high. Soil aeration may influence the availability of nutrients to plants (Miller and Turk, 2002). The bulk density was found similar between agricultural soil (1.15-1.24 g/cm^3) and control soil (1.10-1.22 g/cm^3) Bulk density was similarly described by Yuandong *et al.*, (2006) and Krebs *et al.*, (1999) in soil environment. Moisture content of agricultural soil (3.5-10.7 %) and control soil (3.7-11.06 %) were found similar during the study.

The pH value was observed slightly high (7.11-7.63) in agriculture land, which shows that agriculture land is going to alkaline in nature which confirms that agriculture land again disturbed by its proper pH values whereas due to the decay of organic matter has produced the acidic properties of soil. Soil pH was found slightly alkaline in agricultural soil (7.1-7.6) and control soil (7.2-7.4). Similar trend of pH fluctuation have been described by Kasem and Singh (1999) & Bharti et al. (2013) in agricultural soil environment.

The electric conductivity of agricultural soil and control soil was found in the range of 24.1-27.7 and 23.0-23.7 mho/cm respectively with some minor fluctuations. Electric conductivity has positive correlation with all heavy metals viz. Cd (0.3965) Cu (0.9454), Fe (0.4198), Mn (0.9076), Ni (0.8286), Pb (0.8596) and Zn (0.7586) in agricultural soil. The chloride in agricultural soil and control soil was found 499.5-734.3 and 313.8-529.3 µg/g respectively with some minor fluctuations. Chloride has positive correlation with all heavy metals viz. Cd (0.3654) Cu (0.8479), Fe (0.3249), Mn (0.7254), Ni (0.6603), Pb (0.6972) and Zn (0.7744) in agricultural soil environment.

The potassium in agricultural soil and control soil was found almost in uniform pattern 31.0-36.5 and 30.3-34.5 µg/g respectively with some minor fluctuations. Potassium has slightly positive correlation with many heavy metals viz. Cd (0.6852) Cu (-0.1689), Fe (0.7116), Mn (0.0611), Ni (0.2623), Pb (0.2369) and Zn (-0.6269) in agricultural soil. Korfali and Davies (2004) and Soltan (1999) have been exhibited a clear idea about the fluctuations in potassium concentrations in soil system. The occurrence of sodium in agricultural soil and control soil was found very high 192.0-599.0 and 95.33-380.0 µg/g respectively with some minor fluctuations. Sodium has slightly positive correlation with many heavy metals viz. Cd (0.7499) Cu (0.0853), Fe (0.8436), Mn (0.3169), Ni (0.4813), Pb (0.4876) and Zn (-0.4581) in agricultural soil. Similar observations were made by Soltan (1999), Bharti (2013) and Korfali and Davies (2004).

Cadmium concentrations in soil (0.7-3.4 ppm) turn down in rainy season due to the dilution factor, while in the ground water system its impact seems after monsoon and cadmium concentration reduces. Concentrations of copper in agricultural soil was recorded maximum 36.3 ± 7.4 in summer 2005 and minimum 13.4 ± 6.0 in winter 2005-06 ranged between 5.0 to 42.5 ppm. Iron is one of the most abundant elements of the rocks and soil, ranking fourth by weight. The concentration of iron in agricultural soil was recorded maximum 82.8 ± 18.1 in summer 2006 and minimum 26.8 ± 10.8 in monsoon 2005 ranged between 14.40 to 100.5 ppm. Singh *et al.*,(1994) observed the similar trends in agricultural soil of industrial area.

In agricultural soil, manganese was comparatively low in concentrations (5.8-13.6 ppm) regarding other metals. Mn was found slightly high at experimental sites in the case of soil samples. The concentration of manganese in agricultural soil was recorded maximum 13.6 ± 1.4 in summer 2005 and minimum 5.8 ± 1.7 in winter 2006-07 ranged between 2.0 to 15.0 ppm. Manganese, Iron and potassium may deficient in alkaline soil (Miller and Turk, 2002), while manganese and iron is soluble in acidic soil (Brady, 1995). The concentration of nickel in agricultural soil was recorded maximum 10.5 ± 0.8 in summer 2005 and minimum 5.3 ± 1.1 in winter 2006-07 ranged between 3.8 to 12.1 ppm. Pb was also second most enriched element after iron in agricultural soil (25.1-62.4 ppm) due to the high distribution of these metals in earth crust. Lead is deposited mostly in bones and some soft tissues. High concentrations of lead may create toxicity in human (Kudesia, 1992).

During the study, in all experimental soils zinc concentration was found slightly higher than those at control soil (7.3-16.5 ppm). Positive correlations were found between zinc and temperature (0.8704), electric conductivity (0.2569), Cl (0.7613), pH (0.4955) in agricultural soil. Zinc concentration among all metals studied was found at fourth position in agricultural soil (7.7-19.4 ppm). Zinc is sometimes found in insufficient quantity in soil (Miller and Turk, 2002). Zinc salts are relatively non-toxic, but high concentrations may cause health problems like vomiting, renal damage, etc. (Kudesia, 1992). High amount of Zn may harm to living organism of that ecosystem (Aslam *et al.*, 2004). Correlation between physico-chemical parameters and heavy metals of soil at control site are given in table-8 for each metal. For cadmium correlation was found maximum 0.8706 and 0.7532 with water holding capacity and Electric conductivity respectively. Correlation for copper was found maximum 0.9142 and 0.8290 with temperature and chloride respectively. Correlation for iron was found maximum 0.8397 and 0.8795 with water holding capacity and sodium respectively. Correlation for manganese was found maximum 0.8814 and 0.7925 with temperature and chloride respectively. Correlation for nickel was found maximum 0.7267 and 0.6699 with temperature and water holding capacity respectively. Correlation for lead was found maximum 0.8608 and 0.8055 with water holding capacity and Electric conductivity respectively. Correlation for zinc was found maximum 0.8704 and 0.7613 with temperature and chloride respectively.

In the case of horizontal distribution, the heavy metal concentrations decrease with increasing distance from pollution source. In the circle of 1 Km from pollution source almost heavy metals level was found higher than the outer wide circle in the industrial area. Heavy metals contamination was found to be low in soil at control site and also in outer circle of textile industrial area. However, the area of around 1 Km from textile industrial area was found highly affected by heavy metals in Panipat region (Bharti, 2013).

Table 12.1: Physico-chemical Characteristics of Soil Near Textile Industries

Parameters	Unit	Summer 2005		Monsoon 2005		Winter 2005-06	
		Mean	SD	Mean	SD	Mean	SD
Temperature	℃	27.667	3.456	25.833	2.517	17.160	3.866
WHC	%	42.590	0.476	34.997	4.926	35.800	2.814
Bulk density	mg/cm^3	1.203	0.021	1.273	0.021	1.274	0.048
Soil moisture	%	3.377	1.027	10.600	2.360	5.210	1.166
pH		7.700	0.100	7.800	0.100	7.920	0.084
EC	mho/cm	30.833	1.041	29.667	1.457	26.120	0.944
Cl	µg/g	769.333	140.479	721.000	86.000	551.600	35.211
Na	µg/g	424.000	117.656	100.333	86.489	264.600	159.054
K	µg/g	33.333	1.528	30.333	1.528	33.000	1.581

Table 12.2: Physico-chemical Characteristics of Soil at Control Site

Parameters	Unit	Summer 2005		Monsoon 2005		Winter 2005-06	
		Mean	SD	Mean	SD	Mean	SD
Temperature	℃	27.833	2.701	26.500	2.500	17.500	3.482
WHC	%	44.183	0.742	37.733	5.519	37.500	2.670
Bulk density	mg/cm^3	1.107	0.051	1.207	0.012	1.168	0.076
Soil moisture	%	3.733	1.286	10.683	1.994	5.630	0.972
pH		7.233	0.153	7.467	0.058	7.310	0.167
EC	mho/cm	23.633	0.153	23.100	0.557	23.040	0.182
Cl	µg/g	529.333	114.474	446.667	62.067	313.800	64.317
Na	µg/g	338.000	124.864	95.333	37.005	183.800	143.796
K	µg/g	33.000	2.646	30.333	2.517	33.200	0.837

Table 12.3: Mean Values of Physico-chemical Characteristics of Soil at Control and Experiment Sites

Parameters	Unit	2005-06			
		Control Site	SD	Experimental Sites	SD
Temperature	℃	22.625	5.527	22.558	5.707
WHC	%	39.646	4.205	38.825	4.271
Bulk density	mg/cm^3	1.157	0.066	1.180	0.066
Soil moisture	%	6.242	3.052	6.054	3.163
pH		7.321	0.156	7.361	0.262
EC	mho/cm	23.242	0.380	25.742	1.960
Cl	µg/g	401.583	116.923	601.667	119.654
Na	µg/g	217.667	148.153	386.667	189.092
K	µg/g	32.583	2.193	33.917	2.314

Table 12.4: Heavy Metals in Soil Near Textile Industries

Heavy Metals	Unit	Summer 2005		Monsoon 2005		Winter 2005-06	
		Mean	SD	Mean	SD	Mean	SD
Cadmium (Cd)	ppm	3.533	0.586	0.773	0.560	1.920	0.396
Copper (Cu)	ppm	36.867	7.407	31.300	4.652	15.400	5.439
Iron (Fe)	ppm	77.267	14.408	32.700	11.701	28.460	12.233
Manganese (Mn)	ppm	13.767	0.907	10.967	2.501	6.540	2.221
Nickel (Ni)	ppm	10.400	1.179	7.567	1.079	5.940	1.242
Lead (Pb)	ppm	62.467	9.804	40.833	11.545	26.820	9.166
Zinc (Zn)	ppm	11.267	2.950	16.967	3.037	9.580	2.647

Table 12.5: Heavy Metals in Soil at Control Site

Heavy Metals	Unit	Summer 2005		Monsoon 2005		Winter 2005-06	
		Mean	SD	Mean	SD	Mean	SD
Cadmium (Cd)	ppm	2.233	0.306	0.733	0.473	0.460	0.351
Copper (Cu)	ppm	11.533	15.396	23.000	4.036	9.980	4.141
Iron (Fe)	ppm	68.633	17.539	19.000	11.207	20.940	12.563
Manganese (Mn)	ppm	11.500	1.114	9.200	1.833	4.962	2.028
Nickel (Ni)	ppm	8.433	1.172	6.533	1.026	3.380	1.846
Lead (Pb)	ppm	42.267	3.121	30.633	8.999	19.000	7.316
Zinc (Zn)	ppm	12.100	1.500	15.400	3.830	7.460	2.475

Table 12.6: Mean Values of Heavy Metals in Soil at Control and Experiment Sites

Heavy Metals	Unit	2005-06			
		Control Site	SD	Experimental Sites	SD
Cadmium (Cd)	ppm	1.033	0.819	1.950	1.098
Copper (Cu)	ppm	14.317	9.218	24.100	11.451
Iron (Fe)	ppm	35.267	25.354	43.150	25.433
Manganese (Mn)	ppm	7.984	3.215	9.283	3.850
Nickel (Ni)	ppm	5.675	2.527	7.608	2.161
Lead (Pb)	ppm	29.317	11.729	39.967	17.818
Zinc (Zn)	ppm	10.667	4.148	11.867	5.640

Table 12.7: Correlation Between Heavy Metals of Experimental Soil

	Cadmium (Cd)	Copper (Cu)	Iron (Fe)	Manganese (Mn)	Nickel (Ni)	Lead (Pb)	Zinc (Zn)
Cadmium (Cd)	1						
Copper (Cu)	0.3719	1					
Iron (Fe)	0.7981	0.5348	1				
Manganese (Mn)	0.4834	0.9502	0.6730	1			
Nickel (Ni)	0.6368	0.8904	0.8093	0.9581	1		
Lead (Pb)	0.6911	0.8811	0.7809	0.9274	0.9566	1	
Zinc (Zn)	-0.1615	0.7484	-0.0190	0.5876	0.4374	0.4660	1

Table 12.8: Correlation Between Heavy Metals and Physico-chemical Parameters of Soil at Control Site

	Temperature	WHC	Bulk Density	Soil Moisture	pH	EC	Cl	Na	K
Cadmium (Cd)	0.6763	0.8199	-0.3977	-0.3107	-0.3093	0.7773	0.6980	0.5320	0.0836
Copper (Cu)	0.6307	0.2015	0.2982	0.4074	0.4782	0.0989	0.6089	-0.2909	-0.4336
Iron (Fe)	0.3246	0.8397	-0.6903	-0.6830	-0.6779	0.8251	0.3079	0.8795	0.5500
Manganese (Mn)	0.8814	0.6726	-0.1244	0.0151	0.0432	0.6419	0.7925	0.2525	-0.1647
Nickel (Ni)	0.7578	0.6737	-0.2465	-0.0108	-0.0862	0.6505	0.6530	0.3863	-0.1443
Lead (Pb)	0.6596	0.8608	-0.4316	-0.2208	-0.2642	0.8055	0.6111	0.5749	0.1158
Zinc (Zn)	0.8704	0.1744	0.3951	0.5580	0.4955	0.2569	0.7613	-0.3999	-0.5542

REFERENCES

Aslam, M.M.; Baig, M.A.; Hassan, I.; Qazi, I.A.; Malik, M. and Saeed, H. (2004): Textile Wastewater Characterization and Reduction of its COD and BOD by Oxidation, *Electron. J. Environ. Agri. Food Chem.*, 3(6): 804-811.

Bharti, P.K. (2007): Effect of Textile Industrial Effluents on Groundwater and Soil Quality in Panipat Region (Haryana), *Thesis Submitted to Gurukula Kangri University, Hardwar*, pp: 191.

Bharti, Pawan K., Singh, V. and Kumar, P. (2013): Post Irrigation Impact of Textile Industrial Effluent on the Composition of Soil System at Panipat (Haryana), India. *International Journal of Higher Education and Research,* 2(1): 11-15.

Bharti, P.K., Kumar, P. and Singh, V. (2013): Impact of Industrial Effluents on Ground Water and Soil Quality in the Vicinity of Industrial Area of Panipat City, India. *Journal of Applied and Natural Sciences,* 5(1): 132-136.

Bharti, Pawan K. (2013): Soil Quality Assessment in the Vicinity of an Industrial Area, In: Soil Quality and Contamination (Eds.- Bharti, P.K. and Chauhan, A.), *Discovery Publishing House Pvt. Ltd.*, Delhi, pp: 1-31 (ISBN: 93-5056-361-4).

Bharti, Pawan K. (2013): Assessment of Heavy Metals in Agricultural Soil, In: Soil Quality and Contamination (Eds.- Bharti, P.K. and Chauhan, A.), *Discovery Publishing House Pvt. Ltd.*, Delhi, pp: 87-125 (ISBN: 93-5056-361-4).

Bharti, Pawan K. (2013): Soil and Sediment Quality Assessment Larsemann Hills, Antarctica, In: Soil Quality and Contamination (Eds.- Bharti, P.K. and Chauhan, A.), *Discovery Publishing House Pvt. Ltd*, Delhi, pp: 134-140 (ISBN: 93-5056-361-4).

Bharti, P.K. and Chauhan, Avnish (2013): Soil Quality and Contamination, *Discovery Publishing House Pvt. Ltd*, Delhi, pp: 186 (ISBN: 978-93-5056-361-8).

Gomez-Serrano, Garcia-Macias, A., Espinosa-Mansilla, A. and Valenzuela-Calahorro (1998): Adsorption of Mercury, Cadmium and Lead from Aquoes Solution on Heat Treated and Sulphurized Activated Carbon. *Wat. Res.,* 32: 1-4.

Kashem, M.A. and Singh, B.R. (1999): Heavy Metal Contamination of Soil and Vegetation in the Vicinity of Industries in Bangladesh, *Water, Air and Soil Pollution*, 115: 347-361.

Korfali, S.I. and Davies, B.D.E. (2004): The Relationship of Metals in River Sediments (Nahr-Ibrahim, Lebanon) and Adjacent Floodplain Soil, *the CIGR J. of Scientific Research and Development*, Manuscript LW 04 010, 6: 1-22.

Kudesia, V.P. (1992): Water Pollution, *Pragati Prakashan, Meerut*, pp: 407.

Malik, D.S. and Bharti, P.K. (2007): Soil Quality of Irrigated Agricultural Fields in Textile Industrial Area of Panipat City, *Asian Journal of Experimental Sciences,* 21 (2): 445-451.

Mani, V.; Kaur, H. and Mohini, M. (2005): Toxic Metals and Environmental Pollution, *J. Ind. Poll. Cont.*, 21(1): 101-107.

Millar, C.E. and Turk, L.M. (2002): Fundamentals of Soil Science, Biotech Books, Delhi-35, pp: 462.

Singh, T.B.; Jadon, S.P.S. and Mishra, G.J. (1994): Degradation of Water and Soil Quality of Parwanoo Area with Respect to Heavy Metals, *IJEP*, 14 (4): 282-287.

Soltan, M.E. (1999): Evaluation of Ground Water Quality in Dakhla Oasis (Egyptian Western Desert), *Environmental Monitoring and Assessment*, 57: 157-168.

Trivedi, R.K. and Goel, P.K. (1984): Chemical and Biological Methods for Water Pollution Studies Karad, *Environmental Publication,* pp: 1-251.

Yuandong, Z.; Shirong, L. and Jiangming, M. (2006): Water-holding Capacity of Ground Covers and Soil in Alpine and Sub-alpine Shrubs in Western Sichuan, China, *ACTA Ecologica Sinica*, 26(9): 2775-2782.

Index

• • • • • • •